The Celtic Tige

The Celtic Tiger

The myth of
social partnership in Ireland

Kieran Allen

Manchester University Press
Manchester and New York

distributed exclusively in the USA and Canada by St. Martin's Press

Published by Manchester University Press
Oxford Road, Manchester M13 9NR, UK
and Room 400, 175 Fifth Avenue, New York, NY 10010, USA
http://www.manchesteruniversitypress.co.uk

Distributed exclusively in the USA by
St. Martin's Press, Inc., 175 Fifth Avenue, New York,
NY 10010, USA

Distributed exclusively in Canada by
UBC Press, University of British Columbia, 2029 West Mall,
Vancouver, BC, Canada V6T 1Z2

British Library Cataloguing-in-Publication Data
A catalogue record for this book is available from the British Library

Library of Congress Cataloging-in-Publication Data applied for

ISBN 0 7190 5847 3 *hardback*
     0 7190 5848 1 *paperback*

First published 2000

07 06 05 04 03 02 01 00   10 9 8 7 6 5 4 3 2 1

Typeset in Sabon
by Servis Filmsetting Ltd, Manchester, UK
Printed in Great Britain
by Bell & Bain Ltd, Glasgow

Contents

Tables and figures

Tables

Figures

Abbreviations

AIB	Allied Irish Bank
ASEAN	Association of South East Asian Nations
ATGWU	Amalgamated Transport and General Workers Union
ATTAC	Action pour une Taxe Tobin d'Aide aux Citoyens
CIE	Coras Iompair Eireann
CORI	Conference of Religious in Ireland
CPI	Consumer Price Index
CSO	Central Statistics Office
DIRT	Deposit Interest Retention Tax
ESRI	Economic and Social Research Institute
EU	European Union
FIRE	finance, insurance and real estate
GDP	Gross Domestic Product
GNP	Gross National Product
ICTU	Irish Congress of Trade Unions
IDA	Industrial Development Authority
IFSC	International Financial Services Centre
IMF	International Monetary Fund
INO	Irish Nurses Organisation
ITGWU	Irish Transport and General Workers Union
JMSE	Joseph Murphy Structural Engineers
JR	job rotation
NAFTA	North American Free Trade Area
NCB	National City Brokers
NILP	Northern Ireland Labour Party
OECD	Organisation for Economic Cooperation and Development
OPEC	Organisation of Petroleum Exporting Countries
PAYE	Pay As You Earn
ROCE	return on capital employed

SIPTU	Services, Industrial, Professional and Technical Union
TD	Teachta Dala
UCD	University College Dublin

Introduction

Ireland was supposed to be different. The two main political parties did not divide on left–right lines but were broad catch-all organisations that garnered support from all quarters of society. The elite did not go to private schools and talk with different accents to the rest. They were 'self-made men' who had been to the Christian Brothers schools and followed their local GAA teams. Class was a British thing, associated with grimy factories and aristocrats who spoke with a plum in their mouths. Maybe it was the memories of the War of Independence or the strength of Catholicism, but there was a sense of a 'national community' – not class division.

It was always a myth. The 'self-made' men usually turned out to be the sons of former captains of industry. Despite all the talk of community, all manner of polite signals were used to indicate that people should know their place. It has always been much harder for individuals from a working-class background to 'move up' the ladder in Ireland than it was in Britain. In 1987, for example, only 6.5 percent of individuals rose from the working class to the professional and managerial class. In Britain, it was slightly higher, at 8.3 percent.[1] Not a huge difference, but it serves to show that not only is social mobility limited in modern capitalism, but the scale of class barriers cannot be assessed from superficial social attributes such as accents, titles or lifestyles. There may be few lords and ladies in Ireland and the rulers may talk with broad rural accents, but there was always a tight class structure which militated against workers.

If the classless Ireland was a myth in the past, it has become a hollow joke in the Celtic Tiger. In the 1960s, the Fianna Fail leader Sean Lemass took up the slogan of the US President John F. Kennedy, and promised that a rising tide would lift all boats. His other favourite analogy was the national cake. Instead of seeking a larger share, he urged workers to increase the size of the cake so they got a bigger slice with the same share. Yet few politicians repeat these type of metaphors today. The reason has little to do with a change in the style of the speech writers – the change has occurred in reality itself. It would be hard to find any evidence that the majority of workers have held onto their share of the economy or even seen it expand in the boom. The most the majority of the population are promised is a 'trickle-down effect'. Even if we accept this claim at face value, there are important differences between the metaphors of the 1960s and the 1990s. The latter version assumes that the wealthy can take as much as they like and have no social or moral obligation to share any of that wealth. They need only promise that a few drops will fall from their overflowing cups.

All of this is justified by a form of gritty realism. A mysterious process called 'globalisation' means that market forces have to be given free rein and the desire for profit must be liberated from all constraint. If a comprehensive health service or the claims of older workers to a decent pension gets in the way, then so be it. The Celtic Tiger came out of a jungle of competitive capitalism and brooks few claims for costly reforms. Instead, the population are repeatedly urged to be grateful for the half a million new jobs that have been created. Demands for more money by 'sectional interests' – who never seem to encompass the business elite – are condemned for threatening these new jobs.

Yet it is precisely the theme of this book that class divisions and even class struggle has become more relevant than ever before in Ireland today. The Celtic Tiger elite has gone to great lengths, including forms of illegality, to increase its share of the wealth. For example, one of the mechanisms they have used was the Ansbacher account. Here, 121 of the richest people in the country lodged at least £50 million in a secret account to avoid tax. The pivotal figure was Des Traynor, who is now deceased but who was the chief executive of the Guinness and Mahon Bank, a board member of Cement Roadstone, one of the largest private firms, and also of Aer Lingus, the state airline. Money for the account was often paid to Traynor in cash and then lodged with the Ansbacher (Cayman) bank, where a secret record was kept. Individual account holders were given a code, such as S1 or S9. The purpose of the exercise was to give wealthy individuals access to offshore banking which was beyond the reach of the Revenue Commissioners – even though the money was in fact held onshore. A rich individual could make withdrawals from a bank in Ireland but still evade tax. Even better, he or she could earn interest from the Ansbacher account that was only marginally below that obtained in another bank.

Ansbacher became famous because account holders S8 and S9 were none other than Charles J. Haughey, the former Taoiseach and Fianna Fail leader.[2] However, there were probably many other similar accounts. They represent an attempt by most of the ruling elite to effectively withdraw from the tax system. Ever since the Second World War there was supposed to be an implicit bargain struck in European societies. The wealthy held on to their money, but in the interests of longer term social cohesion they paid a moderate rate of tax to fund public services. The irony of the Celtic Tiger was that while the elite talked of a social partnership with the unions, they had already torn up this implicit social contract. Deprived of valuable resources, hospitals were closed down, class sizes in schools rose and local authority house building virtually ceased. Thatcher may have coined the slogan 'There is no such thing as Society', but the Irish elite took it to heart.

If the Ansbacher account represented one side of an undeclared class war, the first national nurses' strike of 1999 was a signal that dramatic changes were occurring on the other side of the class divide. Nurses could hardly be regarded as battle-hardened trade union militants. Their major union, the Irish Nurses Organisation (INO), used to regard itself as an exclusively professional association and only affiliated to the Irish Congress of Trade Unions (ICTU) in recent years. In 1981, for example, the INO identified itself with the most conservative sections of Irish society by supporting the Pro-Life campaign, which managed to subsequently insert an article into the Irish constitution equating a mother's life with that of the 'unborn'.[3] Yet in 1999 an astounding 96 percent of nurses voted to take strike action to pursue a claim for higher pay. Despite being lectured by numerous experts about their naivity about industrial relations, hospitals were picketed by scores of the mainly female workforce. The strike had followed four years of agitation where nurses repeatedly rejected the advice of politicians, union leaders and the Labour Court to assert their right to pursue their wage claim.

Irish society has sometimes had difficulty facing up to the reality of social class. The idea that nurses, who were once ironically nicknamed Charlie's Angels – the Charlie in question being none other than Charles Haughey – were part of an incipient class conflict seemed strange to some. Were they not decent middle-class women who had been caught up in the trauma of a run-down health service? What possible bearing could their 'special case' have on class conflict in the Celtic Tiger? Yet strangely, the Irish state saw that their struggle was caught up in the wider argument about pay in the Celtic Tiger. The main reason why the Taoiseach, Bertie Ahern, who once wrote blank cheques for his political mentor, Charles Haughey, could not pay the nurses was that it would provoke a pay revolt. The nurses were apparently damaging the whole concept of social partnership which was the foundation of the Celtic Tiger economy.

At least that is what most of official Irish society argued, until eventually some small concessions were made. However, the original question still remains: what has a dispute about nurses' pay got to do with class conflict? It is a question that gets to the heart of this book.

The sustained boom that became known as the Celtic Tiger has transformed Ireland. Undoubtedly many of the elements of these changes were already in place, but the boom has accelerated them in dramatic ways. None more so than the images of what constitutes the working class of today. In the past, it seemed easy to locate the Irish working class on a mainly rural horizon. They lived on council estates; they worked in factories and usually came from Dublin where they professed not to like 'culchies'. The workforce was overwhelmingly male and mostly wore overalls in their daily work. Raising people out of this class and leaving behind the relics of an industrial empire was almost one of the official promises of the newly independent state. To that end, the cultural experience of this social group was virtually ignored until films like *The Commitments* appeared and, ironically, drew on US black soul music as its vehicle of expression.

Yet the forces which go to make up the broader working class are by no means static. If capitalism is such a dynamic system that it can reshape everything so that 'all that is solid seems to melt to air', then why would the dominant image of workers from the 1950s and 1960s still apply today? The primary condition for being a worker is a reliance on wages, on a necessity to sell your labour to survive. There is more to it than simply this, of course, and some of the issues are explored in Chapter 2. But our general approach has been to assume that in terms of one's relation to the wider economy, there is little difference between working in a large office and a factory today. In the case of both white collar and blue collar employees, wages are controlled, whereas the profits of the employer are free to soar. Contract working, job insecurity, constant pressure for flexibility and systematic efforts to reduce 'unit costs' prevail in both fields. These features also apply whether one is working for the state or in private industry. There are, of course, many nurses or teachers who may not see the common situation they share with industrial workers. Irish society after all promotes an image of social ascent for 'better off' families. Yet, it is our contention that it is necessary to start with the actual situation in the Celtic Tiger, rather than how different groups perceive that situation. With that in mind, the book attempts to document how the majority of workers have lost out.

While the details may be new, much of the information contained in the chapters that follow will not come as a surprise to many, because one of the great ironies of the Irish success story is that it has already produced a discontented majority. The term is a deliberate inversion of John Kenneth Galbraith's famous phrase about the 'contented majority'.[4] Ever since his book was written in 1992, the phrase has been widely used by commentators to lament the 'culture of greed' that has grown up among the relatively privileged two-thirds of the population. It has become fashionable to write of the majority of workers as conservative, brainwashed by the media and prey to every opportunist politician who promises tax cuts. Again, however, this is not our approach. Not only can it be demonstrated how the majority of Irish people have lost on the Celtic Tiger, it is also becoming increasingly apparent that there is widespread discontent over this.

We use the term 'discontent' deliberately, as it is not a sentiment that is focused or structured around a particular political outlook. It does not register directly on the electoral figures or find spokespersons who articulate a coherent alternative to the status quo. It is however broad, diffuse and visible in many surprising ways. One sign is the enormous popularity of strikes and other forms of resistance. In the past, it was sometimes argued that strikes were unpopular and that the unions had to find new ways of winning public opinion. Yet, despite the immense hardships caused by the nurses' strike, 66 percent of the population felt it was justified.[5] Similar levels of support were evident during a national strike in the large retail chain, Dunnes Stores. Even when a bar strike occurred during one of Ireland's World Cup fixtures, few passed the pickets. Similarly, the housing crisis in the Celtic Tiger has led to huge levels of support for those who have fought evictions. A struggle at St Ultan's flat complex against developers who wished to evict sitting tenants was so popular that Dublin Corporation was forced to take the whole complex into public ownership. What is sometimes termed 'cynicism' or 'voter apathy' may also be regarded as another expression of this discontent. Declining voter turnout is often decried as a danger to democracy, but it may also be regarded as a withdrawal of legitimacy to political institutions that are seen to be so tarnished with corruption.

Discontent, however, is not normally a permanent state of affairs. It reflects a suspension of past beliefs and an uncertainty about future convictions. Inevitably it contains contradictory elements that pull different ways. The next few years will be important in Ireland, particularly if the Celtic Tiger does not last as long as official spokespersons predict. If the contention of this book about rising levels of discontent is correct, the key issue is: what types of alternatives are available to articulate and focus the latent anger that now exists? Experience in the rest of Europe shows that the centre ground of politics no longer offers the only pole of attraction. Forces are emerging on both the left and the right which are challenging for the allegiances of many. Although Ireland may have had a stable consensus around right-wing politics for several decades, there is no reason to assume that it will remain immune from these developments. If anything, the sharpening of conflicts in the Celtic Tiger make the emergence of new political forces virtually inevitable. In attempting to highlight the common interests of workers, this book is clearly part of a project to promote the left alternative.

Chapter 1 examines why the Celtic Tiger came about. It notes how the Irish economy is held up as a model of development by the International Monetary Fund (IMF), who hail it as a pragmatic example of how neo-liberal politics can be made to work. The chapter challenges the view that the boom was a reward for the fact that the majority of the population took the 'hard medicine' of low wages and public sector cuts in the late 1980s. It looks for an alternative explanation at the set of conjunctures which led to a huge flow of US investment to Ireland.

Chapter 2 takes issue with the notion that the main division in modern Ireland is between a contented majority and an underclass minority. It focuses on the ambiguities contained in the term, 'social exclusion' and argues that a class analysis presents the best way of approaching the Celtic Tiger. It examines some aspects of the recent US boom to argue that class polarisation has become a feature of booms in late capitalism.

Chapters 3 and 4 provide detailed empirical evidence on why the majority of workers have lost out. Chapter 3 looks more specifically at the issue of wages and argues that the social partnership arrangements have ensured that workers received a declining share of the economy. It contrasts the relatively slow growth in wages to the phenomenal increases in productivity that occurred. Chapter 4 examines the practice of cutting taxes to attract multi-nationals and stimulate Irish entrepreneurs. It is sometimes claimed that Ireland's policy of undercutting the tax regimes of other European Union (EU) countries has benefited the country as a whole. The chapter, however, finds that Irish society has borne a considerable cost because of both the legal and illegal forms of tax avoidance.

Chapter 5 deals with one reason why the discontent has not been focused – the relative passivity of the unions before the growing social inequalities. It examines the divergent interests of the union hierarchy and the wider membership. It argues that social partnership has helped to restructure the labour movement so that 'business unionism' has become the dominant perspective of the labour leadership. It finds, however, that the boom has also strengthened the bargaining power of the rank and file and has laid the basis for new conflicts about the future direction of the labour movement.

Chapter 6 examines what has occurred at the other end of the class divide, among the ruling elite. Ireland has been swept by a range of corruption scandals in recent years. Yet the tribunals which were established to deal with them seem to have difficulty explaining exactly why they occurred. The chapter looks at how 'crony capitalism' is not a practice that belongs exclusively to south east Asian countries but finds the roots of this behaviour in the nature of the market itself.

Finally, Chapter 7 looks at the wider context in which the new discontent has grown. The two main pillars of Irish conservatism, Fianna Fail and the Catholic Church have weakened considerably in recent years. This did not occur because of an automatic process of secularisation or liberalisation. Instead, major contradictions have been thrown up by the rapid pace of industrial development and these have only partially been resolved by huge struggles on issues like the 'X' case where a 14 year-old-rape victim won her right to leave Ireland for an abortion.

Throughout this book, we have unashamedly taken the side of those who have lost out on the Celtic Tiger. Far too many other commentaries use the guise of academic neutrality to present a framework whereby profit and exploitation seem an inevitable part of life and accordingly view worker militancy as a problem. Despite or rather because we have taken the side of workers, this book also aims to present its evidence in the most clear and objective form possible.

Notes

1 R. Breen and C. T. Whelan, *Social Mobility and Social Class in Ireland* (Dublin, Gill and Macmillan, 1996) p. 23.
2 S. Smyth, *Thanks a Million Big Fella* (Dublin, Blackwater Press, 1997) p. 141.
3 E. O'Reilly, *Masterminds of the Right* (Dublin, Attic Press, 1988) p. 62.
4 J. K. Galbraith, *The Culture of Contentment* (London, Sinclair-Stevenson, 1992).
5 J. O'Malley and K. Moore, 'Huge Poll Backing for Nurses Strike', *Sunday Independent* (24 October 1999).

1
How the Celtic Tiger was born

Not so long ago a building worker had a ready way of assessing the prospects of the Irish economy. If there were more than a handful of cranes on Dublin's skylines, boom times were coming and jobs were to be found. If there were none, it was time to pack your bags and search for work in London, Berlin or New York.

Today these barometers have been shattered as Dublin's skyline is littered with cranes. No matter where the eye looks, the long steel machines are working ceaselessly to throw up buildings in months rather than years. Ireland is in the throes of its greatest boom ever and is the fastest growing economy in the Organisation for Economic Cooperation and Development (OECD). Throughout much of the 1990s, the recovery of the US economy exercised a fascination for conservative economists. 'Could it get any better' *Business Week* noted 'For two years the US economy has soared ever higher, reaching starry strata last explored in the 1960s'.[1] The cause of this unrestrained celebration was a steady increase of about 2.1 percent per year in Gross Domestic Product (GDP) throughout the 1990s. Yet the rate of growth of the Irish economy has been more than twice that figure.

The Celtic Tiger was baptised in 1994 by an economist working with the Morgan Stanley investment bank.[2] Since the start of the decade the average yearly rate of growth has been 6.3 percent of GDP. There are, however, some difficulties with these bald figures because of the role played by the multi-nationals. Multi-nationals operate across many economies and seek out the best way of minimising their tax bills. One of the principal mechanisms they use is the manipulation of prices within a firm, so that more profits appear to be generated in countries with a low tax regime. The practice, known as transfer pricing, means that components which come from a plant in another country are priced at an artificially low cost so that more profits seem to be made in a country like Ireland. Paul Sweeney, one of the more enthusiastic writers about the Celtic Tiger, cites the example of the Coca-Cola plant in Drogheda, County Louth. Here the 200 workers are reported to have made the company a profit of £400 million in one year.[3] If each worker is creating a profit of £2 million from an annual salary of, say, £30,000 to be generous, this amounts to a staggering rate of profit which Marx never even dreamed of.

This type of problem has led one economist to claim that Irish economic figures have 'about as much empirical status as moving statues, flying saucers and the statues of Elvis-found-on-Mars stories'.[4] This seems, however, to be unduly pessimistic, because one way of getting over the difficulty is to use different measures of growth. Ireland, for example, is unique in Europe in that its GDP is significantly out of line with its Gross National Product (GNP). GDP includes profits, dividends and rent which are removed from the country whereas GNP does not. This is important as the multi-nationals tend to repatriate the profits rather than re-invest them in Ireland. It is estimated that by the 1990s, foreign repatriation approached 15 percent of GDP.[5] If we use the GNP measure, then we can minimise to some extent for the effect of transfer pricing. Between 1990 and 1998, GNP rose at an average rate of 5.7 percent per year which is, again, considerably higher than the growth rate in the US economy.

Another way of assessing the reality of the boom is to simply compare the figures of growth with the reality of people's lives. One of the characteristics of a boom is the manner in which 'reserve armies' of labour are drawn from the countryside, the home and from other countries into the workforce. The Irish state used to hold the unenviable reputation of having one of the lowest participation rates for married women in the workforce in the EU. The combined influence of Catholicism and high levels of unemployment meant that the official constitutional position, that a woman's primary role was in the home, prevailed.[6] Even as late as 1961 just 5 percent of married women were in paid employment.[7] Today that has dramatically changed, as more married women have joined the workforce than in the previous twenty years combined. As a result Ireland has begun to converge with the EU norm.

Take the issue of emigration, which at one stage seemed to be an essential part of the Irish experience. As recently as 1990 one sociologist could write that 'The Irish are a people peculiarly disposed to emigration, so much so that it is easier to explain why they wander rather than remain at home'.[8] Yet today that pattern has been reversed and not only has emigration dried up, but there is now a small stream of both refugees and economic migrants coming to Ireland. This produces its own ironies. Up to 1999, the Government refused to grant refugees the right to work, even though Irish farmers complained that they needed to import foreign labour to help with harvests.[9] Not only has de Valera's rural idyll of sturdy self-reliant farm folk disappeared, but large farmers now feel themselves victims of a labour shortage.

The boom brings its own form of chaos. Streets are snarled with cars and commentators argue that Ireland's infrastructure cannot handle the phenomenal rate of growth. House prices have reached fantasy levels and large queues form outside rented accommodation each September as a huge influx of students compete with others to find accommodation. Employers complain loudly about 'holding onto staff' while employees operate the laws of the market to their advantage. Hospital wards are increasingly staffed by agency nurses, who are used as a temporary stop gap measure to cover for the shortages. Everywhere there is a frenetic buzz – the pubs are full, the new middle classes are packing into ever more exotic restaurants. For some there is an 'irrational exuberance', where traditional constraints are lifted in the belief that the bubble can never burst.[10] Ireland has reached its own modernity at a pace that has left many with a sense of dizziness.

A reward for hard medicine?

It was not always like this. In the late 1980s, Ireland had one of the highest rates of unemployment in the EU, increasing from 10 percent in 1981 to 17 percent in 1986. Debt repayments on borrowing undertaken in the early 1980s constituted a huge burden. One economist, Raymond Crotty, spelled out the pessimistic scenario that awaited it in the 1990s,

> Another peculiar combination of circumstances has enabled Irish government to borrow during the past forty years far more relative to

population and national wealth than the government of any other country . . . But now too Irish society has been forced into a dependence on foreign resources as complete as that of the exotic potato 140 years ago. As failure of the potato was inevitable then, so is the eventual withholding of foreign credit which now alone sustains the economy. Then mass famine ensued; now utter economic, political and social collapse will be the consequence.[11]

Crotty's nationalism led him to apocalyptic predictions, but he was by no means unique. As late as 1995, one writer who saw the Tiger economy as an aberration was still offering a cure for 'the Irish disease'.[12]

So what turned the situation around? One answer is that the Irish state was able to forge a consensus for cutting back on public spending and limiting wage rises. This is the approach adopted by the former government Minister, Ray McSharry, and the former Managing Director of the Industrial Development Authority, Padraic White, in their recent book on Celtic Tiger. They argue that fiscal stability and social partnership were the 'critical pillars' in transforming the economy.[13] It follows that if this approach is maintained then the boom can continue. One of the key economists with the semi-official research institute, the Economic and Social Research Institute (ESRI) has shown how discussions about the origins of the Celtic Tiger has broader implications when he argued that

the development of a political consensus in the 1980s on tackling Ireland's critical fiscal problems was very important in the ultimate success of the Irish economy. Sustaining and reinforcing this partnership approach to income determination so that it survives pressures from rising expectations is vital.[14]

Sometimes economists make the most general pronouncements without any reference to the suffering caused by public spending cuts or even to the political context in which these cuts take place. Neutrality appears to be guaranteed by the use of a technical language about 'tackling critical fiscal problems' without specifying exactly how this is to be done or who is to pay the price of such cutbacks. It is necessary then to fill in the picture somewhat before we explore the argument.

In 1987, Charles Haughey was elected to government office after running an election campaign which denounced public sector cut-backs. Fianna Fail billboards appeared all over the country with the slogan 'Health cuts hurt the old, the sick and the handicapped' and it was by no means an aberration. Haughey spent much of the 1980s attacking monetarist policies which caused 'alienation and widespread unrest'.[15] Yet within six months, the new Fianna Fail Government did an about-turn and introduced a cuts package of £485 million that amazed the opposition with its sheer scale and daring. Hospital wards were closed and more than 20,000 public servants were made redundant. Incontinent old people were even rationed for the amount of protective nappies they might use. Yet, while Haughey spoke of the need for restraint to tackle 'critical fiscal problems', he himself led a life of such unparalleled luxury that he did not need to pay attention to how his own personal finances were organised.[16]

Despite embarking on a stringent policy of 'fiscal rectitude', Haughey managed to keep the unions on board. Claiming that they were more fearful of an onslaught from the 'New Right', the union leaders forged an effective alliance with Haughey to introduce a Programme for National Recovery, which limited wages and accepted large-scale public sector redundancies. Political commentators were amazed with the scale of Haughey's achievement, with one writing that any other government would have found it 'difficult if not impossible' to proceed with apparently contradictory policies, 'one which involved huge cuts in public spending and the other which involved doing a deal with the unions designed to effectively tie them into the process of government'.[17] This then was the political consensus that agreed on the need for 'tackling Ireland's critical fiscal problems'.

It is an argument that can draw on considerable academic currency. The 1980s witnessed a highly orchestrated retreat from Keynesianism, a reassertion of neo-liberal ideas and a wholesale assault from within professional economics on the argument that workers' rights and capital accumulation were compatible. Lal summed up this approach when he argued that 'the case for liberalising financial trade control systems and moving back to a nearly free trade regime is now incontrovertible'.[18] The shift reflected the political atmosphere of the 1980s when Reagan, Thatcher and Kohl were in power. While the central focus of the attack was on the failure of the Third World countries to recover from indebtedness, the argument was generalised through series of reports from the

World Bank and the IMF. The 'counter-revolution' drew its inspiration from neo-liberal economics which saw the market as the most rational way to allocate scarce resources. By rationing goods according to people's ability to pay, it apparently produces a socially efficient process. The market also allocates production according to the criterion of maximum profit and this, it was argued, automatically 'corresponds to social usefulness'.[19] Where economic failures occurred, this was primarily caused by 'rigidities' which distorted the workings of the market.

The primary aim of neo-liberal economics was to 'roll back' the damage that had been caused by the rival school of Keynesian economics. State intervention, it asserted, had not only damaged competition, but also encouraged 'rent seeking' or 'direct unproductive profit-seeking behaviour'.[20] A large state sector encouraged companies to compete for access to state contracts and licences via bribery or appeasement of politicians or unions. It also has led to self-seeking behaviour from public sector employees. Against such rigidities, neo-liberal economics advocated tight budgetary control, privatisation and tax cuts to offer more incentives to individuals.[21] Another important rigidity that had to be removed was union power, as this led to excessive regulation of the labour market and so prevented wages reflecting market conditions. Ironically neo-liberals looked to the state to introduce new laws to curb this activity. It was argued that if rigidities were removed, then each country would gain its own 'comparative advantage' on the world market and expand its economy around those areas where it was most competitive.

Irish economic policies were influenced by this intellectual revolution, but were actually undertaken with their own brand of pragmatism. There was no major programme of privatisation until a decade after the Programme for National Recovery was signed and indeed Haughey promised the unions that Fianna Fail would not sell off any commercial semi-state industry.[22] The excesses of Thatcherism were denounced in stringent tones from almost all sides. Instead of being marginalised, the union leaders were brought centre stage. Officially the Irish state was concerned about the poor and the excluded who were threatened by 'sectional interests'. Nevertheless, after 1987 there was agreement on the three core principles of the neo-liberal argument that: (1) public spending had to be cut back (2) tax cutting was the key to encouraging enterprise by individuals and companies (3) wage costs had to be reduced and union power curbed through legislation. Ireland's more pragmatic approach to applying neo-liberal policies was eventually promoted as an important model for others to follow. Thus, the IMF hailed the experience of both Ireland and New Zealand (where the changes occurred under a Labour Government) in the 1980s for producing 'widespread agreement' on overcoming obstacles in the way of the market.[23] Similarly, the *World Investment Report* has used Ireland as a model for attracting foreign direct investment.[24]

However, there are good reasons for doubting the argument that fiscal rectitude and wage restraint produced the Celtic Tiger boom. For one thing, there is a central irony in the neo-liberal case because it argues, on the one hand, that one cannot 'buck the market' but then cannot explain why if the market is so powerful, so much energy is required from economists to advise states to conform to its 'laws'? More simply, why is the particular matrix of state policies the decisive factor in shifting the allocation of capital?

The series of propositions that make up the neo-liberal case do not hold together as neatly as its supporters might like. It is argued, for example, that the market allows individuals to maximise their profits and this in turn leads to higher levels of investment and employment. Yet, while perfect market conditions may increase profits, it does not necessarily follow that this leads either to a growth in investment or employment. Companies can choose to employ their capital in 'financial instruments' or more general forms of speculation rather than in productive capital or in job creation. For much of the late 1980s and early 1990s Ireland was regarded as being sound on the 'fundamentals' of budget restraint, low wage increases and low inflation, but this did not lead to job creation or to a major increase in investment in plant and machinery.

Past experience also shows that the particular matrix of policies that were developed after 1987 have not always been the key factor in producing a boom. Irish wages have traditionally been lower than elsewhere, but this did not lead to an influx of investment until recently. In 1981 for example, Tony O'Reilly, then president of the US multi-national Heinz, claimed that 'Irish hourly earnings are not yet a deterrent . . . Neither for the most part is trade union activity. Irish workers when properly led are as good as any'.[25] Yet just after this rather patronising pronouncement, the Irish economy succumbed to a dramatic slump and did not recover until 1984. The experience elsewhere shows a similar pattern. Most of the countries of Eastern Europe have carried out structural adjustment programmes which involved cuts in state spending and a deregulation of the market, but the recipe, which apparently worked for Ireland in the 1990s, did not bring results. The cumulative foreign direct investment for the whole of Eastern Europe in the years 1989–96 was around $44 billion. This may sound large but the cumulative foreign direct investment into Britain alone, which had much higher wage rates than Eastern Europe, was some $86 billion.[26]

Conventional economists are therefore faced with a problem. They wish to claim that Ireland's ability to take 'hard medicine' led to the Celtic Tiger, but they cannot explain why the medicine worked at one point rather than at another. They cannot explain why the medicine works in Ireland rather than in most of Eastern Europe, which has complied even more readily with their prescriptions. They can offer no guarantee that restraining wages and cutting public spending will lead to a continuation of the Irish boom. The irony of capitalism is that no sooner is a particular model discovered to be the recipe for success, than the elements which underlay its destruction seem to be in place. Most famously, Will Hutton once championed the German model of the social market and the east Asian models over their British equivalent, yet neither seemed to fare particularly well in the 1990s.[27]

Instead of seeking a national peculiarity which produces temporary success, it may be more fruitful to look at developments in the global economy to see why a particular area becomes attractive. This approach is more relevant in Ireland, because one of the main factors that created the boom was the high influx of foreign investment. However, before doing so, we need to look at how the Celtic Tiger throws light on other theories about development.

Sociologies

Sociological theories of development have traditionally been dominated by the two conflicting perspectives of modernisation theory and dependency theory. Modernisation theory was originally developed by Walter Rostow and was closely associated with the outlook of the USA. Rostow, who outlined the 'stages of growth' schema, served as an advisor to John F. Kennedy and advocated the bombing of Vietnam.[28] Dependency theory, by contrast, emerged as a radical response in Latin America where it was associated with revolutionary nationalist movements. Both theories in a more diluted and depoliticised form have been applied to Ireland.

Modernisation theorists believe that the key factor in economic development is changes in the internal value system, so that entrepreneurship can be promoted. According to Rostow, traditional societies block industrialisation because their value systems are 'fatalistic' and the benefits of technology are not applied. In the second stage of his schema for growth, the value system shifts, so there is a willingness to exploit the fruits of modern science and new types of enterprising men(sic) come forward who are willing to mobilise savings and take risk. This leads to the third 'take-off' stage where there is a high rate of investment, sometimes derived from foreign sources. In stages four and five, there is a drive to maturity as industrialisation spreads beyond its original bases, leading to the growth of mass consumption which stimulates further industrialisation.[29] One question naturally arises from this schema: what causes the value system to change? Rostow answered that, aside from Britain and Western Europe, the value system changed because 'of some external intrusion by more advanced societies. These invasions – literal or figurative – shocked the traditional society and began or hastened its undoing'.[30] The clear implication was that US-based intervention, in either a military or in a cultural form, could play a key role in the modernisation process.

The Irish historian Joseph Lee has taken up the focus of modernisation theory on the value system and saw it as the principal cause of Irish underdevelopment. He argued that 'Irish manufacturers were not psychologically prepared for expansion'[31] and, accordingly, Irish society was characterised by a 'possession ethic' rather than a 'performance ethic' as many wanted to hold on to what they had rather than take risks. This produced 'inherited institutional structures, reflecting a national culture that tolerates attitudes conducive to poor performance (which) still permits minus men to drag down aspiring achievers to a level well below their potential'.[32]

On the left, the Workers Party, which commanded significant working-class support in the 1980s, argued that underdevelopment had been caused by the subjective failings of a 'lazy bourgeoisie'. The party claimed that 'the Irish bourgeoisie were, and are, by any standards the most avaricious and lazy ruling class ever seen in the European polity'.[33] This class refused to put their capital to work productively and invested in banking and property speculation instead. Echoing Lee's notion of their psychological defects, the party argued that the Irish bourgeoisie produced 'speeches instead of steel and oratory instead of ore'.[34]

The manner in which the Celtic Tiger took off casts doubt on many of these arguments. As the economy boomed, the Irish bourgeoisie did not stick to either speeches or a mere 'possession ethic' and instead created a host of new companies. Industrial activity grew once there was a realistic hope of profit, rather than because of any subjective change in the psychology. Nor was there any decisive change in the value system to explain the emergence of the Celtic Tiger. If anything, traditional values seemed to grow stronger in the 1980s with divorce being rejected and a 'Pro-Life' amendment inserted into the constitution.

Dependency theorists reject the notion that underdevelopment is caused by the internal value system of a country and have highlighted the importance of colonialism in dislocating indigenous societies and depriving them of the necessary capital to benefit from economies of scale. However, the nationalist impetus behind the theory means that they tend to equate development with economic independence. Unless a balanced national economy is formed where native capital recycles profit back into the economy, real progress is hindered. Some dependency theorists such as Andre Gunter Frank argued that contact with metropolitan countries produces 'the development of under development'.[35] Others such as Carduso concede that industrialisation has occurred in many former colonies, but argue that it assumes a different form to that of the older advanced industrial countries. There is a 'dependent industrialisation' which has high levels of profit repatriation, indebtedness and a dual economic structure where a modern sector is dominated by multi-nationals who have few 'linkages' with the traditional sectors.[36] For most dependency theorists, these two forms of industrial development mean that the world is divided into 'core' and 'peripheral states', with the former exploiting the latter.

Dependency theory has been popular in Irish colleges, as it offers a seemingly radical critique of capitalism. However, the approach is not necessarily left wing, as the case of Raymond Crotty demonstrates. He argued that 'the continuing underdevelopment of Ireland has been the enduring, pathological consequence of British capitalist colonialism' although he was not opposed to capitalism itself but only to its British variety.[37] According to Crotty, the problem with colonialism was that it led to 'incorrect factor prices' which prevented the smooth running of the market. Among such distorted factor prices were the high price of land, high labour costs and excessively high interest rates. He condemned 'trade unionists (who) have been able to secure privileged positions' and proposed the wholesale privatisation of the public sector, so that each citizen received a 'national dividend'.[38] Once this occurred, the state should cease to support services such as higher education and also set about 'greatly reducing the publicly provided health service'.[39] Far from offering a radical alternative, Crotty's ambiguous book contains ample material for an Irish Thatcherite.

Denis O'Hearn, by contrast, writes from a left-wing republican perspective and produces an important indictment of the inequalities of the Celtic Tiger. He links these equalities to the growth of neo-liberal policies which are associated with the multi-nationals. Yet the Celtic Tiger has thrown his particular version of dependency theory into question, as the scale of the boom has confounded many of his predictions. As late as 1995, O'Hearn wrote that 'there is no longer an Irish economy, just a black hole through which Trans National Corporation profits, jobs and Irish citizens vanish;'.[40] This was just prior to a record expansion of jobs and the virtual ending of emigration. Hindsight will often upset some of the predictions of any particular theory and this does not necessarily render it a fatal blow, but in this case we are referring to core arguments. The predictions of economic doom grew directly from a claim that the domination of foreign capital is necessarily associated with dislocation and that the only real 'economic development' is one where there is economic independence.

More seriously, dependency theorists argue that the real beneficiaries of the boom are foreign capitalists rather than native capitalists. This apparently happens because the Irish state no longer serves national interests but foreign domination. Thus, O'Hearn argues that state development agencies go 'out of their way to attract foreign companies rather than nurturing new Irish enterprises'[41] Yet this begs the question: why should the Irish state be so opposed to the native capital which, after all, fund the dominant parties that govern that state? O'Hearn concedes that this is a complex question, but for others the answer is more clear cut. According to Gerry Adams, for example,

The economy of the 26 counties is dominated by foreign capital; massive proportions of the profit generated in Irish industry are exported in particular to Britain. The resources of the state are controlled and exploited by foreign interests and even the ruling class is not based principally on native capitalism but is an agent class acting as agents of foreign capital. This ruling class put into power by Britain appreciates that its interests lie in the maintenance of partition and feels its interests threatened by popular struggle. Economic dependence on Britain translates in terms of political interest.[42]

There is no empirical basis for Adams' argument that massive proportions of profit in modern Ireland are exported to Britain. The USA has long replaced Britain as the dominant foreign economic interest in Ireland. Nor does it make any sense to claim that the Irish ruling class acts solely as agents of foreign capital, because this ignores how the interests of foreign and native capital converge on almost every issue. Foreign capital uses Ireland as a platform for the export of its goods into the wider EU market and has no interest in uprooting native capital from its own markets. This is why there are no serious splits and divisions on national lines within the capitalist class. It is also why the Irish state is not staffed by foreign agents, but by an Irish elite who run the country in the joint interests of native and foreign capital. Both these sectors enjoy the low rates of tax on company profits and the wage restraint which Irish workers have bestowed for over a decade. Both have equal access to the high levels of grants and subsidies offered by the Irish state and it is no longer true to claim that indigenous industry has been being discriminated against in the allocation of grants. After the publication of a White Paper on Industrial Policy in 1984 there was, as Table 1.1 indicates, an important change in the balance of state funding of industry in favour of indigenous industry.

Table 1.1 Programme supports for industry 1985 and 1989

	1985	1989
	£m	£m
Indigenous	198.1	171.5
Overseas	191.1	145.3

Source: Department of Industry and Commerce, *Review of Industrial Performance 1990* (Dublin, Stationery Office, 1990) p. 43.

All of this has an important bearing for how we should examine the Celtic Tiger. In the past, critical writers on the Irish economy focused on its state of development and Ireland was presented as either a neo-colony, a dependent country or a peripheral state that was exploited by core regions. The key question was: how could Ireland become economically as well as politically independent? This approach unfortunately shifted the focus off the class divisions within Ireland and implied that Irish capital and Irish workers had a common interest in development. It suggested 'real development' would bring gains for the poor and this dovetailed with a republican outlook which argued that workers should at this stage only seek full independence, both political and economic, for their country.

Today this approach is obsolete because it is abundantly clear that the Republic of Ireland has developed and now appears in the top twenty-five richest countries in the world. There are important legacies from its colonial history, not least the continuing issue of partition, and there is also a greater reliance on foreign capital than other countries. Yet there is no ideal model of capitalist development and there is certainly no basis for the claim that native capital has been victimised. The fundamental issue today is no longer how can Ireland develop – but why has development produced such a degree of class polarisation. However, before examining the scale of these class inequalities, let us return to the issue of how the Tiger was born.

How the Tiger was born

The Irish economy needs to be viewed against the background of the global system, because only such a perspective can explain how it received a major stimulus from US investment.

Rates of growth in all the major industrial economies have been lower since the mid-1970s than they were in the Golden Age of capitalism during the long post-war boom from 1948 to 1973.[43] The slower growth rates reflected a tendency for the rate of profit to fall. It is estimated that the average profit rates in both the USA and the EU in the late 1980s were only 60 percent of their level in the 1950s and 1960s.[44] One result of this has been increasing competition both between individual companies and the states which champion their own blocks of capital.

This is most obvious in the case of the USA. Throughout much of the 1980s, the USA engaged in the process of restructuring, as it feared losing out to its competitors. Huge arms spending helped to fuel the Reagan boom of the early 1980s, but this was mainly concentrated in defence industries. Private investment in non-military areas remained low and some commentators feared that the USA was about to be overtaken by Japan in key sectors of the world economy.[45] One response from the US Government was to intensify its attacks on the conditions of its own workers. After Reagan sacked twelve thousand air-traffic controllers who were members of the PATCO union in 1981, a major employers' offensive was launched to increase profit rates. Another response was to expand the scope of US investment abroad. In 1982, US direct investment abroad was running at $207,752 million, but by 1997 this had risen to $860,723 million on a historical cost basis.[46] US multi-nationals had always sought markets and natural resources in other countries, but the USA as a whole had a lower proportion of foreign direct investment than most of the other industrialised countries, as its great size meant that companies were more likely to invest at home. Since the 1980s, however, there has been an increased pressure to invest abroad, if only to take on competitors. Another reason was that the rate of profit on investments outside the USA tended to be higher. The return on assets on non-financial majority owned foreign affiliates is higher than the average return on assets for US domestic non-financial corporations.[47]

The USA is not alone in this pattern and in the last decade there has been a spectacular growth in foreign direct investment around the globe, as capital no longer feels secure in dominating its home markets, no matter how large they are. World foreign direct investment flows are now nearly twice what they were in 1990 and some sevenfold what they were in 1980.[48] Contrary to some myths, the vast bulk of this foreign investment did not go to the developing countries. A small proportion certainly flowed to the emerging markets of east Asia and Latin America in the hope of high rates of return. However, more than three-fifths of all foreign investment went to the advanced industrial economies.

One of the factors which influenced this pattern was the formation of three main trading blocs – the North American Free Trade Area (NAFTA), the EU's single market and the Association of South East Asian Nations (ASEAN) bloc centred on Japan. The formation of these regional blocs was itself the result of growing competitive pressures. The European single market, for example, was supposed to give extra advantages to European firms by allowing them to enjoy economies of scale, unified standards which broadened markets and new synergies based on the pooling of research and design. The aim was to allow these firms to compete with the giant US and Japanese firms in the global economy.

The move to a single internal market in Europe diverted some direct investment away from non-EU countries, as US and Japanese companies rushed to ensure they had a production base behind EU barriers. Foreign investment, for example, declined in Austria and Sweden until it became it was clear they were joining the EU.[49] By contrast, the share of foreign investment going to EU countries rose. In 1985, for example, the EU share of foreign direct investment stock had fallen to 30.8 percent of the global total, yet as moves to a single market accelerated, this rose again to 42 percent in 1990 and remained at 39 percent in 1995.[50] The USA was already well positioned to gain entry to EU markets, as its investment in Europe had increased substantially at the time of the last enlargement in 1973. However, this investment tended to be concentrated in older industries such as automobiles.

As the industrial structure of capitalism changed, many of the new computer companies such as Intel and Apple needed a European base because the continent was one of the key battle-grounds between the global giants. It accounted for 28 percent of world market share and European companies tend to be weak, with the value of EU computer imports being approximately double the value of its exports.[51] By adopting an aggressive strategy of reloca-tion within the EU boundaries, US companies have been spectacu-larly successful in capturing a significant proportion of this market and by 1994 US companies held a 38 percent share of Europe's com-puter and office equipment market, which was exactly double that of their Japanese rivals.[52]

This, then, is the context for the emergence of the Celtic Tiger. In almost every country, the wealthy have demanded wage restraint and public sector cutbacks, but these have not generated economic success. Ireland was lucky, however, because it was able to establish itself as a major location for US investment into Europe and none of this was planned or predicted. The Irish state borrowed from a model of regional development which had been applied in Britain in the 1970s to offer a package of incentives for particular industries.[53] It chose electronics and the full resources of a state bureaucracy were applied to gaining a lead in this area, but few had expected the torrent of US investment that flowed at the end of the 1980s least of all those who advocated the cutbacks. Global capitalism is such a dynamic and chaotic system that no planning is possible. New winners emerge quickly for a short period for reasons that have been unforeseen – and they can also disappear when other forms of restructuring take place.

Ireland offered of a distinct set of advantages to multi-national firms who wanted a European base for their operation because it had a spectacularly low rate of taxation on corporate profits. Profits derived from manufacturing and some services were subject to a tax rate of 10 percent until 31 December 2002. Thereafter a Corporation Tax of 12.5 percent is to apply to all trading profits in all sectors. Figure 1.1 shows how this tax rate significantly undercuts other regimes in Europe.

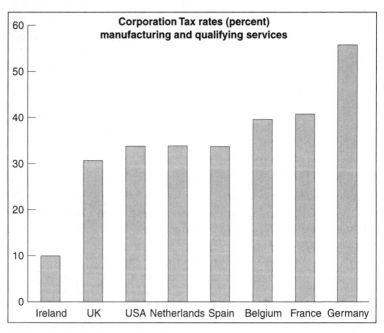

Source: IDA, *Achieve Global Competitiveness in Financial Services* (Dublin, IDA, 1999) p. 4.

However, this is only part of the story. A variety of other allow-ances which we shall consider in more detail in Chapter 3 often meant that the effective rate was lower than 10 percent. One study of tax and US corporate investment found that 'low and in some cases a negative effective tax rate applied'.[54] Ireland's role as a tax haven on the edge of Europe was further strengthened by the way in which the Irish state and the US Government co-operated to promote a pro-business agenda. The tax rate on profits in the USA in the mid-1990s was 34 percent and profits which were repatriated from Ireland to the USA were supposed to be subject to this rate. However, an agreement between both governments allowed US companies to gain credits on higher taxes paid elsewhere and to use these credits to offset charges that could be made against the low tax rate paid in Ireland.

Ireland also offered a young, educated, English-speaking work-force which could be hired at rates of pay which stood at the bottom of the European league. The US Department of Labour estimated, for example, that the total hourly compensation for Irish workers was $14 an hour compared to $28 an hour in Germany in 1998.[55] The use of English meant that executives of US parent companies could work more closely with Irish managers to employ American strategies for raising productivity and preventing union organisa-tion. English also offered considerable advantages in the computer industry, as it is the dominant language of information technology. The Irish state streamlined higher education on vocational lines, so that more graduates were turned out for the computer industry, tele-sales and the lower reaches of financial services. By 1992 only 51 percent of new entrants to third level education were enrolled in the university sector[56] and an increasing proportion were offered courses in computing, business studies and applied languages.

Ireland also provided a stable pro-business climate for the multi-nationals. Irish politics are dominated by right-wing parties who command over 80 percent of the vote and have a long history of sup-porting native capitalism. The legacy of colonialism has been used to promote an ideology of national development, so that what is good for business appears to be good for Ireland. This climate gave the multi-nationals a sense of security that they could enjoy the low tax regime and low wage rates for some time into the future. The Industrial Development Authority (IDA), which is one of the agen-cies seeking to attract foreign capital, makes much of this right-wing climate. In order to reassure the notoriously fickle bankers, for example it claims that one of the unique advantages of the International Financial Services Centre is that it has 'strong political support'.[57]

All of these factors combined produced a huge influx of US capital to a country that has only 3.7 million inhabitants. The key attraction that linked them all together was that Ireland offered a cheap platform for the export of goods into Europe. US investment grew dramatically in the late 1980s and 1990s. In 1983, for example, 36,039 people or 17.5 percent of Ireland's manufacturing workforce was employed by US companies, but by 1996 this had risen to 54,167 or one-quarter of the manufacturing workforce.[58] US investment is concentrated in the most profitable and highly advanced sectors of the economy and its plants are on average six times larger than Irish plants and produce nearly three times as much per employee. As a result, their combined output is greater than the whole of the Irish-owned manufacturing industry.[59] They are also highly concentrated in key areas such as electronics, software and health care and pharmaceuticals, whereas Irish manufacturing is more dispersed. Outside of manufacturing, there has also been a growth of US investment in services, particularly telesales and financial services.

All of this is associated with a strong pattern of what economic geographers call agglomeration.[60] Once particular cost advantages become known, rival firms tend to locate near to each other so that none lose out. In the past, firms from particular sectors of the economy tended to cluster in individual regions of the USA and this pattern is now being replicated in Europe. Many believed that agglomeration would lead multi-nationals to settle in the core regions of Europe where they could enjoy lower transport costs, but if anything the agglomeration of US firms has occurred on the periphery, in the more developed British economy and also in Ireland. The IDA has claimed that 26 percent of all greenfield projects established by US firms in Europe were located in Ireland.[61] Ireland's computer sector certainly includes a significant presence from all the major US companies in the field. They include Intel, which established Europe's largest wafer fabrication plant in Kildare in 1990; Dell, the world's largest personal computer company, which located its sole European plant in Limerick in 1990; Motorola, which opened in 1989 and employs 1,500;

Hewlett Packard, which began a major expansion in 1997 for a 650,000 square foot plant and IBM, which has established a new business campus to employ 3,000 people in customer support.

Today Ireland has by far the highest level of direct US investment per manufacturing worker of any country in Europe. The capital deployed per worker is a full seven times higher than the European average.[62] The Irish economy as a whole is now more dependent on US foreign investment that most other countries. The US Department of Commerce has drawn up a chart, which is reproduced in a modified form in Table 1.2, which shows that Ireland comes top of the league for the contribution that US foreign affiliates make to its overall GDP. Allowance must again be made for how transfer pricing may distort the figures; nevertheless, even if this is taken into account, it is clear that US investment plays a hugely significant role. One way of appreciating this is to compare Ireland to other countries in Latin America. Ireland is more dependent on US investment than, say, Costa Rica and Honduras, which are often described as an American backyard.

Table 1.2   Gross product of US majority-owned foreign affiliates as a percentage of GDP of host country

Country	1989	1996	1997
Ireland	12.4	13.5	16.5
Singapore	8.0	10.6	9.4
Canada	9.5	8.9	9.2
United Kingdom	6.2	7.1	6.8
Honduras	5.6	6.3	6.4
Costa Rica	5.6	5.1	5.5
Netherlands	5.8	4.4	5.5
Malaysia	4.6	4.6	5.0
Australia	4.4	4.4	4.8

Source: R. Mataloni, '*US Multinational Operations in 1996*' *Survey of Current Business,* September (1998), Table 13.

US investment, combined with a huge influx of EU structural funds, provided the motor for growth in the Irish economy. Far from pushing Irish capital out of its traditional locations, US companies created new opportunities for it to expand. Up to 1988, indigenous Irish industry showed a pattern of decline, but this was reversed with the influx of US investment and since then employment in

Irish-owned manufacturing has grown by 9 percent and output has risen considerably.[63] This has occurred against a background of a general decline in manufacturing across Europe. Service industry has also gained significantly, because the 'backward linkages' of multi-nationals have grown and, while the multi-nationals import a high proportion of their components, they are increasingly looking to Irish firms to provide services. These linkages provide an incubator for small businesses and impose a form of quality control on larger firms which enables them to move out of Irish markets. As one writer put it, 'the foreign firms in Ireland play a role somewhat similar to that of the domestic market in wealthier countries, facilitating the transition to export activity'.[64] This may not conform to Arthur Griffith's ideal of an Irish business class dominating its own economy, but it is the most viable form of capitalism available.

The success story of the Celtic Tiger is therefore intimately linked to the way the US economy itself has grown. The latter's growth has produced a barely concealed triumphalism and the 'American model' of deregulated markets is held up as the key to the future. While the EU has stagnated and Japan has been caught in its longest recession since WW2, the USA has forged ahead. Even the comparatively slow rate of growth is considered by some to offer a new way forward. The 'Goldilocks economy' which is neither too hot nor cold but grows steadily is supposed to offer a new paradigm that is far superior to the German or Japanese miracle of earlier decades.[65] Optimists about the future of the Celtic Tiger assume there will be a continual flow of US investment. Even if the multi-nationals have been somewhat reluctant to re-invest their spectacular profits back into the Irish economy, they assume that a steady flow of new investment will help to buoy up its performance.

There are, however, good grounds for doubting these optimistic predictions. For one thing, capitalism has an uneasy habit of tripping up its most enthusiastic supporters. In 1997, for example, South Korea which was still hailed as the miracle Newly Industrialising Economy, was blessed by the most prominent economists and assured of its future. Jeffrey Sachs, the Harvard University advocate of free market economics, claimed there was 'no possibility' of a Mexican-style crash; Paul Samuelson predicted that growth rates in east Asia would be higher than before and the IMF could see 'no problem in Korea's economy in the light of macro-economic indexes'.[66] Yet today the crash of the Asian Tiger has made a mockery of all these learned pronouncements.

The notion that the US economy can grow indefinitely and provide a flow of investment to the Celtic Tiger is dubious in itself, but the assumption that an 'Irish model' based on social consensus and free market economics will guarantee continued growth is blinkered in the extreme. In the meantime, it is worth examining what really happens when there is a capitalist success story. After all, if the rising tide does not lift the majority of boats, then we should be pretty concerned when it starts to run out.

Notes

1 'How long can this last?', *Business Week* (19 May 1997).

2 D. O'Hearn, *Inside the Celtic Tiger: The Irish Economy and the Asian Model* (London, Pluto Press, 1998) p. 1.

3 P. Sweeney, *The Celtic Tiger: Ireland's Economic Miracle Explained* (Dublin, Oak Tree, 1998) p. 47.

4 C. O'Grada, *A Rocky Road: The Irish Economy Since the 1920s* (Manchester, Manchester University Press, 1997).

5 O'Hearn, *Inside the Celtic Tiger*, p. 63.

6 Bunreacht na hEireann, Constitution of Ireland (Dublin, Government Publications, 1992) Article 41, Clause 2.

7 E. Smyth, 'Labour Market Structures and Women's Employment in the Republic of Ireland' in A. Byrne and M. Leonard (eds) *Women and Irish Society: A Sociological Reader* (Belfast, Beyond the Pale Publications, 1997), pp. 63–81.

8 L. Ryan, 'Irish Emigration to Britain Since World War II' in R. Kearney (ed.) *Migrations: The Irish at Home and Abroad* (Dublin, Wolfhound, 1990), pp. 45–69.

9 S. MacConnell, 'Farmers See Refugees as Answer to Labour Shortage', *Irish Times* (4 June 1999).

10 A. Sewn, *Irrational Exuberance: The Myth of the Celtic Tiger* (Dublin, Blackhall, 1999).

11 R. Crotty, *Ireland in Crisis: A Study in Capitalist Colonial Underdevelopment*, (Dingle, Brandon, 1986) p. 80.

12 C. Guiomard, *The Irish Disease: And How to Cure It*, (Dublin, Oak Tree Press, 1995).

13 R. McSharry and P. White, *The Making of the Celtic Tiger: The Inside Story of Ireland's Boom Economy* (Cork, Mercier, 2000).

14 J. Fitzgerald, 'Through Irish Eyes: The Economic Experience of Independence in Europe', ESRI Working Paper, no. 89 (October 1997).

15 C. Haughey, *Spirit of the Nation*, (Cork, Mercier, 1986) p. 820.

16 *Report of the Tribunal of Inquiry (Dunnes Payments) McCracken Tribunal* (Dublin, Stationery Office, 1997) p. 57.

17 S. Collins, *The Haughey File*, (Dublin, O'Brien Press, 1992) p. 128.

18 D. Lal, *The Poverty of Development Economics*, (London: Institute of Economic Affairs, Hobart Paperback, 1983) p. 32.

19 H. Johnson, 'The Market Mechanism as an Instrument of Development' in G. Meir *Leading Issues in Economic Development* (Oxford, Oxford University Press, 1989) p. 517.

20 See J. Mantinussen, *Society, State and Market: A Guide to Competing Theories of Development* (London, Zed Books, 1991) p. 261.

21 A. Harberger, *Economic Policy and Economic Growth*, (San Francisco, International Centre for Economic Growth, 1984).

22 Irish Congress of Trade Unions, *Annual Report and Conference Proceedings (1987)* (Dublin, ICTU, 1987) p. 209.

23 IMF, *World Economic Outlook*, May 1999 (Washington, IMF, 1999) p. 120.

24 UNCTAb, *World Investment Report 1998: Trends and Determinants* (New York, UNCTAD, 1998) p. 102.

25 Quoted in E. O'Malley, *Industry and Economic Development: The Challenge of the Latecomer*, (Dublin, Gill and Macmillan, 1989) p. 217.

26 M. Haynes and P. Glatter, 'The Russian Catastrophe', *International Socialism Journal*, no. 81: (Winter 1998) p. 54.

27 W. Hutton, *The State We're In* (London, Cape, 1995) pp. 262–77.

28 N. Chomsky, *Rethinking Camelot: JFK, the Vietnam War, and US Political Culture*, (London, Verso, 1993) p. 109.

29 W. Rostow, *The Stages of Economic Growth: A Non-communist Manifesto* (London, Cambridge University Press, 1971) Ch. 2.

30 Ibid. p. 6.

31 J. Lee, 'Capital in the Irish Economy' in L. M. Cullen (ed.) *The Formation of the Irish Economy*, (Cork, Mercier, 1969) p. 57.

32 J. Lee, 'Motivation: An Historian's Point of View' in Foras Forbartha (ed.) *Ireland in Year 2000 Towards a National Strategy* (Dublin, Foras Forbartha, 1983) p. 37.

33 The Workers Party, *The Irish Industrial Revolution* (Dublin, Repsol, 1978) p. 15.

34 Ibid.

35 A. G. Frank, *Capitalism and Underdevelopment in Latin America* (New York, Monthly Review Press, 1969).

36 F. H. Carduso, 'Dependent Capitalist Development in Latin America', *New Left Review*, no. 74 (1972) pp. 83–95.

37 Crotty, *Ireland in Crisis*, p. 67.

38 Ibid., pp. 115 and 126.

39 Ibid. p. 126.

40 D. O'Hearn, 'Global Re-structuring and the Irish Political Economy' in P. Clancy, S. Drudy, K. Lynch and L. O'Dowd (eds) *Irish Society:*

Sociological Perspectives, (Dublin, Institute of Public Administration, 1995) p. 104.

41 D. O'Hearn, 'The Irish Case of Dependency: An Exception to the Exception', *American Sociological Review*, 54:4 (1989) p. 581.

42 G. Adams, *The Politics of Irish Freedom* (Dingle, Brandon, 1986) p. 91.

43 E. Hobsbawm, *The Age of Extremes: The Short History of the Twentieth Century* (London, Michael Joseph, 1994) pp. 257–87.

44 C. Harman, *Economics of the Madhouse* (London, Bookmarks, 1995) p. 89.

45 See T. McCraw, *America Versus Japan* (Boston, Harvard Business School Press, 1986). Also D. Ernst and D. O'Connor, *Competing in Electronics: The Experience of Newly Industrialising Countries* (London, Pinther, 1992).

46 Bureau of Economic Analysis, 'Direct Investment Positions on a Historical Cost-Basis 1982–1997', (Washington, US Department of Commerce, 1987).

47 R. Mataloni, 'US Multinational Operations in 1996', *Survey of Current Business* (September 1998).

48 UNCTAD, *World Investment Report 1998,* p. 8.

49 R. Baldwin, R. Forslid and J. Haaland, 'Investment Creation and Investment Diversion: Simulation Analysis of the Single Market Programme', CEPR Discussion Paper, no. 1308 (1995).

50 R. Barrell and N. Pain, 'The Growth of Foreign Direct Investment in Europe', *National Institute Economic Review*, no. 160 (1997) p. 63.

51 European Union, *Panorama on EU Industry* (EU, 1997) Section 14, p. 9.

52 Ibid.

53 F. Ruane and H. Goreg, 'The Impact of Foreign Direct Investment on Sectoral Adjustment in the Irish Economy', *National Institute Economic Review*, no. 160 (1997) p. 78.

54 M. McCutcheon, 'The Tax Incentives Applying to US Corporate Investment in Ireland', *Economic and Social Review*, 26:2 (1995) p. 165.

55 Figures from USA Bureau of Labour Statistics quoted in National Competitiveness Council, *Report on Costs*, (Dublin, Forfas, 1999) p. 6.

56 P. Clancy, 'Education in the Republic of Ireland: The Project of Modernity' in P. Clancy *et al.*, *Sociological Perspectives,* pp. 467–95.

57 Industrial Development Authority, *Promotion Pack: Achieve Global Competitive Advantage in Financial Services* (Dublin, IDA, no date).

58 Central Statistics Office, *Census of Industrial Production 1983 and 1996* (Dublin, Stationery Office) Table 6.

59 Ibid.

60 G. Ottaviano and D. Puga, 'Agglomeration in the Global Economy: A survey of the "New Economic Geography"', *World Economy*, 21:6 (August 1998) pp. 707–32.

61 IDA, *Annual Report 1998* (Dublin, IDA, 1998) p. 12.
62 F. Barry, J. Bradly and E. O'Malley, 'Indigenous and Foreign Industry: Characteristics and Performance' in F. Barry (ed.) *Understanding Ireland's Economic Growth* (Basingstoke, Macmillan, 1999) p. 46.
63 Ibid. p. 65
64 Ibid.
65 M. B. Zuckerman, 'A Second American Century', *Foreign Affairs*, 77:3 (May/June 1998) p. 18.
66 Quoted in S. Gyoung-Lee, 'The Crisis and the Workers Movement in South Korea', *International Socialism Journal*, no. 78 (Spring 1998) pp. 39–54.

2
A discontented majority

Someone walking through the small working-class enclave of East Wall in Dublin during the summer of 1999 could not but help notice the posters in almost every window. 'No High Rises' proclaimed the message from the residents' association. The area is hemmed in by a constant stream of traffic and parents complain they can barely hear their children when they walk them back and forth to school because of the noise. Many are also worried about the rising levels of asthma, which they attribute to the exhaust fumes. Yet plans were drawn up by the Spencer Dock Development Company to build office blocks nearby in a £1.2 billion development that looked set to rival the first phase of London's Canary Wharf. The office complex was to include a huge car park which would act like a magnet to Dublin's traffic. The protests ensured that the planning board eventually turned down most of the proposed development.

Across the river Liffey in another working-class area, Ringsend, there have also been regular protests. Here generations of families have lived side by side, for a period in local authority housing and later in houses they bought themselves, but this pattern is now changing. The 'gated communities' have arrived complete with intercoms, and high earners in more flash cars come and go with little connection to the surrounding area. House prices have rocketed as a location near an inner city waterway becomes desirable. The residents have organised several marches to protest that there are no longer 'affordable houses' for their sons and daughters. According to one community activist, the working class are being 'economically cleansed' from the inner city.[1]

Community activism often cuts across political boundaries and is highly specific, but there is a new edge to the protests in East Wall and Ringsend because both areas feel they have missed out on the Celtic Tiger. Any reference to the Tiger is met with hoots of derision. 'We never seen it around here.' 'It's passed us by' are remarks that, in some contexts, are almost as common as the traditional Irish conversation openers about the weather. It is not particularly hard to see why. Cheek by jowl with both areas is the most potent symbol of the Tiger economy – the International Financial Services Centre. Here an elaborate network of financiers take 'positions' on interest rates in different economies or assess the prices of commodities or credit in the next decade as part of a 'futures' market. The gleaming offices of the banks and insurance brokers house a host of employees who operate the finance markets to generate enormous profits, but few people from the surrounding areas work there. Even fewer have seen even a trickle from the vast wealth contained in the bank vaults. For the vast majority of East Wall and Ringsend, it is simply a different world.

The Irish boom has produced a powerful sense of unease. This unease is at its sharpest when the two sides of Ireland are located side by side, but it is also more widespread. When unemployment and emigration soared in the 1980s, many felt they had to accept belt tightening and pay restraint. The refrain that the 'country cannot afford it' was the greatest put down of any argument for a redistribution of wealth. This changed in the 1990s, but many complain that only the rich have gained from the boom years. Social scientists have often remarked that absolute deprivation has never been such a powerful stimulus to revolt as a sense of 'relative deprivation'.[2] Constant poverty can often lead to a feeling of resignation or despair, but this can shift quickly when expectations rise because of small improvements in living standards. The conspicuous consumption of the rich in the last decade in Ireland has also heightened this appetite for change and created a mood of discontent and unease. The incessant talk of success has raised everyone's expectations and has led to a more acute awareness of how the majority of the population have fallen behind. These discontents are not confined to 'traditional' areas or regions, but pervade Irish society today.

Yet the unease rarely finds public expressions in the official institutions of Irish society and there have been few voices in the media, the research institutions and the universities who have articulated a feeling that the majority are losing out. There have certainly been dire warnings about the need for economic discipline. The ESRI was reported to have advised employers to cut back on growth lest employees feel too powerful and demand more.[3] Even when the modest proposal for a minimum wage was debated, there were some official voices arguing that it should be set at a very low rate, despite the boom. Indeed, without a trace of embarrassment, well-paid economists advised that a high minimum wage would be damaging for young people.[4]

One of the reasons for the official silence about the discontent is that few have questioned the principles of social partnership which have become the official ideology of the Irish state, much as republicanism or Catholicism were in the past. From this vantage point, all social groups have a common interest in co-operation and talk of class conflict is an anachronism or, worse, a British import. Where discontent is recognised among Pay As You Earn (PAYE) employees it is often seen as a form of 'consumerism' or pursuit of 'sectional interests'. Demands for higher pay which are advanced by workers to gain an extra share of the boom are seen as a form of 'selfishness' that will damage 'the economy'. Against these pressures, the majority of Ireland's intelligentsia advocate a form of social partnership which purports to give a voice to the excluded and the marginalised. From this perspective, Ireland seems to have escaped the rigours of neo-liberalism and has even pioneered a successful and caring approach to the market place.

This chapter will seek to challenge this ideology because the promised trickle-down effect of wealth has hardly materialised and instead there has been a steady stream going the other way. The term 'ideology' is used advisably. An ideology can be defined as a set of ideas shared by large number of people which forms some kind of coherent-related system and is connected to the maintenance of power and economic privilege. Dominant ideologies typically work by masking conflicts of interest and by presenting their outlook as the most practical, rational and feasible for the good of society as a whole. As Eagleton has pointed out, 'dominant ideologies help to unify social formation in ways convenient for its rulers . . . it is not simply a matter of imposing ideas from above but of securing the complicity of the subordinated classes'.[5] One of the ways this occurs is by securing the ideological co-option of intellectuals associated with movements of subordinate groups. It also occurs through

exercising hegemony over leaders thrown up by workers' organisations, so that they see no alternative but to work through the existing social order.

Social exclusion

All ideologies pick up on aspects of reality and configure them in
ways which buttress the outlook of our rulers. As evidence mounts
of the growing disparities in income, few could deny there are major
inequalities in Irish society. However, the dominant way of seeing
this inequality in Ireland is to conceive it as a form of 'social exclusion'. The booming economy is supposed to have benefited the
majority, but to have left behind a residual category, the 'socially
excluded'.

The term 'social exclusion' has an interesting background. It orig-
inated in France in the mid-1970s when there was a concern about
various categories of people who were unprotected by social insurance, 'the marginal, asocial persons and other social misfits'.[6]
Official French society had long placed an emphasis on a social solidarity that cut across the classes and the sociology of Emile
Durkheim can be regarded as giving theoretical expression to the
solidarisme movement of the late nineteenth century.[7] In this tradition, inequalities are supposed to result from people being left out
of the organic bond of society rather than because of the way capitalism works. The term social exclusion was picked up by the
European Commission in 1988 and appeared in the preamble to the
Social Chapter the following year, when there was a promise that 'in
the spirit of solidarity it is important to combat social exclusion'.[8]
Once again the term had an important political ring. Despite the
growing disparities of wealth, it was claimed that the EU was built
on the ethos of social solidarity and that a relatively small number
of unfortunate people had lost out.

Within certain limits the term social exclusion can convey an
important meaning. Long-term unemployment involves more than
the grinding experience of low income, because people are excluded
from all sorts of social activity. The children of unskilled manual
workers are excluded from access to higher education by a host of
informal mechanisms. Cities are increasingly structured so that
ghettos of poverty are created in the suburbs. As Brendan Bartley
has shown in one case study, the poor in modern Ireland are often

moved to 'invisible suburbs' that are out of sight of residents of the more prosperous parts of the city.[9]

Nevertheless, there are also huge difficulties with the use of the term social exclusion. For one thing, the poor are conceived as objects of a most general process. So one hears about 'the marginalised' and the 'socially excluded', but there is little discussion on *who* is excluding or marginalising them. It seems to be a process with no active subjects. If references are made to groups who are 'excluding' others, they are usually couched in the most general form possible. So one writer argued that 'exclusion arises from the interplay of class, status or political power and serves the interests of the insiders'.[10] Yet who these insiders are or how they are structured in class terms is never quite explained. It would seem that no defined group has a direct interest in the maintenance of poverty or exclusion.

The term social exclusion also contains an important ambiguity at its very core. It can imply that the structures of society exclude the poor or that the poor themselves hold particular values which lead to their marginalisation. In practice, both meanings are used simultaneously, giving the term an ambiguous meaning which allows it to be used by both the political elite and anti-poverty campaigners. The effect is that the focus shifts from looking at the inevitable class inequalities under capitalism to looking at mechanisms to re-integrate the poor into the labour market. As a result, some writers who discuss social exclusion tend to propose minor structural reforms to facilitate access to the labour market, but also to insist that the poor have duties as well as rights.[11]

Most crucially, in this ideological use of the term social exclusion, the interests of the poor are conceived to be in opposition to the majority of society. This arises from the currently fashionable view that there is a three-tier society where two-thirds have a direct stake in the maintenance of inequality. Here, for example, is how one writer characterises the division of the Irish labour force

> The first of these are 'tenured employees' who have job security, form the back bone of the trade union movement and are concerned to protect their own jobs. Secondly, there is a large body of temporary employees who have jobs without traditional life time security associated with these jobs. This group is growing in number and is engaged in contract, temporary, part time and casual employment. The third group are permanently unemployed. This group finds it very difficult

to get any form of paid employment and becomes trapped in a vicious cycle of poverty and idleness.[12]

What is interesting here are the very formal barriers that appear to exist between the three tiers. There is no sense of movement between the unemployed and those in temporary and contract employment. The trade union movement is supposed to cater only for those with job security, as if a considerable amount of its time was not spent fighting over contracts and rights for part-time workers. The implication is that the 'tenured employees' have interests that are opposed to the rest because they occupy privileged positions. This opposition between the 'deserving poor' and organised employees bent on class struggle is a familiar one in Catholic social teaching which tends to draw on a corporatist model of society. Corporatism was originally advocated by the Catholic Church in the 1930s as a way of upholding traditional society in an unfolding capitalist economy. It was argued that if people are integrated into an organic entity built on partnership and solidarity, the twin dangers, individualism and class conflict, could be avoided.[13]

A similar emphasis on championing the poor while opposing the militant activities of organised labour has played an important role in the populist politics of Fianna Fail. When the party was first formed it decided to 'lean on the economic side' and present itself as a defender of the poor.[14] Yet it was opposed to any class programme that would destroy the common good and saw militant trade unionism as a decidedly British import. During the heyday of trade union militancy in the late 1960s, the party sought to draw sharp contrast between harsh industrial militants and the policy of Fianna Fail which looked after 'the social welfare classes'.[15] An important policy theme of the party was to present itself as a 'compassionate' defender of the underprivileged while working actively to expand indigenous capital.

Rejection of class conflict and a purported opposition between the interests of the socially excluded and the wider working population is still central to the ideology of the Irish Republic today. It provides the intellectual framework for opposing wage increases as 'sectional demands' which destroy the common good and helps underpin social partnership, which is supposed to both provide a necessary discipline for trade unionists and also gives a voice to those who lobby for the poor.

Much of this argument gains sustenance from the notion that the working class has declined in the current 'post-industrial' society only to be replaced by a privileged middle class who espouse sectional outlooks. The book *Understanding Contemporary Ireland* may serve as an example of this approach. Written by researchers who worked for the ESRI, it draws on the classical sociologist Max Weber to acknowledge the existence of inequality, but to conceptualise it in terms of a privileged 'middle class' who dominate the state structures. The class system is seen in terms of a series of empty places which are filled by the basic market capacities – capital, educational skills and labour skills. These are the attributes with which individuals 'can bargain in the markets of capitalist society in exchange for an income'.[16] The writers claim that the growth in educational qualifications has produced a system of 'credentialism' where over one-half of the workforce has become 'middle class'.[17] They argue that 'the class position of most families had already been established in the 1960s and 1970s. This depended by and large on the ability to take advantage of the opportunities for education opened up in those decades and consequently to secure access to a favoured niche in the class system'.[18]

The description of the majority of the Irish workforce as a 'middle class' who occupy 'favoured niches' allows the ESRI writers to develop an ambiguous argument. On one hand, there is a concern for the poor and those who do not enjoy social mobility and considerable data is produced to show there are major obstacles to the social mobility of the unskilled manual groups. Yet the overall framework in which the concern is expressed does not offer a major challenge to Irish society, because there is nothing in this approach which departs from the traditional ESRI demand for more public sector cuts. Indeed as those at the receiving end of these cuts are the 'middle class' public sector employees, the cuts may even be seen to advance the fight for equality.

Another less subtle and more direct argument about the polarity between the socially excluded and the majority of employees appears in John Kenneth Galbraith's book, *The Culture of Contentment*. It would be difficult to overestimate the impact of this book on Irish supporters of social partnership. Although Galbraith pointed to the growing inequalities of American society, he argued that the majority were not merely complicit but had a vested interest in these inequalities. According to Galbraith, the fundamental division in modern society is between a 'contented majority' and a 'functional underclass'. The contented majority are comparatively privileged and believe that, not only are they 'receiving their just desserts', but they are very articulate about what seems to invade their sense of self-satisfaction.[19] This majority, which includes 'a certain if diminishing number who were once called proletarians' employ highly convenient social and economic doctrines that were once used by a handful or aristocrats or capitalists to justify their position.[20] In contrast, an underclass is excluded from the modern political structures and poses an ever-present hazard of inner city violence and drug use which threatens to embrace the whole of society.

The debt which modern Catholic social teaching owes to Galbraith is acknowledged in the reports of the Conference of Religious in Ireland (CORI) which are one of the leading advocates of this intellectual tradition. Galbraith's notion of a selfish majority helps to transmute class conflict into a conflict over moral values. Thus one recent CORI report noted that the demands for social change are blocked because of

> the present shroud over our western world where the majority of the people live in comfort and relative affluence. In the past the 'contented' class (the well off and privileged) were a small minority of the population. Now however they constitute a majority of most voting populations and consequently are in a position to ensure their societies are run in their own interest.[21]

CORI have provided an important intellectual influence especially when their reports have highlighted the dramatic levels of inequality in the Celtic Tiger. Indeed at times when the Labour Party had entered into coalition governments with right-wing parties, it often seemed that CORI was the only official voice highlighting the interests of the poor. On the other hand, however, CORI have also been among the most vociferous supporters of social partnership and the Government has given them scope to operate some experimental schemes to help overcome social exclusion. They have therefore played a crucial role in aligning lobby groups for the poor with structures that are designed to lower wage rises for the majority of workers. One of the reasons for their influence is that they operate at a meeting point between the elements of traditional Irish society, with its mixture of social Catholicism and nationalism, and the new language of social exclusion that has arisen from the Brussels bureaucracy.

Where is the contented majority?

Many objections can be raised to the supposed obliteration of class conflict in Ireland and its replacement by an opposition between a contented middle-class majority and an excluded or underclass minority. The term 'middle class' which is used to define a major section of society is extremely vague, because it lumps together people who have different relationships to ownership of companies or power in state bureaucracies. The mere fact that someone works in an office as against a factory or a garage hardly means that they belong to the same class category as those who command vast amounts of wealth. The term middle class even disguises the differences of interest that exist within occupations labelled 'white collar'. It might be asked why, for example, are a routine white-collar clerical employee and a Chief Executive assigned to the same class groups? As Stanley Aronowitz has pointed out, the term '"white collar" is a label that presupposes an essential difference between the structure of labour in the factory and the office. It is a category of social ideology rather than of social science'.[22]

Even if we concede that there is a tendency for the number of blue-collar manual workers to decline there are still huge problems with the notion of a contented middle class. In 1958, the British sociologist David Lockwood produced his celebrated work *The Blackcoated Worker* which offered an account of a 'socio-economic group that had long been a discomfort to Marxist theory: the growing mass of lower non-manual or white collar employees'.[23] He argued that the situation of white-collar employees differed from manual workers as regards their 'market situation' in three main respects – the size of their income, their degree of job security and their opportunity for promotions. These arguments were taken up by other sociologists such as John Goldthorpe, who has had an important influence on discussions about the Irish class structure.[24]

Yet this perspective fails to take account of the enormous changes that have occurred in white-collar, 'middle class' jobs. In the early part of the twentieth century there was an enormous difference between clerks and manual workers, as office workers sought to emulate their employer in many ways. They hired domestic servants, ensured their wives did not work and lived in the better parts of town. The difference in their situation helped to account for their widely divergent political outlooks. In Germany in the late 1920s, for example, a high proportion of office workers looked to Nazi-led unions, in contrast to manual workers who stayed loyal to socialist unions.[25] The numbers of white-collar employees were comparatively small and they undertook essentially managerial tasks, which involved them in a close, personal relationship with their employers. Lewis Corey summarised the traditional position of the clerk as an 'honoured employee'. 'His position was a confidential one, the employer discussed affairs with him and relied on his judgement; he might, and often did, become a partner and marry the employer's daughter.'[26]

Weberian sociologists tend to play down the process by which capitalism transforms the occupational structure and turns the majority into wage earners, no matter what their own subjective views are. As capitalism expanded it needed more sophisticated systems of accountancy, more complex forms of record keeping and more developed sales techniques. As the numbers involved in these activities grew, their social situation began to change. Managerial functions were separated off from clerical work and later the office itself became subject to the same process of rationalisation and subdivision that had affected the factory floor. Instead of seeing the clerk as both a subordinate and an ally, the employer became concerned to raise his or her productivity levels and cut back on unit costs. Braverman drew out the implications of this process of proletarianisation

> the labour market for the two chief varieties of worker, factory and office, begins to lose some of its distinctions of social stratification, education, family and the like. Not only do clerical workers come increasingly from families of factory background, and vice versa, but more and more they are merged within the same living family. The chief remaining distinction seems to be a division along the lines of sex.[27]

Lockwood's own criteria on white-collar differences are useful benchmarks to show what has changed. First, the wages of skilled manual workers overtook those of routine white-collar employees in the mid-1930s and by the 1960s, a factory worker was on average earning more than the routine office worker. By 1971, Braverman had shown for the USA, the median wages of white-collar employees was lower than every type of so-called blue-collar work. Second, job security for white-collar employees has diminished. An opinion poll in the *Sunday Times* in 1994 found, for example, that 35 percent of its 'middle class' readers were worried about losing their jobs in the coming twelve months, while one in five families had that recent experience.[28] Jobs in colleges, banks and in computing are increasingly part time or part of the growing army of contract labour. As Will Hutton puts it in the British context, 'The new jobs for Britain's middle classes – and even more worrying for their children – are part-time, self-employed or fixed contract'.[29]

Finally, the issue of promotion is more complicated because of the ambiguities involved in the category of white-collar employee. On one hand there has been a big growth in posts concerned with the management and administration of people. Heads of school, university professors and consultants are all being paid more and are also managing more staff. Entry into these grades is of some importance as it involves not only a shift to higher pay, but more autonomy in one's own job and the right to hire and fire other white-collar employees. Those in these positions are more aptly described as belonging to the 'new middle class', or as Wright puts it, people who occupy 'contradictory class locations'.[30] They operate mainly as semi-autonomous employees who are not subject to the discipline imposed by the dictates of capital and are normally involved in organising the exploitation of other white-collar employees. However, for the mass of white-collar employees, there is a ceiling put on promotions and regrading. This arose as clerical work shifted from being male dominated to being female dominated. In 1900, for example, three-quarters of all clerical employees in the USA were male, but ninety years later four-fifths of these occupations were female.[31] For the vast majority of female white-collar employees and for most of the men who work alongside them, promotion into the ranks of the new middle class has about as much reality as blue-collar workers making it into management.

This brings us then to the key problem with the notion of a contented majority: it ignores how growing numbers of white-collar employees are involved in some form of class conflict with their employers. Ever since the 1960s, white-collar trade unionism has been the major growth area for Irish unions. In 1965, only 22 percent of union members belonged to white-collar unions, but a decade later this stood at 31 percent and was rising.[32] A recent survey on attitudes to unions, which unfortunately employed the categories for social class normally associated with advertising,

nevertheless found that more than half of those who belong to the
ABC1 groupings – clerical, professional, managerial groupings –
would like to join a union.[33] Moreover, it has often been white-
collar employees who have been to the fore in pressing for militancy.
Nurses, who once accepted the Florence Nightingale image, treated
it with contempt as they embarked on a four-year campaign to win
higher pay. Sometimes the higher grades in white-collar occupations
occupy many of the leading union positions because they have
greater autonomy and resources to organise – the executive of
Ireland's largest teaching union, for example, is still composed overwhelming of teaching principals – and this leads to pressures to
adopt moderate stances. However, there are also the countervailing
pressures to resist the incessant demands for flexibility, evaluations
and more productivity.

The issue of an excluded, underclass minority may be dealt with
more briefly because, as Adonis and Pollard point out, few people
confess to opinion pollsters to belong to this category.[34] The groups
which apparently constitute the underclass vary greatly depending
which writer has constructed the category. In Galbraith's case it
seems to refer to a working poor who take on jobs which others find
distasteful.[35] Other writers use the terms to refer to the poor generally, minority ethnic groups or even occasionally, women.[36] On the
political right, the term 'underclass' is associated with a form of
moral decay. Thus Charles Murray argues, rather bizarrely, that illegitimate births are a leading indicator of the underclass and violent
crime also provides a proximate measure of its development.[37]

However, poverty is a state which affects sections of the working
class rather than constituting the basis of a class itself. Sometimes it
is a temporary state as people move in and out of jobs, but on other
occasions it is a near permanent condition as people are trapped in
low-paid employment and experience all the cumulative disadvantages that come with it. The fluid nature of the experience of poverty
was underlined in one study of the figures for the late 1980s,
'Significant numbers are escaping poverty and are being replaced,
approximately the same proportion, by others who fall below the
poverty line for the short term. The critical factor in regard to
income mobility seem to be labour market conditions and related
changes in employment status of the head of household . . .'.[38]

The exact constitution of the groupings who fall below the
poverty line varies according to political pressures, the state of the

economy and the level of working-class organisation. About one in five low-paid workers may be classified as being in poverty.[39] Others are retired workers whose poverty levels vary according to how pension and social welfare payments keep up with inflation. In 1973, the retired and those engaged in home duties made up over 43 percent of the poor but by 1987 this had fallen to 17 percent.[40] Whatever the figures, however, becoming old hardly constitutes a change of class position and the bulk of the aged are workers who are surplus to the requirements of capital. The biggest group who constitute the poor are the unemployed, who make up about one-third.[41] Ireland has had traditionally a higher proportion of long-term unemployed, but again this varies according to the state of the economy. In the late 1970s the majority of the unemployed were classified as long term, defined as being out of work for one year or more, but this has now declined significantly. All of this indicates that the concept of the 'underclass', with all its imagery of inner city denizens who live permanently on social welfare and crime, reflects more the latent fears of the privileged. Far from the socially excluded being a different class to the majority of working class, they belong to the poorest section of workers. Moreover, the gap between them and the majority of workers, both blue collar and routine white-collar, is much less than the gap between workers and the ruling class.

The US model

The most convincing case for rejecting the argument that class conflict has been replaced by a conflict between a contented majority and an underclass minority comes from the USA. The US 'miracle economy' provides an important model for the Celtic Tiger. Despite the official pronouncements of social partnership, the Irish Government has picked up on the theme about cutting business taxes and creating flexible labour markets.

However, the USA also showed that workers' experience of an economic boom in the 1990s was quite different to that in the 1960s. During the Golden Age of capitalism, the living standards of workers rose with the expansion of capital so that, as Hobsbawm asked 'what meaning could the Internationale's "Arise, ye starvelings from your slumbers" have for workers who now expected to have their car and spend their annual paid vacation on the beaches of Spain?'.[42] However, when a boom occurred in the 1990s, it was more likely to be associated with an attack on living standards. Lester Thurow has noted

> The rapid and widespread increase in inequality in the United States in the last two decades has traditionally been the province of countries experiencing a revolution or a military defeat followed by an occupation. Indeed this is the first time since the collection of income data began that the median real wages have consistently fallen over a twenty year period. And never before have the majority of American workers suffered real wage reductions while the real per capita gross domestic product (GDP) was increasing.[43]

All indicators point to a growing gap between the majority of workers and the corporate rich. Corporate profits which totalled $330 billion in 1989, the last business-cycle peak, had grown to $631 billion in 1996.[44] This 90 percent increase in profits in the seven-year period was not reflected in a greater willingness to pay taxes to finance the infrastructure which made expansion possible. A 1993 study by the Government Accounting Office found that more than 40 percent of corporations doing business in the USA with assets of $259 million paid Income Tax of less than $100,000.[45] The wealthy elite in the USA are instead paying out greater dividends to themselves as they became more confident that the American state would increase its subsidies to them.[46] Brenner explains how this emerged

> Capitalists and the wealthy accumulated wealth with such success during the 1980s largely because the state intervened directly to place money in their hands – enabling them to profit from their own business failures through lucrative bailouts, offering them massive tax breaks which played no part in the recovery of corporate balance sheets and providing them with an unprecedented array of politically constituted opportunities to get richer faster through fiscal, monetary and deregulation policies – all the expense of the greater mass of population.[47]

Increasingly, wealth was invested in finance, insurance and real estate (FIRE) rather than investment geared to raising production. By the mid-1990s, 23 percent of the private sector's net capital stock was deployed in FIRE which was more than any other industry and represented a 50 percent increase over 1977.[48]

By contrast, conditions for the majority of workers have deteriorated on a variety of fronts. CORI themselves pointed out that 'four out of five people are worse off today than they were in 1980', but unfortunately this did not lead them to question the contented majority thesis.[49] The majority of US workers have suffered from what one economist called 'a silent depression'[50], as real hourly wages peaked in 1973 and declined ever since then, with every major settlement less than in the preceding year. In 1978 the average hourly earnings of America's 77.5 million workers who occupy non-supervisor positions stood at $8.40 an hour but by 1994, they were down to $7.41 an hour.[51] The boom in the 1990s led to a continuation of this trend with real family incomes declining by 6 percent between 1989 and 1995.[52]

The decline in wages has been only one aspect of a change for the majority of US workers. The top 100 companies laid off no less than 22 percent of their workforce between 1978 and 1995 and the overwhelming number of those who returned to work with other companies accepted a wage cut.[53] The flexible, disposable employee with no benefits has become an increasing reality. So while the Fortune 500 companies reduced their workforce by 30 percent between 1993 and 1998, the number of temporary employees grew by nearly 19 percent in the period from 1995 to 1998 alone.[54] The ideal of most companies has been to create a category of 'contingent workers' – non-union employees who are hired for a limited short period to complete a particular job and who are subject to the maximum levels of exploitation.[55] On top of the job insecurity, many find that work is longer, harder and more stressful. Juliet Schor's study of *The Overworked American* found that employees were working an average of 163 more hours a year, or an extra month, than they were twenty years previously.[56]

US politicians claim that the boom has brought unemployment down to under 5 percent of the workforce. However, the real increase in jobs has been in poorly paid service jobs and self-employment where a downsized worker starts up as a cleaner or a labourer. While the manufacturing workforce fell by 830,000 between 1990 and 1996, service employment grew by 8.6 million in the same period.[57] Interestingly, the growth in non-manufacturing labour productivity fell to a shocking low of 0.2 percent a year because US employers found that wages were so cheap that there was little need to invest in extra equipment.[58] Clinton's campaign to 'end welfare as we know it' assisted the employers greatly, because it helped to define welfare rather than poverty as the central problem facing the USA.[59] Through a host of cuts in welfare programmes, many recipients have been forced to join the new servant class who clean the homes of the rich, protect their property, look after their children and wait on them in the big hotels. Instead of an underclass permanently dependent on welfare, there is an impoverished section of the workforce which moves in and out of temporary jobs.

It should be stressed that the USA provided the major model for a capitalist boom in the 1990s. All other 'models' of capitalism, whether they are the European 'social economy' or ones based on 'traditional Asian values', have failed to produce a sustained boom. The face of modern capitalism should therefore be clear. Far from a contented majority facing a deprived underclass, most workers face growing insecurity, reduced real wages and witness a transfer of wealth to those who are already privileged. In 1969, the top 1 percent of US society owned one-quarter of the wealth, but today that has risen to 40 percent.[60] No wonder *Newsweek* produced a marvellous parody of John F. Kennedy's famous promise during the boom of the 1960s that 'a rising tide would raise all boats'. One of its headlines in May 1993 was 'A Rising Tide Lifts the Yachts'.[61]

Late capitalism and class polarisation

Other approaches are clearly needed to assess what is happening in modern capitalism and, fortunately, the late 1990s produced a new questioning about the present social order. One of the reasons for this is that the experience of economic instability has undermined the confidence of even the system's own supporters. When the world economy seemed to be on the point of a generalised economic collapse in 1998, one of the leading financial speculators, George Soros, was moved to write that 'The global capitalist system that has been responsible for such remarkable prosperity is coming apart at the seams'.[62] All of this has led to a renewal of interest in the writings of Marx[63] because his analysis placed so much stress of booms and slumps and his predictions about class polarisation seem more relevant then ever. The Marxist concepts of late capitalism and class conflict present a far more useful framework from which to analyse the Celtic Tiger than any of the other approaches we have encountered so far.

The term 'late capitalism' indicates that there is a continuity in the economic dynamic of society in recent decades. For Marx, capitalism was a system built on the general production of commodities and wage labour, which is subject to exploitation. Capital contains within it a tendency to self-expansion and being 'fanatically bent on making value expand itself, he [the capitalist] forces the human race to produce for production's sake . . . Accumulation for the sake of accumulation, production for production's sake'.[64] This drive to accumulate leads to both economic chaos, when frenetic periods of expansion are followed by wasteful slumps, and also to a permanent pressure to intensify the rate of exploitation. Ireland may be an important base for producing the new information technology, but this hardly means that we are living in a post-industrial age where the possession of 'theoretical knowledge' has replaced the possession of capital in importance.[65] The market system and the huge inequalities that accompany it mean that the use of this technology is dictated by the needs of capital rather than by any altruistic pursuit of knowledge. However, there are also important differences in performance of late capitalism compared to the Golden Age of capitalism in the 1950s and 1960s.

Late capitalism is characterised by slower rates of growth and the Celtic Tiger is very much the exception, which should be seen as such. In the core of the system, growth rates have fallen consistently. From the early nineteenth century to the 1970s, the US economy grew by an average of 3.8 percent a year, which meant that real economic output doubled roughly every nineteen years, but today the growth rate in the USA has slowed to 2.1 percent a year and at that rate it would take nearly thirty-six years to double output again.[66] Table 2.1 illustrates the general decline in the growth rate of Western capitalism since 1973.

Table 2.1 Gross domestic product, various countries 1960–96 (average annual percentage change)

GDP	1960–73	1973–79	1979–90	1990–96
United States	4.0	2.6	2.4	2.1
Japan	9.2	3.5	3.9	1.6
Germany	4.3	2.4	2.1	1.7
G7	4.8	2.8	2.55	1.6

Source: R. Brenner, *The Economics of Global Turbulence* (London, New Left Review, 229 Special Issue, 1998) p. 235.

Second, generalised recessions occur at more regular intervals and as a result they cannot be explained away simply by conjunctural factors. The first major slump of the modern era occurred between 1973 and 1975 and dragged industrial production in the core zones down by 13 percent.[67] The main explanation offered by conventional economists was that the Organisation of Petroleum Exporting Countries (OPEC) oil cartel had held the world to ransom. The fact that the downturn in the world system had begun before the increase in oil prices was virtually ignored. When another slump occurred in 1980, this time after the OPEC oil cartel was broken up, the explanation offered by Milton Friedman and others was that public spending was to blame.[68] Yet public spending had increased in all industrial countries after the Second World War and still a long boom ensued. After a decade when Friedman's monetarist policies held sway in most industrial countries, another major recession struck in 1989. Then, after most parts of the world recovered, a major slump broke out in east Asia in the 1997, affecting up to 40 percent of the world.

Third, as industrial production faced a more unstable future, there has been an explosion in financial and share speculation. Despite the sluggish growth of the US economy, for example, the paper value of equities has risen from 0.7 times annualised income to 2.1 times annualised income.[69] The main reason for this has been an unprecedented bull run on share prices which rose to a 125 year high – at least until recently.[70] Overall there has been an explosion of financial instruments on the world economy, with an equivalent value of the US economy passing through the global financial exchanges each day. Between 1986 and 1997, for example, the market for 'financial derivatives' such as interest rates futures, currency options and stock-market index futures has grown from $618 billion to $12,207.3 billion.[71]

Fourth, the internationalisation of capital has meant that states can no longer exercise the same degree of control over their national economies as they did in the past. In most countries, exchange controls have been removed and capital can leave the country more easily when it disapproves of government policy. When the Mitterrand Government in France, for example, tried to operate a Keynesian policy of reflation in the 1980s it was severely undermined when capital began to leave the country. As Mitterrand refused to take more radical action to deal with this outflow, he was

eventually forced to retreat from his own policies. The internationalisation of capital does not to mean that companies do not seek the
protection of a nation state. Nor does it mean that because of 'globalisation' capital can move around the world at will.[72] Nevertheless,
it does suggest that individual states are in a weaker position to
adopt reflationary or protectionist measures.

In brief, late capitalism is characterised by a high degree of
instability and this in turn means that there are important changes
occurring in the relationship between the contending classes. One
baseline definition of social class is 'A group of persons in a community identified by their position in the whole system of social production, defined above all by their relationship (primarily in terms
of degree of ownership or control) to the conditions of production
(that is to say, to the means and labour of production) and to other
classes'.[73] It should be noted that this definition makes no reference
to forms of lifestyle, consumption patterns or status gradation, but
focuses on objective conditions. It follows, that, as Callinicos points
out, the term 'working class' does not necessarily imply solely
manual workers.[74] If the sale of labour is qualified by the absence of
control or autonomy over the conditions of work, then the majority of those currently classified as white-collar may be assumed to
be part of an expanded working class. The point of this discussion
is not to trade possible definitions or categorisation systems, but to
point to some connection between the changing nature of late capitalism and the behaviour of different social groups in modern
society. The connection is best captured by the concept of class polarisation.

Class polarisation may be deemed to operate at both a structural
and a political level. At the level of the state, governments of all hues
are more likely to help to redistribute resources away from the
working population and towards the owners of capital. In brief,
instead of a trickle-down effect there is a steady stream flowing the
other way. This may be achieved in a variety of ways, including cuts
in social spending to make way for increased subsidies for the
wealthy. At the level of the broader economy, Marx's traditional categories on how capitalism responds to its difficulties are relevant.[75]
One way, he argued, that capitalists respond to threats to their rate
of profit is to increase 'relative surplus value'. This means extracting more value from workers during the course of the existing
working day. The emphasis on 'flexibility' or removing 'downtime'

reflects this tendency to intensify work effort. Far from being neutral concepts that flow from the needs of modern technology, they reflect a drive to increase the rate of exploitation. Another way that Marx argued that capitalists respond is to increase 'absolute surplus value' by lengthening the number of hours worked. The demands for 'annualised hours' which attempt to undermine the notion of a weekend break or set periods of holidays are relevant here. So too is the introduction of more complex shift patterns or the pressure for compulsory overtime work, which sparked a major strike in General Motors plants in the USA. Finally, Marx pointed to a pattern of 'immiseration' of sections of the working class. The pressure to reduce pay for new entrant grades even when they do the same work as older workers reflects this.

The term 'class polarisation' does not just imply a changed objective relationship but a prediction about the actual behaviour of different social classes. Many have generalised from the Reagan–Thatcher years to assume that there would be no response from a working class that was believed close to extinction. However, the removal of long-term expectations such as the belief that one's sons and daughters should expect better economic standards than their parents, that people have a right to be cared for while sick, regardless of their income, or that the average Irish worker could aspire to own his or her own home, implicitly carries with it the possibility of greater social conflict. New struggles in a variety of countries would tend to confirm the re-emergence of forms of class conflict. The waves of strikes in the USA and Canada, the general strike in France in 1995 and the extensive resistance to downsizing in South Korea all testify to growing resistance by workers. Even at a more muted level the return of social democratic governments to every country in Europe in the late 1990s, with the exception of Ireland and Spain, may also be an indicator of growing awareness of class division. Contrary to some impressions, it would appear that the reported death of class conflict has been greatly exaggerated.

All of this therefore provides the background for an examination of the Celtic Tiger. Over the next two chapters we shall examine evidence to show the degree of polarisation between the social classes. Although the Irish economy is an exception in terms of its growth rates, the corporate elite who dominate are more than aware that it is an exception. Their behaviour is shaped by the knowledge that as Ireland makes up a tiny part of the global economy, they face a highly unstable world. This means that the pressure for a transfer of wealth to those who already possess an abundance of it is as relentless as elsewhere.

Notes

1 *Socialist Worker* (21 July 1999).
2 J. Davies, 'Towards a Theory of Revolution', *American Sociological Review*, 27:1 (1962) pp. 5–19.
3 B. Sheehan, 'Reaction to ESRI's Call for Restraint May Have Missed the Real Issue', *Industrial Relations News* (11 March 1999).
4 *Report of National Minimum Wage Commission* (Dublin, Stationary Office, 1998) p. 58.
5 T. Eagleton, *Ideology: An Introduction* (London, Verso, 1991) p. 30.
6 C. Cousins, 'Social Exclusion in Europe', *Policy and Politics*, 26:2 (1997) pp. 127–45.
7 K. Thompson, *Emile Durkheim* (Milton Keynes, Open University, 1982) p. 45.
8 Quoted in J. Berghman, 'The Resurgence of Poverty and the Struggle Against Exclusion: A New Challenge for Social Security in Europe', *International Social Security Review*, 50:1 (1997) pp. 3–21.
9 B. Bartley, 'Spatial Planning and Poverty in North Clondalkin' in D. Pringle, J. Walsh and M. Hennessy (eds) *Poor People, Poor Places: A Geography of Poverty and Deprivation in Ireland* (Dublin, Oak Tree Press, 1999) pp. 225–63.
10 H. Silver, 'Social Exclusion and Social Solidarity: Three Paradigms', *International Labour Review*, 133:5/6 (1994) p. 543.
11 Berghman, 'Resurgence of Poverty', pp. 17–18.
12 S. Healy and B. Reynolds, 'The Future of Work: A Challenge to Society' in B. Reynolds and S. Healy (eds) *Work, Unemployment and Job Creation* (Dublin, Justice Commission, Conference of Major Religious Superiors, 1990) p. 66.
13 G. Esping-Andersen, *The Three Worlds of Welfare Capitalism* (Cambridge, Polity Press, 1990).
14 de Valera to Ruttledge (n.d.). Quoted in T. Ryle Dwyer, *de Valera: The Man and the Myth* (Dublin, Poolbeg, 1991) p. 134.
15 K. Allen, *Fianna Fail and Irish Labour: 1926 to the Present* (London, Pluto Press, 1997) p. 137.
16 R. Breen, D. Hannan, D. Rottman and C. Whelan, *Understanding Contemporary Ireland: State Class and Development in the Republic of Ireland* (London, Macmillan, 1990) p. 11.
17 Ibid. p. 59.
18 Ibid. p. 68.

19 J. K. Galbraith, *The Culture of Contentment* (London, Sinclair-Stevenson, 1992) p. 18.

20 Ibid. p. 19–20.

21 Conference of Religious in Ireland, *Growing Exclusion* (Dublin, CORI, 1993) p. 15.

22 S. Aronowitz, *False Promises: The Shaping of American Working Class* (New York, McGraw Hill, 1973) p. 33.

23 D. Lockwood, *The Blackcoated Worker* (London, Allen and Unwin, 1989) p. 218.

24 See J. Goldthorpe, *Social Mobility and Class Structure in Britain* (Oxford, Clarendon Press, 1987) and R. Breen and C. Whelan, *Social Mobility and Social Class in Ireland* (Dublin, Gill and Macmillan, 1996).

25 D. Gluckstein, *The Nazis, Capitalism and the Working Class* (London, Bookmarks, 1999) p. 85.

26 Quoted in H. Braverman, *Labour and Monopoly Capital: The Degradation of Work in the Twentieth Century* (New York, Monthly Review Press, 1974) p. 294.

27 Ibid. p. 353.

28 Quoted in W. Hutton, 'Bad Times for the Good Life', *Guardian* (2 August 1994).

29 Ibid.

30 E. O. Wright, *Classes* (London, Verso, 1985) Ch. 2.

31 N. Stockman, N. Bonney and S. Xuewen *Women's Work in East and West: The Dual Burden of Employment and Family Life* (London, UCL Press, 1995) p. 70–1.

32 W. K. Roche and J. Larragy, 'The Trend of Unionisation in the Republic of Ireland' in Department of Industrial Relations, UCD (eds) *Industrial Relations in Ireland* (Dublin, UCD, 1987) p. 25.

33 ICTU, *What People Think of Unions* (Dublin, ICTU, 1968) p. 15.

34 A. Adonis and S. Pollard, *A Class Act: The Myth of Britain's Classless Society* (London, Penguin Books, 1997) p. 9.

35 Galbraith, *Culture of Contentment*, p. 33.

36 D. Gallie, 'Employment, Unemployment, and Social Stratification' in D. Gallie (ed.) *Employment in Britain* (Oxford, Blackwell, 1990) pp. 465–93.

37 C. Murray, *The Emerging British Underclass* (London, IEA, Health Welfare Unit, 1990)

38 J. Williams and B. Whelan, 'Poverty: Temporary or Permanent' in B. Nolan and T. Callan (eds) *Poverty and Policy in Ireland* (Dublin, Gill and Macmillan, 1994) p. 93.

39 B. Nolan, 'Low Pay and Poverty' in Nolan and Callan, *Poverty and Policy in Ireland*, p. 129.

40 T. Callan, B. Nolan and C. Whelan, 'Who are the Poor?' in Nolan and Callan, *Poverty and Policy in Ireland*, p. 70.
41 Ibid. p. 70.
42 E. Hobsbawm, *The Age of Extremes: The Short History of the Twentieth Century* (London, Michael Joseph, 1994) p. 267.
43 L. Thurow, 'Almost Everywhere: Surging Inequality and Falling Real Wages' in C. Kaysen (ed.) *The American Corporation Today* (New York, Oxford University Press, 1996) p. 383.
44 *Economic Report of the President* (Washington, US Government Printing Office, 1997) p. 401.
45 K. Danagher, *Corporations are Going to Get Your Mama* (Monroe, Maine, 1996) p. 40.
46 R. Brenner, *The Economics of Global Turbulence* (London, New Left Review 229 Special Issue, 1998) p. 209.
47 Ibid. p. 207.
48 Ibid. p. 211.
49 Conference of Major Religious Superiors in Ireland, *Growing Exclusion* (Dublin, CORI, 1993) p. 17.
50 W. Petersen, *Silent Depression: The Fate of the American Dream* (New York, WW Norton, 1994).
51 L. Elliot and D. Atkinson, *The Age of Insecurity* (London, Verso, 1998) p. 240.
52 Ibid. p. 243.
53 Brenner, *Economics of Global Turbulence*, p. 200.
54 S. Weber, 'The End of the Business Cycle', *Foreign Affairs*, 76:4 (July/August 1997), p. 72.
55 Brenner, *Economics of Global Turbulence*, p. 201.
56 J. Schor, *The Overworked American: The Unexpected Decline of Leisure* (New York, Basic Books, 1992) p. 29–30.
57 Brenner, *Economics of Global Turbulence*, p. 204.
58 Ibid. p. 205.
59 J. O'Connor, 'US Social Welfare Policy: The Reagan Record and Legacy', *Journal of Social Policy*, 27:1 (1998) pp. 37–62.
60 Elliot and Atkinson, *Age of Insecurity*, p. 244.
61 Quoted in J. Geier and A. Shawki, 'Contradictions of the "Miracle" Economy', *International Socialism Review 2*, Fall (1997) p. 8.
62 L. Elliot, 'The Silence of the Sushi Bar', *Guardian* (19 September 1998).
63 See J. Cassidy, 'The Next Big Thinker', *Independent on Sunday* (7 December 1997).
64 Quoted in C. Harman, *The Economics of the Madhouse* (London, Bookmarks, 1997) p. 30.
65 D. Bell, *The Coming of the Post-Industrial Society* (Harmondsworth, Penguin, 1976).

66 B. Bluestone and B. Harrisson, 'Why we can Grow Faster', *The American Prospect*, no 34, p. 63.

67 N. Harris, *Of Bread and Guns: The World Economy in Crisis* (Harmondsworth, Penguin, 1983) p. 76.

68 E. Butler, *Milton Friedman: A Guide to His Economic Thought* (Aldershot, Gower, 1985) Ch. 9. See also, M. Friedman, *There's No Such Thing as a Free Lunch* (La Salle, Open Court, 1975).

69 M. Wolff, 'Threats of Depression', *Financial Times* (26 August 1998).

70 D. Henwood, *Wall St* (London, Verso, 1998) p. 3.

71 IMF, *International Capital Markets: Developments, Prospects and Policies*, September 1998 (Washington, IMF, 1998) p. 99.

72 P. Hirst and G. Thompson, *Globalization in Question* (Cambridge, Polity, 1996)

73 G.E.M. de Ste Croix, *The Class Struggle in Ancient Greek World* (London, Duckworth, 1981) p. 43.

74 A. Callinicos, 'The New Middle Class and Socialist Politics' in A. Callinicos and C. Harman, *The Changing Working Class: Essays on Class Structure Today* (London, Bookmarks, 1987).

75 K. Marx, *Capital Volume 3* (London, Lawrence and Wishart, 1959) pp. 232–40.

3
Who got the main share of the Celtic Tiger?

The Ryanair company is a powerful symbol for the Celtic Tiger. It presents itself as a trusting, dynamic concern that cuts through the red tape of state bureaucracy. An aggressive, 'no frills' airline which prides itself on cheap fares, it is also immensely profitable. When the company's shares were floated on the Stock Exchange, the Ryan family who founded the company gained £117 million for selling a quarter of the shares, while Michael O'Leary, the chief executive, received £17 million for his shares.[1] O'Leary was quite forthright about how he deserves this money and once informed a business magazine that 'I'd love to spend the rest of my life in Barbados, with a load of babes'.[2]

Yet Ryanair presents a different image to many workers. When thirty-nine baggage handlers joined Ireland's largest union, Services, Industrial, Professional and Technical Union (SIPTU), the company refused to recognise them or even go to the Labour Court to discuss their grievances. When the workers took industrial action their security passes were withdrawn, effectively locking them out of the airport. Within a short period of time, other workers in Dublin airport struck in solidarity and scores of union activists ran up the runway to block airplanes taking off. The media denounced the 'anarchy at Dublin airport' but it was a sudden and unexpected illustration of the power of workers.[3] However, after two days when the airport was closed, the SIPTU leadership persuaded the Ryanair workers to lift the pickets. Soon afterwards one of the leading union activists in Ryanair was sacked and the union failed to win recognition.[4] 'It was a case of defeat being snatched from the jaws of victory' is how one activist put it.[5]

If Ryanair is a symbol of the success of the Celtic Tiger, then it is also a symbol of the bitter class polarisation that lies underneath it. It raises questions about how we are to assess the economic inequalities that have grown with the boom. The extraordinary personal wealth that Michael O' Leary and the Ryanair family have accumulated may be exceptional, but just how exceptional is it? While official Irish society barely recognises the reality of class, many are acutely aware of the growing disparity of incomes, yet research on the scale of class inequality in Ireland is still in its infancy.

The most important source of information on poverty and wealth is the official statistics, because only governments have the resources to measure flows of money, trends in taxation or social welfare. Moreover, they can exercise some degree of compulsion to ensure that at least part of an individual's income enters the public domain. This is why the publications of the Central Statistic Office (CSO), the Central Bank, the Revenue Commissioners and various government reports are an essential tool for examining the degree of inequality. However, there is also a problem with these sources, as official statistics are gathered according to the needs of a state which rules over a class society. They originally emerged with the rational accounting culture of capitalism and were designed to serve its needs. According to one study, it was 'only when commodity production became widespread that recognisably statistical activity emerged but it is with the domination of industrial capital that statistics became universal'.[6]

Sometimes government statistics are blatantly biased and one former British Government Minister, Ian Gilmour, has acknowledged that measuring poverty was very difficult under Margaret Thatcher because of the 'deliberate obfuscation of government statistics'.[7] Similar considerations apply to Irish statistics on wealth. While there have been many studies done on the poor, very few have appeared on exactly how the Irish rich operate. One reason is that statistics provided by the state provide little help in making scientific assessments about the concentration of wealth. In 1989 Sean Byrne noted that 'much interesting data which could be collected about the personal distribution of wealth is not collected or if collected, not published to preserve confidentially. The wealthy generally do not wish attention to be focused on their wealth or the means by which they acquire or retain it'.[8] Many of his points are still relevant today. There is no information provided on bank deposits at various levels. One can calculate exactly how many people receive

Family Income Supplement or a Lone Parents Allowance but there is no information on how many people have banks accounts of more than, say, £30,000 or £40,000. Typically the CSO agglomerates data which has the effect of hiding particular figures. Byrne cited the example of farm holdings where the largest acreage published in the *Statistical Abstract* was 150 acres and holdings beyond this were not categorised for reasons of 'confidentiality'.[9] A decade later, the largest farm size category is over 100 hectares but there is no breakdown beyond this. Statistics on national income combine figures for profits with figures for professional earnings, dividends and income from land and building. All of these are derived from some form of capital but there are no figures for the numbers of individuals receiving dividends at particular levels. Similarly, while there are overall statistics which show how many individuals have private insurance, these figures are not broken down to see how many take out the more expensive plans which yield higher tax benefits. At best therefore, the available figures give only crude indications of the inequality between classes, but they are nevertheless the only ones we have.

Redistribution to the wealthy

The year 1987 was supposed to be the start of a new era when management and unions co-operated to get the Irish economy out of the doldrums and share the wealth between them. The Programme for National Recovery committed the social partners to 'seek to regenerate the economy and improve the social equity of our society through their combined efforts'.[10] The year therefore serves as a useful benchmark for assessing how the major classes fared in the following decade.

Even the most cursory glance at the official National Income and Expenditure figures for the decade after 1987 shows there has been a systematic transfer of wealth to the better-off sections of Irish society. As Table 3.1 illustrates, the share of the national economy going to wages, pensions and social security has declined by 10 percent. By contrast, the share going to unearned income in the form of profits, interest, dividends and rent has risen by 10 percent. This transfer of wealth is unprecedented and could only have occurred because, as one US labour leader put it, there has been a 'one sided class war'.[11] Behind these statistics lies a determined strategy to increase profitability through an unprecedented drive to raise pro-

Table 3.1   Changing factor prices of non-agricultural income

	1987 %	1992 %	1997 %
Profits, interest, dividends, rent	31	36	41
Wages, pensions, social security	69	64	59

Source: Central Statistics Office, *National Income and Expenditure Release*, 30 June 1999, Table 2, various years.

ductivity. Tax rates of capital have also been cut and the wealthy have taken advantage of numerous state subsidies to increase their wealth. Yet at the same time wage increases have been pegged down, despite the unprecedented boom.

One of the key results of social partnership was that any claimed link between profits and wages was severed. In the past, workers in the private sector made wage claims either to catch up on awards granted to other workers or to gain a share in increased profits. However, while profits have grown quite quickly in the Celtic Tiger, wages have been held in check. Industry provides the most dramatic example of the divergence between the growth of profits and remuneration for employees. Between 1990 and 1997, industrial profits have increased by 144 percent while wages have grown by 59 percent.[12] In other areas such as agriculture, transport and distribution, the rise in profits has not been so large and as a result this lowers the overall discrepancy between the rise of profits and wages. However, the average profit growth for every year between 1990 and 1998 was 50 percent above the rate of growth of wages.[13]

In some ways this is not surprising as Ireland claims to offer US multi-nationals one of their highest rates of profit in the world. Officially, US companies are making a 25 percent rate of return on their investment in Ireland and this is more than double the return from Portugal, three times Spain and five times Britain.[14] These figures undoubtedly contain an important degree of exaggeration, because multi-nationals manipulate their internal pricing structure to benefit from Ireland's status as a tax haven. Nevertheless, even if multi-nationals are only receiving half the rate of profit they claim, they are doing exceptionally well. Moreover, they are not alone because, contrary to some impressions, the profit levels of indigenous companies have also risen substantially. Forfas, the development agency for indigenous industry, does not calculate profits as a percentage return on the capital employed (ROCE) but rather uses figures based on profits as a percentage of sales. They also do not maintain a consistent table over a ten-year period and comparisons can only be taken as general indicators. Nevertheless, it is clear that the profitability in Irish-owned companies stood at 3.3 percent of sales in 1987, whereas a decade later this had nearly doubled to 6.1 percent of sales.[15]

One remarkable feature of the Irish boom is that this high level of profits was not reflected in a surge in investment. In fact the ratio of fixed investment to GDP almost halved between 1980 and 1994[16] and capital intensity of output is among the lowest in Europe.[17] Fixed capital in the form of machinery and equipment, for example, has fallen in manufacturing from £691 million to £525 million in constant prices between 1990 and 1995.[18] This occurred despite the huge flow of foreign direct investment and the build up of EU structural funds. After 1995, the level of investment picked up somewhat, but this did not signify a major shift in the pattern. Much of it came from an accelerated influx of US capital and from a dramatic rise in investment in building and construction. The overall investment ratio remained at under 20 percent of GDP, which was lower than it was in the early 1980s. The low level of investment has meant that the huge profits levels went elsewhere.

Where did the wealth go? One answer is that a considerable proportion of it flowed out of the country. Since the early 1990s, the outflow of funds from Ireland has accelerated dramatically and one way this shows up in the official figures is in payments for royalties and licenses. Multi-nationals, who engage in transfer pricing, often recoup some of their money that was officially used in Ireland by charging their Irish branch plants a high price for the use of equipment that was developed elsewhere. Between 1991 and 1998 the outflow of money on royalties and licenses grew by a staggering 443 percent. However, the other major growth area has been the re-export of dividends and profits which grew by 210 percent over the same period.[19] In all, the actual outflow revealed in the balance of payments figures for 1998 is near to £12,000 million which is, as Colm Rapple points out, 'about £3,700 for every man, woman and child in the country'.[20]

Another destination for the new wealth has been the Irish Stock

Exchange. Traditionally, this was a small exchange where a few institutional investors from pension and insurance funds followed the movements of well-established Irish firms. However, this has changed dramatically in recent years as a series of tax cuts has opened the way to a surge of new investors. Between the mid-1980s and 1997, the Capital Gains Tax fell from 60 to 20 percent and this has offered a considerable incentive to the wealthy to engage in speculation on share price movements in the hope of windfall profits. The shift towards a single European currency and the relaxation of exchange controls has also brought a surge of foreign investors seeking Irish stocks and today overseas institutions account for nearly 40 percent of the stock market.[21] All of this has helped to drive the Stock Market to giddy heights. Since 1993, the stock exchange has experienced a 'bull run' where shares seem to rise effortlessly. The baseline of the Stock Exchange index is set at 1,000 for the prices that were available on 4 January 1988 and between 1988 and 1993, the index only moved by 262 points. However, since then the index has increased a full 3,810 points.[22] As one of Ireland's major unions has pointed out, share values increased by a phenomenal £14 billion in 1997 alone.[23] Of course these were paper values, but if you had the paper and chose to sell, you could have made a fortune. Figure 3.1 illustrates the enormous growth of Irish share prices.

Speculation on share prices has also been a predominant feature of the US Goldilocks boom of the 1990s. Supporters of the stock markets claim that they play an important role in raising capital for industry and so supporting jobs but it is doubtful if this is the case to any significant degree. Henwood in his study of Wall Street estimated that stocks only financed 5 percent of real investment between 1945 and 1979[24] and since then the share of corporate profits paid out in dividends has grown dramatically. During the long post-war boom in capitalism, US firms typically paid out 44 percent of their after-tax profits as dividends, but by the 1990s non-financial corporations were paying out 60 percent in dividends.[25] Much of that was recycled onto the Stock Exchanges, where it chased after shares which rose in price in a way that was often unrelated to any increase in real production or even sometimes to profit levels. The Internet shares which surged in price even though no profits were returned are a more than eloquent testimony to the growth of this bubble economy.

A similar pattern of share price speculation has emerged with the

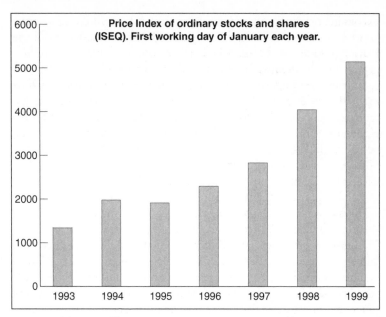

Source: CSO, *Monthly Economic Series*, June 1999, Table 8.28.

Celtic Tiger and the level of dividends payments is also quite high. According to one estimate, dividends and interest payments took up between 60 and 70 percent of all profits made in Ireland between 1990 and 1997.[26] Many of these dividend payments also found their way back onto stock exchanges, where they sought a return on capital employed, or a ROCE according to the jargon of the financial journalists, that was higher than was generated in the real economy. The spectacular performer of the Irish Stock Exchange was Elan corporation, which gave its investors a 2,043 percent rate of return over a ten-year period.[27] The search for phenomenal profits from share dealing has also led to some extraordinary forms of behaviour. Powerscreen, for example, saw a huge surge in share prices, until it was discovered that one of its subsidiaries, Matbro, lost £47 million in a bookkeeping error. Replacements for defective tractors it sold were apparently counted as new sales![28]

The Stock Exchange is only one part of an aggressive financial sector that has mushroomed with the Celtic Tiger. Ireland always had a highly developed banking system and even after the great famine of 1847 there was an extensive banking network that siphoned funds off to the metropolitan centre of the British Empire. When Fianna Fail was first established it denounced the banks as satellites of the Bank of England and Sean McEntee, one of the party's chief spokesperson on economic matters, even claimed that, 'The banks which have been bleeding the Irish farmer, crushing Irish industry, investing Irish money abroad, jeopardising it in British securities want to retain the present (Cumman na Gaedheal) government in office for their purposes . . . A Fianna Fail government would not be tied up with the old Unionist Party and the banks'.[29] Fianna Fail however soon learnt that the logic of the market allowed for no simple distinction between productive capital and the financial sector, as the wealthy demanded to invest when and where they pleased.

Far from the new republican elite distancing themselves from the banks, they soon learned to embrace their interests and concerns. The admiration was clearly mutual and in the 1970s, the Allied Irish Bank (AIB) allowed the debt of the rising Fianna Fail star Charles Haughey to increase to just over £1 million, even though this figure represented a considerable proportion of the bank's funds at the time.[30] Fianna Fail leaders were not the only recipient of AIB's generosity, as they also wrote off a £140,000 bad debt for Garrett Fitzgerald, the former Fine Gael leader after he left office. The National Irish Bank also wrote off a debt of £263,540 in return for a mere £20,000 for a Fianna Fail Teachta Dala (TD), John Ellis. Ellis was in danger of being declared bankrupt and his withdrawal from the Dail might have caused the collapse of the Haughey Government in 1990.[31] On top of supporting the personal lifestyle of prominent politicians, the AIB also funds all the major political parties in proportion to their votes.

The close relationship between the banks and the political elite has paid off – for the banks. Profits at the two main Irish banks, the AIB and the Bank of Ireland, have risen astronomically, so that they are now making over £2 million per day. The after-tax profits of the Bank of Ireland have grown by 570 percent since 1990, while the AIB which used to make £65 million in after-tax profits in 1987 made £535 million in 1998. The surge in profits reflects the growth in the Irish economy, but it also indicates that the banks are taking a bigger slice of the surplus. This occurs because Irish banks have the highest interest margins in Europe.[32] Under the 'productivity clauses' of the various partnership agreements, the wages of the majority of workers also go directly to the banks and this captive market means that banks can impose relatively high charges for normal transactions. By portraying themselves as an essential component of the nation, the banks have also been able to call on state support. In 1984, for example, the Irish Government organised a rescue package for an AIB insurance subsidiary to prevent the whole bank facing bankruptcy. Yet it failed to take out any shares in the return for this rescue package even though, according to one former minister, those shares would have been worth in excess of £1 billion today.[33] The AIB initially refused to make any contribution to a second tranche of funds for the rescue package in 1989 and when it eventually did so, it made a relatively derisory offer and claimed the right to write off these expenses for tax purposes.[34]

The development of Ireland's financial sector culminated in the formation of the International Financial Services Centre (IFSC) in 1987. The proposal for the Centre came from a Dublin-based stockbroker, Dermot Desmond, who worked closely with Charles Haughey and one of the first initiatives of the Haughey Government was to establish a 10 percent rate of tax for finance houses who used the Centre. By 1989, a road show was organised to promote the IFSC in New York because US companies needed to gain access to a head office that was regulated by the Central Bank of one of the twelve EU states if they were to operate in this market. Ireland was promoted as their most effective tax haven and since then the IFSC has established itself as a major rival to other offshore centres such as the Cayman Islands, Luxembourg and the Channel Islands. Its particular advantage is that it combines a low tax haven inside the EU with a liberal regime of regulation.[35] According to one survey over $116 billion of funds were being administered or managed at the IFSC on 30 April 1998. Yet despite this enormous wealth, the Centre still pays some of the lowest wages in the financial world. According to the recruiting agency Merc Partners, 'in most sectors and job categories, salaries in Dublin are near the bottom of the scale'.[36] Indeed so low are the salaries that the annual turnover of staff was running at an amazing 21 percent in 1998.[37] One of the largest employers at the Centre is Citibank who aim to recruit another 1,300 employees over the next few years. Six out of every ten new employees will take up employment with an annual salary of £10,000, which means that their take home pay will be only slightly more than the minimum wage of £4.40 an hour.[38]

Another section of the rich who have done extremely well in the

Celtic Tiger are property owners and builders because the owner-ship of property has traditionally been heavily subsidised and there are myriad tax breaks for the discerning investor. Although major cities are crammed with cars, there are tax allowances available for multi-storey carparks which act as magnets for ever more cars. There are also even schemes for building seaside resorts where the initial investment and rental income can be written off for tax pur-poses. Investors in commercial property benefit from incentives available under the Urban Renewals schemes which began in 1984. These established designated areas in parts of the city, such as Temple Bar in Dublin where over £8 million was advanced of public funds to reconfigure the area as Dublin's Latin Quarter.[39] Yet Temple Bar forms only part of Dublin's south inner city and a few minutes walk from the kitsch bohemian restaurants lie parts of the Liberties which are wracked by heroin, yet this area has not bene-fited from a similar injection of funds. Overall it is estimated that the subsidies paid out to property developers in the Urban Renewal areas has amounted to approximately £461 million.[40]

These subsidies only added to the high returns that building firms and the large property owners have made. Ireland's largest building firm, Sisks, has seen its profits grow six times between 1994 and 1997, while the profits of one of its rivals, G & T Crampton, trebled in 1997 alone.[41] One of the main reasons has been the escalation of prices in both commercial and residential property. In the year up to March 1999, capital values in the office sector grew by 35 percent and in the retail sector by 31 percent.[42] The main reason why the capital values escalated is that rent on such property has risen to astronomical heights. Prime office rents in the Celtic Tiger are now in excess of £247 per square metre.[43] Prime retail units can command an annual rent of £2,150 per square metre while £1,290 is charged for an equivalent space in new shopping areas.[44] In the residential sector, builders are virtually guaranteed high rates of return because of the escalation in house prices. One senior planner at the South Dublin Council has estimated that builders are getting a 100 percent profit on every house they build.[45]

Here then are some of the main beneficiaries of the Celtic Tiger. The multi-national companies and the Irish corporate elite, the directors of the banks and the growing financial sector, the large property owners and building firms all possessed money to begin with and state policy has been designed to ensure they made more in the vague hope that there might be a trickle-down effect. 'What's good for business is good for Ireland' has become the motto of all the main parties. The very vocabulary of the Celtic Tiger reflects the self-affirmation of this class as the 'entrepreneur' has replaced the rebel as the hero of modern society. No school board, government agency or charity can do without the 'entrepreneurial spirit' that is supposed to guarantee efficiency by subjecting everything to 'market forces'. Discussion of the scale of their wealth is dismissed as 'begrudgery' or the 'politics of envy'. Yet the owners of capital have forged themselves into a tight network which measures every action of the state in terms of how it serves their interests.

These are not, however, the sole beneficiaries of the booming economy. The striking thing about the very wealthy is often their very invisibility, their concern to 'get on with the job' of making money while avoiding the public eye. Few actual capitalists, for example, sit in Parliament, they tend to leave it to members of the professional classes to represent their interests. Advanced Western industrial societies have produced a wider layer of managers, accountants and barristers who directly or indirectly aid the process of exploitation, while formally living off salaries themselves. As we have seen in Chapter 2, a number of writers have referred to this grouping as a 'new middle class'. They tend to live on very large salaries and to occupy positions where they are not subjected to the dictates of capital in a direct way. Their working lives are self-directed, often geared to managing people and facilitating the process of extracting surplus value. Unlike the old petty bourgeoisie, they do not necessarily possess property in terms of shop, pubs or farms – although they have increasingly speculated on the property boom – but are often inserted into the upper echelons of white-collar grades.[46]

They also, however, comprise a relatively small number of people. One of the useful features of the Revenue Commissioners' reports is that they attempt to categorise the population into a number of income ranges for tax purposes. There is obviously a problem here, as a recent inquiry has found that the wealthy illegally used fake non-resident accounts to hide parts of their income. The new middle class are more likely to find ways of underestimating their income through the use of accountants or through measures which ensure they receive payments in non-wage forms – for example, benefits in kind, vouchers for child care or holidays. Nevertheless, even if we take this into account and measure the new middle class by a rough baseline salary, their number still appears strikingly small. The last Revenue Commissioners' report which covers the tax year 1995–96 shows that only 57,227 people or just 4 percent of Income Tax payers earned over £40,000. If we push that baseline figure down to include some higher paid workers, we still find that only 6 percent earned over £35,000 or 9 percent earned over £30,000.[47] Even if we take into account the widespread practice of placing unearned income into non-residential accounts to avoid tax, the segment of the population which includes owners of capital and the new middle class amounts to something between 15 and 20 percent of the Irish population.

The growing gap between these social classes and the rest of the population is reflected in some interesting patterns of consumption. As O'Hearn has pointed out, one of the extraordinary features of the Celtic Tiger is that its phenomenal growth has been accompanied by a fall in the share of GDP going to private consumption. So while private consumption accounted for 59.3 percent of GDP in 1987, it had decreased to 52.2 percent in 1997.[48] This fall reflects that fact that GDP is artificially inflated through transfer pricing, but it also provides an additional indication that while the general mass of the population may have seen some benefits, they are in fact receiving a declining share of the overall economy. However, if there has been a fall in the share of the national economy going into general consumption, the luxury consumption of the rich and the new middle class has increased quite dramatically. Prestige cars, for example, have typically functioned as a symbol of conspicuous consumption for the wealthy and sales of cars with price range from £26,000 to £50,000 have grown dramatically (see Table 3.2).

Another form of luxury consumption is the growth of private education. Traditionally, Ireland has had a finely tuned class system in education. Vocational schools were geared to the children of skilled and unskilled manual workers and were often underfunded. In almost every provincial town, there was a 'good school' which educated the sons and daughters of higher professionals. The religious managers had an acute sense of class distinction and all manner of informal entrance tests were used to check that children came from both the right address and had parents with the right occupations. Yet the vast majority of the children of the upper professional grades still went to a state school system and the elaborate system of public schools – or more precisely fee-paying private schools –

Table 3.2   Sales of luxury cars 1987–97

Year	Audi	BMW	Mercedes	Other	Total
1987	432	468	490	216	1606
1988	402	609	385	195	1591
1989	678	910	568	251	2401
1990	648	935	799	272	2653
1991	640	814	804	220	2478
1992	863	744	649	267	2523
1993	635	596	606	252	2089
1994	813	808	1,126	404	3151
1995	1,055	1,052	1,059	447	3613
1996	1,470	1,174	1,452	478	4574
1997	1,563	1,780	1,869	597	5789

Source: Society of Irish Motoring.

which characterised the British class system seemed to be absent. However, this is now changing. The wealthier sections of the population still mainly rely on publicly funded primary schools and the numbers attending private primary schools have only fluctuated between 7,000 and 8,000 throughout this decade.[49] The main reason is that the teachers in these schools do not receive the equivalent salaries of state teachers and as result tend to be less qualified. At second level, however, this does not apply and there has been a growth in private education. Top schools such as St Andrews College, Blackrock and Belvedere now have waiting lists that stretch into the year 2010.[50] In the five years between 1993 and 1998, the numbers attending fee-paying schools has jumped by 8 percent and 24,503 children are now enrolled in this form of segregated education.[51] Table 3.3 illustrates some of the costs the new middle class are now bearing for private education.

There is overwhelming evidence, then, to suggest a very small and highly contented minority have gained from the boom and the Celtic Tiger has not only served their needs but expanded their appetites for more. Yet the experience of the majority of workers who produce the wealth is very different. In the following section we look at how they have lost out in one important aspect, on the direct income and salaries they receive. In the next chapter we will examine how the low level of state spending of basic services has affected them.

Table 3.3   Fees at Ireland's top private schools

School	Boarding fee	Day fee
St. Columba's College, Dublin	£6,675	£3,855
Sutton Park, Dublin	£4,800	£2,000/£3,000
Blackrock College, Dublin	£4,700	£2,000
Castleknock College, Dublin	£4,700	£1,670
The King's Hospital, Dublin	£4,600	£2,100
Newtown Park, Waterford	£4,584	£2,010
Our Lady's School, Wicklow	£4,090	n/a
Cistercian College, Roscrea	£3,950	n/a

Source: C. Hogan and A. O'Reilly, 'Private School Survey', *Sunday Business Post*, 16 August 1998.

How workers have lost out

The way one measures how workers are faring can be deeply ideo-logical. One method, for example, is to look at the consumption of particular items as indices of generalised wealth. Thus, Paul Sweeney points to the huge increase in cars to claim that the major-ity are benefiting from the Celtic Tiger.[52] Yet individual items of con-sumption can be easily subject to distortion. In the case of cars, for example, the Government offered a special scrappage scheme to replace old cars with new ones and many took out loans to take advantage of this. Even if we take a range of consumer items, there are still problems with this approach. Thus, one might argue that the combined growth in sales of mobile phones, video recorders, hi-fi equipment shows that people have never had it so good. Yet this approach often relies on a certain awe about new forms of technol-ogy. The widespread use of mobile phones today may be quite novel, but in a few years it will cause as much wonder as the fact that the overwhelming majority have television sets.

An exclusive focus on consumption can therefore produce quite a superficial analysis. There is often an implicit assumption that the working class can be equated with a certain form of lifestyle and any shift from this indicates a movement towards 'the middle class'. In the past, working-class people were supposed to smoke untipped cigarettes, to drink tea rather than coffee and to use takeaways rather than restaurants. Yet today this sort of image is easily recog-nised as a caricature. Unfortunately this does not prevent people equating cappuccino and cafe con latte with being middle class, while using instant and milk is working class. An alternative to this approach is to start from the fact that people are producers before they are consumers. Moreover, in modern society the labour of just a few can produce items which it took thousands to produce a few decades ago. If this is the case, it makes little sense to marvel at the fact that most people have shoes, or that they eat a little more or even go on more holidays than in their grandparents' day. The real issue is, surely, the relative share that workers are getting from the immense wealth they are creating today.

Looked at from this point of view, there are two measures which show that the majority of workers are losing out in the Celtic Tiger. One we have already touched on in Table 3.1. This showed that the share of the national income going to wages, pensions and social security has fallen by 10 percent in the decade since social partnership began. In other words, workers are receiving a lower share of the wealth they are producing than before. However, even this bald statement underestimates what is happening. In 1988, there were 1,091,000 at work but a decade later this had risen to nearly 1,500,000. There has also been a shift from employment in agriculture to other sectors, where workers are more productive. In other words, more workers and, indeed more productive workers, are sharing out a smaller portion of the national wealth. One trade union has attempted to quantify what this might mean for individual workers claiming that 'if wages had maintained the same share of national income in 1997 as it had in 1987, each worker would be better off by over £2,500'.[53]

Another useful way of looking at pay levels in the Celtic Tiger is to contrast the criterion used for assessing fair pay norms in the past with the situation today. During the long post-war boom in capitalism, it was often assumed that there were two key criteria for assessing wage rises. One was that workers had a right to keep abreast of the rate of inflation. The other was that pay rises had to be tied to productivity increases. In 1964, for example, a White Paper 'Closing the Gap' outlined the Fianna Fail Government's approach to pay by arguing that pay rises had to be tied directly to a growth in productivity. In order to facilitate this, the National Economic and Social Council was established shortly afterwards to produce objective assessments on how wage rises might be linked to the wider growth in the economy. So even by confining ourselves to the past logic of capitalism, we might say that workers have a certain entitlement to get wage increases which both match the rise in inflation and their own productivity.

Neither of these criteria is being applied today. Let us take the issue of inflation. The rate of inflation is calculated by a Consumer Price Index (CPI) which is drawn up by the CSO. In the twelve months to May 1999, for example, the CPI rose by 1.5 percent. It might be assumed that even though wages have been capped under social partnership agreements so that they rise by approximately 1.2 percent per annum,[54] workers are more or less keeping abreast with inflation. However, this is not necessarily the case because of the way the CPI is constructed. The CPI in use in Ireland fails to take adequate account of the costs of accommodation for many workers. An explanatory handout from the CSO even claims that 'there is no contradiction between rapidly rising house prices and low inflation'.[55] House purchase is considered to be a 'capital acquisition or investment' rather than a consumer expenditure and so is not included in the CPI. The index, however, does reflect changes in the mortgage interest cost but as interest rates generally have declined, this leads to a bizarre situation whereby the housing component of the CPI actually indicates a fall. To return to our inflation figure for 1998–99, for example, the inflation rate is actually reduced by 0.9 percent because of this factor.[56]

This approach is unsatisfactory for a number of reasons. Housing is one of the most basic needs that workers have and one of the main costs that young workers face. Traditionally, Irish workers have met this need through home ownership and the country has one of the highest levels of home ownership in Europe. As house prices rise, many have found that an ever-increasing share of the wages is being spent on mortgages. Any measure of inflation which excludes these costs is therefore highly artificial. In other countries such as Denmark, Germany, Japan, The Netherlands, Norway, Portugal and the USA, an 'imputed rent' method is used to calculate the actual cost of housing. Yet this is not used in Ireland. Moreover, the rise in house prices has also a knock-on effect upon those workers who do not own a house, because it clearly pushes up rents. Yet even the rise in rents is not fully reflected in the CPI because the CSO assumes that Ireland has a relatively small rental sector. In the basket of items that make up the CPI rents are assigned an overall weighting of 1.8 out of 100. To put that in perspective, expenditure on newspapers comes closely behind with a weighting of 1.1.[57]

The other problem with the CPI is that, according to the CSO, 'it is specifically designed *not* to take into account changes made by households'.[58] Yet the Celtic Tiger has produced important changes in the consumption patterns of Irish households. To take one obvious example, with the increase in the number of women working, more households will tend to rely on relatively expensive pre-prepared meals purchased in supermarkets. The experience in other countries also shows that there is a greater reliance on fast-food outlets or restaurants. Moreover, the overall growth in employment will be reflected in the consumption of more luxury items. By explicitly ruling out a concern about changes to the pattern of expenditure, the CSO can again underestimate inflation. One journalist, who noted that the basket of food items used by the CSO includes items like smoked kippers and Swiss Roll, remarked 'The last Swiss Roll was surely bought circa 1978. And honestly, tinned pear halves?'.[59]

One other, albeit crude, way of looking at inflation figures is to contrast the value put on GDP at constant market prices with the actual value gained in current market prices. Statisticians sometimes refer to this method as producing a 'implied price inflation'. If we use this method on the figures for 1997–98, we get an inflation rate of 6.2 percent. At the time the CPI was showing up an inflation rate of 2.1 percent, which was nearly three times below our alternative measure. Not only does this add some support to our contention that official figures in a class society need to be treated with caution, it also suggests, more importantly, that considerable numbers of workers are receiving pay rises which fall seriously behind the actual cost of living they face.

The other major criterion that was used to assess how workers were faring was the pay–productivity relationship. Here we find that workers have fallen back even further than on the pay–inflation comparison. The growth in productivity in the Celtic Tiger has been quite dramatic. Overall the output of manufacturing industry grew by 170 percent in volume, while employment rose by 19 percent in the decade after social partnership began.[60] This indicates that Irish workers are producing far more than before. There are of course many reasons why productivity has risen. A shift from agriculture to non-agricultural employment will, for example, tend to be associated with a rise in productivity. So too will a modernisation process which shifts investment from traditional sectors to the new hi-tech industries. Nevertheless, the remarkable feature of Ireland's boom is that the huge rise in productivity has not been associated with a major investment in machinery and capital stock by the wealthy. It has however managed to depress real unit labour costs much more substantially than its rivals. According to Sweeney, real unit labour costs have fallen by 19.5 percent in Ireland, 10 percent in Japan, 2.4 percent in the UK and 14 percent in the EU.[61]

A major element in this has been the huge growth in labour productivity. Irish workers are more educated and more skilled than they were a decade ago and are therefore more efficient. They are also working faster and in more stressful ways. One study calculated, for example, that labour productivity rose by 10 percent a year in 1994 and 1995 in the modern sector compared to 3 percent a year in the more traditional sector.[62] In both cases, this represents an increase that is far higher than the equivalent increase in wages. Hannigan has attempted to put some monetary value on this spectacular rise in productivity in manufacturing. He claims that the net output of each employee has increased by over £97,000 in the ten years between 1987 and 1997.[63] If we remember again that this was not caused by a major increase in the concentration of capital, we get some idea of the higher productivity that workers are not giving to their companies.

One of the reasons why labour productivity has risen is that the unions have gone along with a management agenda of introducing forms of lean production in order to increase competitiveness. Lean production is defined by the Canadian Auto Workers as a philosophy whereby, 'all costs associated with non-value added functions are waste and are to be eliminated, whether it is buffers between operations, slack time, waiting time, walking space at work stations or more generally indirect labour such as skilled trades'.[64] In brief, it involves a constant pressure to cut 'downtime' so that the maximum number of seconds of a working day are directly applied to the production of profit. This is often associated with a Human Resources approach which uses the language of 'empowerment' and 'participation'. However there is nothing in this language which contradicts the overall aim of management adopting forms of 'competitive bench-marking' where they seek out the quickest, cheapest and fastest techniques and production practices.[65] While 'team-working' is sometimes hailed as a progressive non-Taylorist approach where workers' talents are engaged in production, the reality is that it often comes as part of an overall strategy of 'management by stress' where workers put considerable pressure on each other to achieve group bonuses.

One interesting study of workplace innovations in Ireland found that 90 percent of surveyed establishments were using at least one of the high performance work-organisation techniques to some degree.[66] The most common was the practice of Total Quality Management which often involves extra stress as workers are obliged to take responsibility for quality control, while often working at a faster pace. The other most popular technique used by 57 percent of the survey was job rotation (JR) or 'multi-skilling' as it is sometimes known. The writers explain that JR

> exposes 'insider' wages to competitive pressures, threatening incumbents of privileged position with material and social losses. The most obvious interpretation of this finding is that a proportion of reported JR refers to ad hoc deployment of workers in simple tasks (e.g. janitorial). For these establishments the motive is not flexibility or involvement, but cost cutting; downtime and indirect labour can be eliminated using this strategy.[67]

It should be stressed that the reference to privileged insiders does not refer to those who occupy managerial positions but rather to shop-floor employees. It is also clear that the general approach of companies has been to involve the union hierarchy in endorsing these changes. After all, few of the full-time officials who negotiate changes with the most bland sounding names actually work for them. The fact that they are presented as an inevitable adaptation to modern flexible conditions also helps to delegitimise resistance. As the writers remark, 'The message is that the greater the trade union voice in corporate change, the lower the probability of worker resistance'.[68]

The pressure for higher profits has also led to a major restructuring of the Irish workforce. Originally social partnership was supposed to offer some protection from the type of deregulated market system that had been championed by the New Right. It was argued that if unions co-operated closely with employers in raising productivity, this would obviate the need for a casualised and unprotected labour market. Yet a decade after the first social partnership agreements were implemented, the inequalities in the Irish labour market resemble most closely those in the deregulated labour markets of the USA.

Despite the claims that Ireland has resisted the worst effects of neo-liberalism, it comes second only to the USA in having the highest proportion of its workforce categorised as low paid. The share of the workforce earning less than two-thirds of median earnings is now 23 percent, one of the highest rates in the OECD.[69] Social partnership was supposed to bring particular benefits to the low paid. However, the real hourly earnings of the lowest decile of the workforce have stagnated or fallen slightly while those of the top decile, which mainly includes the managerial elite, has grown by an average rate of 4 percent annually. As a result, the ratio of earnings of the top decile to the bottom for men working full-time has increased from 3.5 to 5 times between 1987 and 1994.[70] The Celtic Tiger has quite simply one of the worst records on earnings dispersion in the developed industrial world.

One of the reasons why this has occurred is that the fastest growth area for employment is in services, where a higher proportion of low-paid employees are hired. The other reason, though, is that many productivity agreements entered into by unions include a provision for the hire of younger workers at lower pay rates. Known as 'yellow pack' grades, this often produces a divisive situation where workers are paid less for carrying out equivalent or similar work. The burgeoning growth in low pay means that minimum wage legislation has become a hugely popular issue. But the Government has set the figure at a comparatively low level of £4.40 an hour and even that figure is hedged with a host of get-out clauses for employers. Yet one of the reports of the Minimum Wage Commission showed that a full 30 percent of the Irish workforce would have benefited if a minimum wage of £5 an hour had been inaugurated in 1998.[71]

The other pattern that shows a close affinity to the US labour market has been the growth of part-time contract employment. Instead of strongly resisting the casualisation of the workforce, the union leaders have accepted that a degree of 'atypical employment' is not only necessary but even has a vaguely progressive quality. The result has been, rather ominously, that casual labour has increased most in the modern sectors of the economy where American labour market practices are promoted. Thus the development agency Forfas has noted that part-time, temporary and short-term contract employment has risen by 164.5 percent between 1988 and 1997. Yet in internationally traded and financial services companies, temporary forms of employment have grown by a staggering 1,083 percent.[72] Indeed as the decade progressed, the overall rate of casualisation seems to

have increased with the numbers in part-time, temporary and contract employment rising by 19 percent in 1997 alone.[73] One in eight
Irish workers is now officially classified as part time.[74] Supporters of
atypical employment claim that EU legislation prevents the abuse of
workers. Yet the legal protection is often vague and employers have
little difficulty in surmounting it. Thus, it is common for employers
to present workers with eleven month contracts so that there is a
break in their years of service and legal protection is denied.

Another emerging pattern is pressure on workers to seek private
pension arrangements. Most previous societies have celebrated lon-
gevity and shown a respect for the aged. For modern capitalism,
however, increased life expectancy has become a major problem
with the tabloid press often warning about the 'pensions time-
bomb'. Why the growth of a more dependent ageing population is
a problem in an immensely more productive society is rarely
explained. This ethos has meant that a desire for a 'pensionable job'
is scorned as a rigid old-fashioned notion. At the moment only 38
percent of private sector employees are covered by an occupational
pension.[75] Yet there are indications that this may represent a high
point and that employers are pushing the coverage down further.
One study found, for example, that the percentage of pension
scheme members among workers aged below 29 is quite small.[76]

The declining share of the Irish economy going to wages, the
growth of low-paid casual workers and the tendency for wage
increases to fall behind rises in productivity all indicate one thing:
class polarisation is increasing in the Celtic Tiger. The rich are
getting richer, the poor are still confined to poverty and the bulk of
workers are losing out. A recent Human Development report produced by the United Nations shows that even though the Irish
economy is expanding, it has fallen down on the Human
Development Index. One of the main reasons is that it has the
second highest level of poverty in the developed world.[77] That more
than anything bears eloquent testimony to the fact that even when
the market appears successful, it does not benefit the majority.

Notes

1 'Ryan Family Receive £117 Million for Share Sales', *Irish Times* (29
   May 1999).
2 'My Mistakes at Ryanair', *Business Plus* (April 1998).

3 'Anarchy at Dublin Airport', *Irish Times* (9 March 1998).

4 *Report of Inquiry into the Industrial Dispute at Dublin Airport (Flynn/McAuley Report)* (Dublin, Stationery Office, 1998) Chs 4 and 6.

5 Interview with author.

6 M. Shaw and I. Miles, 'The Social Roots of Statistical Knowledge' in J. Irvine, I. Miles and J. Evans, *De-Mystifying Social Statistics* (London, Pluto Press 1979) p. 35.

7 I. Gilmour, *Dancing With Dogma: Britain Under Thatcherism* (London, Simon and Schuster, 1992) p. 112–13.

8 S. Byrne, *Wealth and the Wealthy in Ireland: A Review of the Available Evidence* (Dublin, Combat Poverty Agency, 1989) p. 9.

9 Ibid. pp. 9–10.

10 *Programme for National Recovery* (Dublin, Government Publications, 1987) p. 5.

11 Doug Fraser, former United Auto Workers President. Quoted in K. Moody, *Political Directions for Labour* (Detroit, Labor Education and Research Project, 1979) p. 29.

12 Central Statistics Office, *National Income and Expenditure Release,* 30 June 1999, Table 2.

13 Ibid.

14 A. Burke, 'Why Ireland is so Attractive to Foreign Direct Investors', *Finance* (October 1997).

15 Forfas, *Annual Survey of Irish Economy Expenditures: Results for 1993* (Dublin, Forfas, 1993) p. 17 and *Annual Survey of Irish Economy Expenditures Results for 1997* (Dublin, Forfas, 1997) p. 6.

16 European Commission, *The Economic and Financial Situation in Ireland* (Brussels, European Commission Reports, 1996) p. 13.

17 Ibid. p 1.

18 National Economic and Social Council, *Private Sector Investment in Ireland* (Dublin, NESC, 1998) p. 17.

19 CSO, *National Income and Expenditure* (Dublin, Stationary Office, 1997) Table 30a.

20 C. Rapple, 'Inequality Grows as Wealth Soars', *Sunday Business Post* (4 July 1999).

21 Finance Special Issue, *The Irish Stock Exchange: A Guide to Investment in the World's Fastest Growing Economy* (Dublin, Finance, 1998) p. 6.

22 CSO *Monthly Economic Series*, June 1999 (Dublin, CSO, 1999) Table 8.28.

23 Amalgamated Transport and General Workers Union, *A New Agenda for Economic Power Sharing* (Dublin, ATGWU, 1999) p. 21.

24 D. Henwood, *Wall St.* (London, Verso, 1998) p. 73.

25 Ibid.

26 CSO, *National Income and Expenditure*, Tables 1 and 12.

27 Finance Special Issue, *The Irish Stock Exchange*, p. 39.

28 K. Barrington, 'Powerscreen: Focus on 2,000 Tractors', *Sunday Business Post* (1 February 1998).

29 Sean McEntee papers, P 67/350/10, University College Dublin Archives.

30 M. Brennock, 'Impeding Haughey's owe and grow approach', *Irish Times* (20 February 1999).

31 K. Rafter, 'No Evidence of Phone Call or Letter to NIB, says Reynolds', *Irish Times* (15 October 1999).

32 'Irish Banks Most Profitable in Europe', *Finance* (April 1998).

33 Desmond O'Malley quoted in V. Browne, 'AIB: Devouring the Hand That Fed It', *Magill* (November 1988).

34 Ibid.

35 D. O'Sullivan, 'Choosing the Right Offshore Centre', *Finance Dublin* (June 1998).

36 'IFSC Remains Low Cost Labour Market', *Finance Dublin* (March 1997).

37 'IFSC: Cause for Concern Over High Staff Turnover', *Finance Dublin* (April 1998).

38 E. Micheau, 'Dublin's Citibank', *Business and Finance* (12–18 November 1998).

39 KPMG, *Study on Urban Renewal Schemes* (Dublin, Stationary Office, 1996) p. 75.

40 Ibid. p. 103.

41 B. Carey, 'Who Is Driving the Boom', *Sunday Tribune* (18 April 1999).

42 J. Fagan, 'Return of 6.8 Percent Points to Gradual Slowdown', *Irish Times* (29 April 1999).

43 'Exceptional Growth Will Continue Says Agency', *Irish Times* (1 April 1999).

44 Ibid.

45 L. Reid, 'Minister Slates Wealthy Developers', *Sunday Tribune* (29 August 1999).

46 See C. Harman and A. Callinicos, *The Changing Working Class* (London, Bookmarks, 1989) Ch. 2.

47 Revenue Commissioners, *Statistical Report 1997* (Dublin, Stationery Office, 1999) p. 68–9, Table IDSI.

48 D. O'Hearn, *Inside the Celtic Tiger* (London, Pluto Press, 1998) p. 126. For updated figures see CSO, *National Income and Expenditure* (1997) Table 5.

49 See Department of Education, *Statistical Report 1997* (Dublin, Stationery Office, 1998) p. 4, Table 1.1.

50 C. Hogan and A. O'Reilly, 'Private School Survey', *Sunday Business Post* (16 August 1998).

51 Figures supplied to author from database of the Department of Education.
52 P. Sweeney, *The Celtic Tiger: Ireland's Economic Miracle Explained* (Dublin, Oak Tree, 1998) p. 65.
53 ATGWU, *A New Agenda* p. 23.
54 Ibid.
55 CSO, 'Information Notice: House Prices and the Consumer Price Index: Explanatory Note' (Dublin, CSO, no date) p. 1.
56 CSO, *Statistical Release: Consumer Price Index* (15 June 1999) Table 3.
57 CSO, *Consumer Price Index: Introduction of Updated Series,* Appendix 1, pp. 16 and 18.
58 CSO, *House Prices and Consumer Price Index*, p. 1.
59 D. Walshe and P. Leahy, 'Inflation Gets Trendy', *Sunday Business Post* (18 July 1999).
60 K. Hannigan, 'Manufacturing Productivity Double Other Sectors', *Finance* (June 1998).
61 Sweeney, *The Celtic Tiger*, p. 61.
62 OECD, *Economic Survey: Ireland* (Paris, OECD, 1997) p. 17.
63 Hannigan, 'Manufacturing Productivity Double Other Sectors', *Finance*, p. 33.
64 Canadian Auto Workers, *Work Re-Organisation: Responding to Lean Production* (Toronto, CAW, 1993) p. 4.
65 K. Moody, *Workers in a Lean World* (London, Verso, 1997) p. 91.
66 J. McCartney and P. Teague, 'Workplace Innovations in the Republic of Ireland', *Economic and Social Review*, 28:4 (1997), pp. 381–99.
67 Ibid. p. 385.
68 Ibid. p. 391.
69 A. Barrett, T. Callan and B. Nolan, 'The Earnings Distribution and the Return to Education in Ireland', ESRI Working Paper, no 85 (June 1997) p. 8.
70 B. Nolan and G. Hughes, *Low Pay, the Earnings Distribution and Poverty in Ireland, 1987–1994* (Dublin, ESRI, 1997) p. 6.
71 *Report of the National Minimum Wage Commission* (Dublin, Stationery Office, 1998) p. 9.
72 Forfas, *1997 Employment Survey* (Dublin, Forfas, no date) p. 9.
73 Ibid.
74 CSO, *Quarterly Household Survey, First Quarter 1999* (Dublin, CSO, 1999) Table 1.
75 G. Hughes and B. Whelan, *Occupational and Personal Pension Coverage 1995* (Dublin, ESRI, 1996) p. 41.
76 Ibid. p. 45.
77 P. Cullen, 'Poverty Here 2nd Worst in Developed World', *Irish Times* (12 July 1999).

4
Taxes and social spending

In 1998 Dave McMahon, a 23-year-old bricklayer from Tallaght in Dublin, became one of the first people to be jailed under the Industrial Relations Act. The law had been introduced in 1990 by Bertie Ahern, the current leader of Fianna Fail, and was modelled on a number of anti-union laws in Britain which curbed the rights of workers to picket. Dave McMahon was jailed alongside Willie Rogers, a builder's labourer, for picketing the O'Connor's site in the exclusive Dublin Four district. He had started work in July but was informed that he had to work as a sub-contractor, despite the fact that the Bricklayers and Allied Trade Union have a policy of opposing sub-contracting. They argued that employers should pay PAYE tax, social security, holiday entitlements and wet time, and throughout much of 1998 there had been a series of sporadic strikes over this issue. An unofficial rank and file grouping, known as Building Workers Against the Black Economy, mobilised workers from across the city to close down sites which attempted to use contract labour. Confrontation was inevitable, then, when O'Connors attempted to put some of its staff into a sub-contract regime.

As soon as Dave McMahon was jailed, a wave of solidarity strikes broke out. In Limerick, nearly a thousand building workers downed tools and marched. In Waterford, bricklayers blocked the main bridge into the city for a period. Strikes also took place in Galway, Cork and Carlow. In Dublin, hundreds of building workers congregated outside the High Court and marched around the city, bringing traffic to a standstill. Within a few days, Dave McMahon and Willie Rogers were brought before the court to 'purge their contempt', but they refused to apologise for any of their actions. According to Dave McMahon, 'It should have been the employer, the Construction Industry Federation and the government who were apologising for putting us in jail'.[1]

One of the most popular slogans of the protests was 'Jail the Bankers: Free the Workers'. It was a reference to an extraordinary series of revelations that had appeared in *Magill* magazine just before the confrontation at O'Connor's. The magazine discovered internal documents from the AIB which suggested that '75% of the money in its non-resident accounts was "funny money"'.[2] In other words, most of it had come from Irish residents who had falsely declared themselves to be non-residents in order to avoid Deposit Interest Retention Tax (DIRT). It is estimated that £100 million was owed to the Revenue Commissioners.[3]

These revelations had a particular poignancy for the building workers. One of the activists from the Building Workers Against the Black Economy explained

> A few blocks down from O'Connor's site is the headquarters of the Allied Irish Bank. In the week after it was revealed that this bank had directly been involved in fiddling millions in taxes, these two building workers were jailed. What more do we need to know about how the country is run. Two ordinary blokes were jailed because they wanted PAYE employment – but the bankers who ran a tax scam are walking free.[4]

The Atlantic tax haven

Taxation is one of those explosive issues that emerge quickly in the Irish Republic, only to disappear without leaving significant traces of change. On 20 January 1980, 700,000 people staged a general strike over the tax burden that fell on PAYE workers and 300,000 took part in a street demonstration in Dublin. The BBC claimed it was the 'largest peaceful protest in post war Europe'[5] and, relative to the size of the Irish population, this was fairly accurate. Unlike other tax protests in America, for example, the complexion of this protest was not shaped by the political right. Instead of advocating cuts in public spending, the PAYE revolt focused on the need to shift the tax burden onto the wealthier sections of society. Many felt that the failure of the farmers and big business to pay their 'fair share' meant that workers were forced to pay an excruciatingly high rate of tax.

Yet twenty years after the PAYE protests, Income Tax makes up

37 percent of all tax revenues in contrast to the 12 percent which comes from Corporation Tax and 5 percent which comes from other capital taxes.[6] The heavy burden on employees means punitive tax rates with a single worker on an income of £100 a week starting to pay tax at the rate of 24 percent. This high level of taxation on workers helps to explain the popularity of resistance to other forms of 'double taxation'. When water charges were introduced, many refused to pay, despite the threat of being brought before the courts and the Government was forced to relent. The legitimacy of the protests stemmed from the fact that workers did not feel they should pay any more in tax.

Ironically, successive governments have sought to turn this resentment to their own advantage. The ideology of partnership is premised on the fact that the low pay rises that workers receive are compensated for with tax relief. The Partnership 2000 agreement, for example, specified that the 'government will introduce personal tax reductions to the cumulative value of £900 million on a full year cost basis'.[7]

There are, however, a number of difficulties with the logic behind this approach. First, partnership agreements are apparently forged between a collective body of trade unionists who offer restraint from their membership, yet the tax benefits that apparently follow are dispensed to everyone, no matter whether they are members of a union or not. Second, the tax benefits are distributed in a way that is highly inequitable and disproportionately benefits the higher paid. Research carried out by the Amalgamated Transport and General Workers Union (ATGWU) on the cumulative tax benefits that grew out of social partnership indicates that a single high earner received twice as much benefit as a low-income worker, while a high-earning couple received more than four times the benefit of a low-income couple.[8] Table 4.1 illustrates the union's findings.

There is, however, an even more fundamental difficulty with the notion of a trade-off between low pay increases and tax concessions. In the decade after social partnership began, Ireland set itself up as the prime tax haven for capital on the edge of Europe. In 1987, the top tax rate on company profits stood at 50 percent, but a decade later that had declined to 32 percent. It is proposed to reduce it by a further 4 percent a year to achieve a Corporation Tax rate of 12.5 percent in 2002. This will be the lowest rate in Europe and has caused resentment from other governments, who feel Ireland is

Table 4.1 Net tax benefit (%) 1987–98

Tax Unit	Annual income			
	£7,5000 (Half the average industrial wage)	£15,000 (Average industrial wage)	£30,000 (Twice the average industrial wage)	£60,000 (Four times the average industrial wage)
Single	18.8%	25.1%	32.4%	36.1%
Couple	10.2%	15.4%	29.1%	34.1%

Source: ATGWU, *A New Agenda for Economic Power Sharing* (Dublin, ATGWU, 1999) p. 23.

bidding tax rates down to suit multi-nationals. However, it also highlights an extraordinary paradox: workers had to offer wage restraint in exchange for tax relief, yet companies could vastly increase their profits and still benefit from tax cuts that made the adjustments for the PAYE sector look microscopic.

The reduction of taxes on profits has occurred without much debate. This in itself is a testimony to the strength of the consensus that had been established around the social partnership ideology. The justification for these tax cuts is often articulated in terms of the interests of Ireland conflicting with a meddling EU bureaucracy which seeks to hamper its entrepreneurial spirit. The bidding down of tax rates by nation states is assumed to be a necessity because of globalisation. Attempts by the former German Finance Minister Oskar Lafontaine to advocate tax harmonisation as a way of reducing this pressure was regarded as an affront to the Irish nation itself. From this perspective, tax cuts provide a positive-sum gain, whereby all sections of the Irish population benefit by 'coaxing' investment away from other countries. Yet in reality the sole beneficiaries of this ideology are a wealthy elite, because the reduction in Corporation Profits Tax is only the headline figure for a variety of other measures which increase their privileges. Like a famous New York millionairess, they seem to believe that taxes are only for the little people.

The pressure from the rich to reduce taxes has taken three main forms. First, there have been strong political campaigns to eliminate taxes on unearned income. Second, lobbying behind the scenes before the annual Finance Acts has lessened the official rate of tax on capital. Lastly, wholesale evasion of tax has occurred with official connivance. Let us look at examples of each of these in turn.

Ireland has had a long history of populist political campaigns to eliminate taxes on wealth and property. In the mid-1970s the Fine Gael Minister Ritche Ryan was pressurised by the Labour Party to introduce wealth tax, but when he did so he was promptly dubbed 'Red Ritche' by the press and a successful campaign was mounted to remove this tax.[9] A similar movement developed over the Residential Property Tax. Ireland has one of the lowest rates of tax of property in the OECD and it was hoped that this tax would help to redress the balance.[10] It imposed a tax rate on properties valued over £75,000 where the income of those living there exceeded £30,000. The low-income threshold, particularly where two adults were working, meant that the tax affected some higher paid workers and this provided the main base for popular opposition to it. Nevertheless, the real threat posed by this tax was that the rates increased with the value of the property and on properties valued at over £200,000, the owners were due to pay a tax rate of 2 percent a year. This modest proposal met such a storm of opposition, particularly from the *Independent* group of newspapers, that it was abolished in 1997 just before the property boom reached dizzy heights.

The lobbying by the wealthy for tax relief in the annual Finance Acts is more difficult to describe precisely because it is so immensely detailed. This is by no means accidental, as a practice has grown up whereby the accountancy profession assists business groups to formulate intricate proposals for new reliefs to be included in the post-budget legislation. In modern capitalist societies information is theoretically available to everyone, yet some of the really significant information, that can affect the fate of large amounts of money, is often so highly specialised as to be normally of interest only to a tiny minority. The assumption is that this sort of information needs to be bought by those who can afford the accountants. Given this limitation, we can only provide a few examples to illustrate how this method of tax reduction works.

One of the key concerns of the wealthy is inheritance taxes. Officially modern societies are supposed to be based on a meritocracy where the brightest are rewarded for their own efforts with elite positions. This explains why books such as the *Bell Curve* which purported to provide a biological basis for this award system were so popular.[11] Yet the threat of death brings this pretence to an end, because the wealthy go to extreme lengths to pass their bequests onto their children. Ireland, however, happens to offer more relief than most. The market value of agricultural land, for example, is automatically reduced by 90 percent for tax purposes if the son or daughter is a farmer. A similar relief of 90 percent also applies to business property.[12] All of this helps to keep the ownership of property highly concentrated in the hands of a few. Table 4.2 uses the recent Probate Tax which imposed a 2 percent tax levy on all estates to illustrate the very small amount of tax that is paid on inheritance. It shows that the percentage taken in tax has declined since 1994, even though estates have grown in value.

Table 4.2   Inheritance Tax as an estimated value of estate 1993–97

Year	Value of estates	Inheritance Tax	Inheritance Tax as a % of estate value
1994	£477,643,600	£42,041,444	9
1995	£614,205,800	£39,947,125	6.5
1996	£720,124,950	£48,141,932	6.6
1997	£851,963,450	£64,006,109	7.5

Source: Revenue Commissioner, *Statistical Report 1997*, Table CAT 2.

The other tax that has been undermined through a constant campaign for reliefs is Capital Gains Tax. This was introduced to tax some of the windfall benefits that the wealthy received from disposal of their assets and was originally set at 40 percent. However, a special reduced rate of 26 percent for shares was established afterwards and there were numerous other exemptions. So, for example, those who bought and sold paintings or who held Irish Government securities were made exempt from the tax under certain circumstances.[13] Finally, in December 1997, the Capital Gains Tax was cut to 20 percent. The main beneficiaries of this change were directors of companies who often received share packages as part of their salary. In 1998 the directors of New Ireland Assurance, for example, saved themselves £1 million in tax when they sold some of their shares as a direct result of the change.[14]

The other major tax on wealth, the Corporation Profits Tax, contains such a host of reliefs that most companies have paid well below the official rate. Originally the biggest relief was the 10 percent rate for sales of manufactured exports, but there was also relief for investment in film, for fish farming, and for Section 84 leasing arrangements which enabled the banks to reap considerable rewards. The indications are that the cost of these reliefs to capital have risen rapidly. In 1987, it was estimated that the total cost of subsidies to the corporate sector amounted to £712 million, but the following year this had risen to £1,189 million. While the basis of these estimates seems to have changed, the latest figures from the Revenue Commissioners put the cost of this form of relief much higher. See Table 4.3 for tax-relief provisions.

Table 4.3 Some tax-relief provision on capital (£m)

Tax relief	1994–95	1995–96
Investment in corporate trades (BES)	25.1	37.2
Capital allowances:		
Urban relief	46.0	62.8
Other	841.2	810.3
Rented/Residential accommodation	21.5	24.4
10 percent rate of Corporation Tax on manufacturing and other activities	1256.1	1393.0
Section 84 loans	33.0	9.5
Double taxation relief	74.5	96.4
Investment in films	38.3	19.1
Group relief	139.0	113.0
TOTAL	2474.7	2565.7

Source: Revenue Commissioner, *Statistical Report 1997*.

Even these figures understate the scale of the tax subsidies granted to capital in the Celtic Tiger, as the figures presented by the Revenue Commissioners do not include the tax foregone on the IFSC. Reliefs here include a provision for a 'double rental allowance', whereby companies can write off double their very expensive rents for tax purposes. The Revenue Commissioners also claim that myriad of other reliefs are 'not quantifiable' and so do not appear in the above figures. They include relief for items such as stallion stud fees, income from foreign trusts, commercial woodlands and investment in research and development.[15] The latter provision ensured that the pharmaceutical company Elan Ltd, which is the highest performer on Dublin's Stock Exchange, paid a tax bill of only 2.6 percent on its profits in 1998.[16]

The third way the Celtic Tiger elite apply pressure on the Exchequer is by avoiding or evading tax. One of the traditional mechanisms used by the very wealthy was to open offshore accounts. These play an important role in the activities of the multi-nationals in Ireland but they are also used by the indigenous elite. The tiny island of Sark has become one popular location for wealthy Irish clients who seek to avoid tax. According to the chairman of the Sark Association of Corporate Administrators many of its members earn between £20,000 and £40,000 a year as directors for Irish firms, many of whom are connected to the International Financial Services Centre.[17] It is estimated that Irish accountancy firms, banks, solicitors and company formation groups are earning between £40 million and £60 million a year servicing this form of tax avoidance.[18]

Most of this activity is legal, but there are other mechanisms which are not. The revelations in the *Magill* article about the AIB set off a chain of events which has thrown some light on the sheer scale of tax evasion which expanded with official connivance. In 1986 a special tax on interest known as Deposit Interest Retention Tax (DIRT) was introduced and it was later agreed that if individuals opened a special savings account they were only liable for a 10 percent rate of tax. The initial tax yield to the Exchequer from DIRT was £253 million in 1987, but just over ten years later in 1998 it had fallen to £188 million, even though the economy was booming.[19] One reason was that, again, a special series of tax-relief measures were introduced in the intervening period. However, a report by the Comptroller General also shows that the fall was due to illegal tax evasion on a gigantic scale.

DIRT was not payable on non-resident accounts because these were, according to IDA, 'an important but not essential element'[20] in attracting foreign investment. However, this provided an important loophole to the Irish rich as well, because the Revenue Commissioners had assured the Irish Bankers Federation that 'completion of the non-resident declaration alone will be regarded as sufficient to absolve the bank concerned from any obligation to include details of interest'.[21] In other words, someone who wanted to evade tax had only to fill in a declaration that they were not resident in Ireland and the banks were under no obligation to check up on this. It was an open invitation to avoid the tax and by 1998, 29 percent of the total £54.5 billion deposited in the Irish banking system was classified as non-resident. The small town of Miltown Malby in County Clare may serve as an example of the scale of tax evasion. In 1991 the Revenue Commissioners discovered that nine individuals had illegally used non-resident accounts in the Bank of Ireland to evade £1,098,732 in tax and that 'the bank had colluded with tax payers in tax evasion on a large scale'.[22]

The Department of Finance and the Revenue Commissioners were aware of the extent of tax evasion for some time. According to the Comptroller General's report 'the official files are liberally sprinkled with references like "half the non-resident accounts are thought to be bogus" and "at least £1 billion of non-resident deposits are thought to be held by Irish residents"'.[23] In 1992 the state's own bank, the Agricultural Credit Corporation, was even made aware of a tax liability for £17 million because of bogus non-resident accounts used by its mainly farming clientele. Yet nothing was done until the scandal broke in *Magill*. The first instinct of state officials was to bow down before the anonymous power of money. They assumed that any attempt to inquire into the these illegal practices would lead to a flight of money. One senior official in the Department of Finance put the matter succinctly, 'I know of no way of detecting bogus non-residents which would not involve checking on genuine non-residents. Given the size of non-residents' deposits, £4,100 million we remain opposed to measures which could put this volume of money at risk'.[24]

Armed with their own appreciation of the awesome power of money, the bankers made repeated representations to government agencies to protect the anonymity of non-resident accounts. For example, on 20 May 1987 the bank representatives met the Minister for Finance to seek assurances that the Revenue Commissioners would not use their powers to inspect the non-resident forms. The Minister stated he was 'sympathetic' to their requests 'but was unable to make any changes at present'.[25] However, this statement should be treated with a certain caution, as it is taken from a carefully crafted civil servant's minute of the meeting. More significantly, a special memorandum appeared from the Superintending Inspector of Taxes informing tax inspectors that they had a right to examine any notice of non-residence held in a bank but that, 'further instructions on the examination of declaration forms will issue in due course and Inspectors should not call for any declaration forms from relevant deposit takers pending receipt of these instructions'.[26] Yet no further instruction ever appeared and not a single declaration of a non-resident account was inspected until 1998 when the scandal broke. Later at a parliamentary inquiry, officials from the Revenue Commissioners claimed they were not able to find the anonymous author of the ingenious instruction for total passivity.

What a stark contrast with the treatment of social welfare recipients! Almost every aspect of the life of an unemployed person is subject to public scrutiny by the state. They can be forced to produce bank accounts, to explain where they were on particular hours and days, to explain the exact nature of their relationship with anyone else in their households. Yet the banks demanded that non-resident account holders had an absolute right to privacy from the gaze of the state, and they received that guarantee in practice. The failure to inspect a single form of a single non-resident account holder between 1986 and 1998 is an eloquent testimony to the class divide in the Celtic Tiger. These events also show how Irish democracy is constantly undermined by the power of money. Officially Parliament debates and passes laws which are supposed to be implemented. Yet, leaving aside the inherent bias of some of these laws, few are even aware of consequences of the studied inaction on the part of state agencies. These invisible practices are rarely the subject of debate in a parliamentary chamber – although instructions written in bureaucratic double talk are often far more important than the public discussion.

All of these practices have helped to establish Ireland's reputation as the Atlantic tax haven, but not everyone is a winner. Because the wealthy pay so little in taxes, PAYE workers pay more than they should. Tax breaks also mean severe cutbacks to public spending programmes. Essential facilities which are freely available in other countries are sometimes non-existent or are of a poorer quality in Ireland. Individuals find themselves under intense pressure to ensure there is a privatised provision for these services. Four brief examples indicate how tax cuts have had a detrimental effect on public services.

Underfunded public services

Education
At one level education and the achievement of educational credentials are valued very highly in Ireland. There is a high overall participation rate and the country compares favourably with others in the

EU. The political establishment has accepted the arguments of the 'human capital' school of economics. Here it is assumed that investment in education leads directly to an enhancement of overall productivity in the economy.[27] However, crude participation rates can disguise a tendency to restrict the range of education. They also tell us little about how there may be a sustained attempt to carry through mass education on the cheap. These issues are important, as the growth of educational qualifications can also be accompanied by informal barriers which militate against the performance of the poorest.

Two key groupings have lost out because of the restricted range of education – pre-school children and adult learners who want a second chance to gain access to universities and colleges. The case of pre-school children illustrates most dramatically the pressure on people to use privatised options rather than providing a state service. Just 1 percent of three-year olds in Ireland gain access to pre-school education compared with 60 percent in Germany, 98 percent in Belgium and even 45 percent in Britain.[28] It appears that the Irish state takes literally the injunction that a woman's place is in the home and makes no provision for crèches, nurseries and forms of pre-school learning. The result has been an almost totally privatised and deregulated facility where many parents pay for childminders in the black economy. The National Childcare Strategy report estimates that 38 percent of parents with children up to the age of 4 avail of paid childcare.[29] The absence of state provision means that Irish parents spend a higher proportion of their income on childcare than other countries in the EU. Full daycare for children costs an average of £71 a week in a childminder's home or approximately 20 percent of a parent's earnings.[30] This reliance on an unofficial private market or wider family arrangements leads to increased stress levels for working parents and poorer facilities for very young children. Just over half of nurseries operate from converted homes and only 13 percent use purpose-built facilities.[31]

Not surprisingly, childcare has become an explosive issue in the Celtic Tiger as the number of working mothers soars. Supporters of the market are faced with a major dilemma, because on one hand they want more women to enter the labour force in order to avoid labour shortages, but on the other they wish to keep public spending low to reduce taxes on the wealthy. The result of this dilemma has been another proposed 'Irish solution for an Irish problem'. The

Expert Working Group on Childcare which commissioned the National Childcare Strategy report suggested that more tax cuts be given as a way of stimulating the market. The suggestion is that there should be extra tax reliefs for the nursery providers to help upgrade their premises and also personal tax relief should be dispensed to parents who pay for these facilities.[32]

However, there is no guarantee that even with these tax reliefs the market will provide adequate childcare for the growing number of mothers who wish to take up paid employment. Caring for children may not be sufficiently profitable to lure capital from other areas such as property speculation. Moreover, the emphasis on personal tax relief rather than free provision is deeply discriminatory. Two high earners will gain far more from tax relief than, say, a single parent who may be trapped between a desire for work and an uncertainty about the costs of childcare. Few people would argue that the education of four to six-year olds should be turned over to private companies, but this only begs the question of why this mechanism is used for children of an even more delicate age.

At the other end of the educational spectrum, adult learners have also lost out as Ireland has the second lowest rate of mature student entry into third level education in the OECD. Only 2.3 percent of entrants to universities were aged over 26 compared to an OECD average of 19.3 percent.[33] These low figures do not occur because a lack of a desire for second-chance education as demand for places is increasing rapidly and for every one mature student who entered third level education five others were denied a chance.[34] There is simply little special provision for the needs of those who lost out because of an educational system that was overcrowded and biased against the poor.

Aside from restricting the range of learning, tax cutting has led to pressure to organise schooling on the cheap. Ireland has one of the highest pupil:teacher ratios in OECD countries, with only Turkey, Mexico and Korea in a worse position. Inside the EU, Ireland has the lowest expenditure per primary school student relative to GDP.[35] These crude figures, however, only tell part of the story. There is an inadequate number of remedial teachers to deal with the children who cannot cope with the high class sizes. There is an over-reliance on traditional 'chalk and talk' methods, as these tend to be more adaptable to a situation with few resources. Only 11 percent of the annual teaching hours for children aged 10 is devoted to the human and natural sciences, which is the lowest proportion in the EU outside of Luxembourg.[36] There is no provision for foreign languages. Languages such as French, German or Spanish are taught privately to those who can afford it, and poorer children are deprived of this valuable cultural resource.

The past underfunding of education means that Ireland stands out among countries in Northern Europe as having the highest proportion of its workforce without second level leaving qualifications.[37] One-quarter of the Irish population has a very low level of literacy skills which means, for example, they may have difficulty identifying the correct amount of medicine to give to a child from the written information on the package.[38] One study of people with difficulties with literacy related this back to their early education

> the majority of people interviewed did not express happy memories of their time in school. They remember being 'shouted at' being 'beaten something brutal', 'having fear instilled' into them, being told they were 'stupid' or 'thick' or 'not bright'. They described large classes, overcrowded classrooms, severe corporal punishment when homework was either not done or was incorrect, being allowed to sit at the back of the class knitting or sewing while other children were doing written work, or being sent out to clean toilets.[39]

The present underfunding of education works to the disadvantage of poorer children at every level. The pressure to seek extra help in grinds, the absence of adequate resources, the encouragement to teachers to engage in forms of rote learning all mean that educational disadvantage is piled on educational disadvantage. One of the more visible signs of this is the way Irish universities are dominated by the children of the professional groupings. Participation rates in third level institutions are almost 90 percent for the higher professional groups in contrast to only 13 percent for unskilled manual groups.[40] There is also a tendency for the children of professional groups to concentrate in universities, while the children of manual workers focus on the Regional Technical Colleges.

Housing

For a long period, the market seemed to meet Ireland's housing needs and the country had one of the highest rates of home ownership in Europe. While manual workers in Europe were more likely to live in apartments, their counterparts in Ireland often owned a

house with a front and back garden. Although the conservative
economists may not have admitted it, state intervention was one of
the key reasons why home ownership was high. Many workers
bought their first home through tenant purchase schemes whereby
local authority housing was sold off cheaply to those who previously paid rent. As Tony Fahey has pointed out, these former local
authority houses accounted for one in four owner-occupied homes
and were one of the main reasons why the overall level of home
ownership constituted 80 percent of all housing.[41]

Yet the Celtic Tiger has changed all that. A rip-roaring boom has
sent house prices rocketing to enormous figures as the wealthy
engage in speculation. Small two up–two down houses can barely
be purchased in Dublin for less than £100,000. In 1994 at the start
of the boom, the ratio of house prices in Dublin to the average
industrial wage was 4.3:1. Four years later this had doubled to
8.2:1.[42] The price of property did not increase because of any major
escalation in the cost of raw materials. It was driven purely by the
anarchy and chaos of a market that rose with the lure of profit in a
booming economy. House prices in fact grew three and a half times
faster than house-building costs over the same four-year period.[43]

The effect of these price rises on Irish society has been quite dramatic. A process has begun whereby home ownership no longer
stretches evenly across all classes and, as in mainland Europe, it is
becoming more associated with the professional and managerial
groupings in society. As Table 4.4 illustrates, over half of all mortgage borrowers were drawn from the professional and managerial
groups in 1997, compared to just over a third a decade earlier. By

Table 4.4 Percentage of different categories of mortgage borrowers,
selected years 1988–97

Year	Professional managerial employer	Salaried non-manual	Skilled semi-skilled manual	Unskilled manual	Farmer fisherman
1988	34.4	27.4	28.0	7.9	2.2
1991	38.2	28.0	25.9	6.7	1.2
1994	37.7	26.5	26.5	7.3	2.0
1997	52.2	19.5	20.3	4.4	3.7

Source: Department of Environment Annual Housing Statistics Bulletins
1989–98 (Dublin, Stationery Office, various years).

contrast, the number of skilled and unskilled workers who hold mortgages has dropped from over a third to under a quarter. As this modern form of social clearance gets under way, more white-collar and manual workers are being forced into the rented sector. Unlike the rest of Europe, this is largely unregulated and the preserve of the small property owners who form the core support for many of the main right-wing parties. The result has again been a major escalation of rent, as landlords have used the lack of security of tenure to evict tenants who are not willing to accept substantial increases. Although landlords are supposed to register with the local authorities, few have done so and even fewer have been prosecuted for this breach of the law. Instead many rest secure in the knowledge that an inspection designed to examine the quality of the building and the compliance of the landlord with a registration fee is as rare as a summer without rain.

As property and rents escalated, more people turned to the local authorities to provide social housing, yet they found that this sector had been run down dramatically. In order to cut taxes on the wealthy, the Haughey Government of 1987 implemented a huge series of cuts in public spending and one of the areas that was hardly noticed at the time was the devastation of the local authority house-building programme. In 1975, for example, the local authorities built 8,794 houses for those on the waiting lists but by 1989, this had dropped to a mere 768.[44] Planners sometimes justified these cuts by claiming that a process of 'residualisation' had occurred on council estates so that only the poorest remained in these areas, creating an atmosphere of cumulative deprivation. Yet the previous government had encouraged this very process by encouraging paid employees to leave these estates in return for a housing grant. No viable alternative was ever provided to local authority houses and even when the building programme picked up again in the 1990s, local authority houses still only amounted to 7 percent of all houses built in 1998.[45]

The result of all these processes is a housing crisis of large proportions. The hostels that cater for the homeless are crammed and many sleep in doorways in the major cities. Although the Irish family is changing dramatically, many have been forced to return to their parents' homes with all the attendant stress and frustration. It is estimated that in 1999 approximately 135,000 people were in need of appropriate housing.[46] However, the Government shows no sign of breaking from the policies that caused the crisis in the first place. The Bacon Report, which was supposed to provide solutions, did not attempt to move beyond market mechanisms and only advocated a slight curtailment of the Government's tax policies.[47] Instead of a rational programme of providing local authority housing on a planned basis, the Government has instead, without much debate, adopted a policy of subsidising the very property owners who helped cause the crisis. The poor have increasingly been shunted into the private rented sector, with the state covering the bulk of the rent. In 1989 just £6 million was paid out on rental supplement under the Supplementary Allowance to private landlords but by 1998, this had jumped to £96 million and provided a significant ballast for landlords who were intent on raising rents.[48]

Transport
The other area which has borne the brunt of the tax cuts is the transport service. The boom/slump cycle that is associated with market economies makes planning transport difficult, but the sudden growth of the Irish economy has thrown traffic projections into chaos. In 1991, for example, the Dublin Transport Initiative produced a forecasting model for 2001 where they attempted to predict how many cars would be in the city, how many passengers would come through Dublin airport and how much tonnage would be unloaded in Dublin Port. Yet all the key assumptions on population size or employment levels were cast aside by the boom and most of their projections were exceeded by 1996.[49] Today the major cities are gridlocked with traffic after a surge in car ownership that has taken Ireland near to the EU average. As most people expect gridlocks, they attempt their journey earlier but this only spreads the chaos for a longer period of the day. The result has been a rapid deterioration in the quality of life as the length of the working day increases and stress levels rise. This is not even to mention the appalling effects of car accidents, pollution and asthma levels.

All of these issues have been exacerbated by a conscious policy to run down spending on public transport in the 1980s. Dublin Bus, for example, has been starved of funds because politicians believed that the longer term effects of spending cuts would not be noticed until years after the decisions were made. In 1987, the annual subvention by the Government to Dublin Bus stood at £16.4 million, which is the equivalent in today's terms of £22 million. Yet it now

Table 4.5 Grants/subsidies to bus companies in selected European cities

City	Grant/subsidy %
Athens	50.0
Barcelona	39.4
Dublin	4.4
Helsinki	55.3
London	14.5
Paris	57.4
Rome	74.5
Strasbourg	46.0

Source: Jane's Urban Transport System, 16th edition, 1997/98.

stands at only £9 million and the staff has been reduced by 1,300 since then.[50] As Table 4.5 indicates Dublin Bus has received the lowest subsidy of any other capital city in Europe. These cuts have produced their own unique form of chaos. As the bus service was forced to seek funds for re-equipping its fleet from its own meagre resources, it tended to purchase single deckers and even mini-buses rather than double deckers. Yet even this form of cost cutting did not prevent the fleet becoming older and the average age of buses is eight years.[51] More buses break down, they come less frequently than they did before and when they arrive they are often crammed to sardine point. Many commuters simply voted with their feet, or more accurately their cars, and the share of bus passengers entering the inner city cordon bounded by the two canals has declined from 29 percent in 1980 to 26 percent in 1997.[52]

The poorer income status of bus users made the service more vulnerable to cutbacks. A Coras Iompair Eireann (CIE) discussion paper noted that

> Traditionally public transport was expected to cater for the access and mobility requirements of captive users i.e. travellers who do not have an alternative mode. Increasingly however the public transport modes are expected to provide an attractive and viable alternative for choice users i.e. travellers who would otherwise largely use a car.[53]

The suggestion that a service should only now become 'attractive and viable' for the new 'choice users' rather than 'captive users' indicates the bureaucratic neglect accorded to half of Dublin's population who relied on the service. Interestingly, the one area where public sector investment was increased in the 1980s was on the sub-urban DART service, where passenger numbers have grown sub-stantially. This borders some of Dublin's wealthier areas and this may help to account for why the shrill cries to cut this service were resisted.

If Dublin suffers from an appalling transport chaos, the under-funding of the rail network has become positively dangerous. Even the management of CIE noted in a recent annual report that 'a short-fall in investment ... is now impacting on safety'.[54] After a major derailment in Knockcroghery in November 1997, the dangers posed by the pattern of underinvestment could no longer be ignored. A special review of rail safety found unacceptable levels of risks that arose from inadequate signalling facilities, bridges in need of renewal and an old and decrepit track. Five hundred and forty miles of the 1,170 mile network is composed of old jointed track that rests on timber sleepers. Much of this rail is fifty years old and was built by the original private companies that were established under the British Empire.[55] The result of this extraordinary neglect is that trains on the Westport and Sligo lines have had to reduce speed con-siderably to avoid accidents. The calamitous deterioration of the rail service has meant that an investment programme of £642 million has had to be undertaken simply to guarantee its safety.[56]

Health

In common with most other industrial countries, the Irish state has cut the overall proportion of the national economy that is spent on health. The worst of the cuts began just after 1987 and initially there was huge opposition. An estimated 20,000 people demonstrated, for example, in Limerick against the closure of Barrington's Hospital, which had been in the city since 1830.[57] Yet these protests never escalated to the level of industrial action because union leaders had agreed that the cuts could be phased in, provided redun-dancies took place on a voluntary basis. This was the price paid for establishing partnership agreements and the Haughey Government took full advantage of it. At one point Ireland topped the OECD record for cuts in admission to acute hospital facilities per head of population. It cut the number of acute beds per 1,000 of the popu-lation by 43 percent and the average length of stay by 295 percent between 1980 and 1993. From a situation in 1980 where it had the highest rate of admissions in the OECD, it moved to one of the lowest.[58] Delays for public patients became exceptionally long with cardiac patients waiting for up to twelve months to get a bed. One of the most extraordinary practices that developed has been the closure of hospital wards over the summer periods.

The policy of cutbacks was lessened after 1992, but the overall proportion of national income going to health spending remained lower than it was in the 1990s. Today a higher component of health spending is now derived from additional burdens imposed on PAYE employees. Since 1991, for example, a special health levy of 1.5 percent has been in place. In addition, hospitals introduced a bed and breakfast charge of approximately £20 for overnight stays in hospitals. The run down of the public service has also led to an increasingly privatised tier of medicine, as the numbers taking out private health insurance has increased to over 40 percent of the population.[59] Higher paid earners again benefit more directly from the way health insurance is organised according to various plans, as they gain greater tax relief on the more expensive plans which give access to private hospitals.

Overall, then, health policy is driven by more rigorous budgetary considerations, with continual attempts to reduce spending in order to facilitate tax cuts. Hospitals are now involved in a 'case mix budget model'[60], where they compete for funding. This has led to increased pressure on individual families who have to look after patients who have been discharged early. Families also bear the brunt of other forms of care. A survey of the carers of Alzheimer's Disease found that a full 87 percent complained about the low level of support from the formal services.[61] Similarly, parents of children with mental handicap have pleaded most eloquently for relief respites and support from society at large. All of this, however, barely figures on registers of the Celtic Tiger elite who organised tax evasion on a huge scale, even though it robbed many of access to properly funded public services.

In conclusion, it should be noted that after 1987, Ireland joined the neo-liberal revolution as taxes on capital and wealth were drastically cut. This was presented as if it would benefit all the population because it increased the level of foreign investment. However, the evidence suggests that the majority did not benefit. First, the tax burden was more heavily loaded onto the PAYE sector, so that even low-paid workers paid comparatively high rates of tax. Second, public services were run down so that the basic quality of life deteriorated for many people. In brief, social vandalism was the price paid for the low level of taxes on capital and the wide scale and organised tax evasion colluded in by the state. In the decade between 1987 and 1997, there was little public debate on the costs that grew with Ireland's status as an Atlantic tax haven. However, the revelations about corruption among the political elite have led many to re-examine this history.

In addition, some conventional economists also realised that the scale of the cuts had created problems for the booming economy. In 1999, the ESRI produced a report which argued that there was an infrastructural deficit, where the underfunding of the public services created bottlenecks for the economy.[62] Yet this represented more of an adjustment in the dominant mindset rather than any fundamental break from what went on before. The proposals for investment in education, transport and even the growing acceptance of the need to 'do something' about housing were motivated by considerations of how best to serve the interests of capital rather than from a real concern to improve the overall happiness of the majority. Unless these proposals for tackling the 'infrastructural deficit' are linked to measures to tax the wealthy, they could remain pious aspirations that are not sufficient to reverse the decade of social vandalism.

Notes

1 'Jailed Building Worker Speaks Out', *Socialist Worker* (5–19 November 1998).
2 U. Halligan, 'Revenue Turned a Blind Eye to Tax Fraud', *Magill* (October 1998).
3 Ibid.
4 'Jailed Building Worker Speaks Out', *Socialist Worker* (5–19 November 1998).
5 Quoted in S. Cody, *Parliament of Labour* (Dublin, Council of Trade Unions, 1986) p. 237.
6 Revenue Commissioners, *Statistical Report 1997* (Dublin, Stationery Office, 1999) p. 7.
7 *Partnership 2,000 Agreement* (Dublin, Stationery Office, 1996) p. 14.
8 ATGWU, *A New Agenda for Economic Power Sharing* (Dublin, ATGWU, 1999) p. 23.
9 P. Bew, E. Hazelkorn and H. Patterson, *The Dynamics of Irish Politics* (London, Lawrence and Wishart, 1989) p. 162.

10 M. Mulreany, 'Taxation: Ireland and the New Europe' in K. Murphy and M. Mulreany, *Taxation: Ireland and the New Europe* (Dublin, IPA, 1993) p. 22.

11 R. Herrenstein and C. Murray, *The Bell Curve: Intelligence and Class Structure in American Life* (New York, Free Press, 1996).

12 T. Cooney, J. McLaughlin and J. Martyn, *'Taxation Summary Republic of Ireland 1998/1999* (Dublin, Institute of Taxation in Ireland, 1998) pp. 242–5.

13 Ibid. pp. 266–7.

14 K. Barrington, 'Capital Gains Tax Cut Prompts Executives to Realise Profits', *Sunday Business Post* (18 January 1998).

15 Revenue Commissioners, *Statistical Report 1997*, p. 61.

16 N. Webb, 'Top Irish plcs Slash Corporation Tax Rates', *Sunday Tribune* (27 June 1999).

17 S. Creaton, '"Sark Lark" Residents in Money Spinner', *Irish Times* (5 June 1998).

18 S. Creaton, 'Financial Services Sector Benefits by £40–60 Million', *Irish Times* (13 February 1998).

19 *Report of Investigation into the Administration of Deposit Interest Retention Tax and Related Matters During the Period 1st January 1986 to 1st December 1998 (Comptroller General's Report)* (Dublin Stationery Office, 1999) Table 2.1, p. 11.

20 S. MacCarthaigh, 'IDA Ireland says IRNRs are not Vital to Multinationals', *Irish Times* (27 February 1998).

21 *Comptroller General's Report*, p. 17.

22 Ibid. p. 81.

23 Ibid. p. 31.

24 Ibid. p. 48.

25 Ibid. p. 44.

26 Ibid. p. 91.

27 S. Drudy and K. Lynch, *Schools and Society in Ireland* (Dublin, Gill and Macmillan, 1993) p. 214.

28 European Commission, *Key Data on Education in the European Union* (Luxembourg, EU Commission, 1997) p. 144.

29 Partnership 2000 Expert Working Group on Childcare, *National Childcare Strategy* (Dublin, Stationery Office, 1999) p. 12.

30 Ibid. p. 17.

31 Ibid. p. 13.

32 Ibid. pp. 57–71.

33 Conference of Heads of Irish Universities, *Guaranteeing Future Growth* (Dublin, CHIU, 1999) p. 27.

34 Ibid. p. 27.

35 OECD, *Education at a Glance* (Paris, OECD, 1997) pp. 101–2.

36 European Commission, *Key Data on Education*, p. 154.
37 ESRI, *National Investment Priorities for the Period 2000–2006* (Dublin, ESRI, 1999) p. 59.
38 Department of Education, *Education 2000 International Adult Literacy Survey: Results for Ireland* (Dublin, Stationery Office, 1997) p. 43.
39 I. Bailey and U. Coleman, *Access and Participation in Adult Literacy Schemes* (Dublin, National Adult Literacy Agency, 1999) p. 11.
40 CHIU, *Guaranteeing Future Growth*, p. 26.
41 T. Fahey, *Social Housing in Ireland* (Dublin, Oak Tree 1999) p. 3.
42 Drudy Commission, *Housing a New Approach: Report of the Housing Commission* (Dublin, Labour Party, 1999) p. 6.
43 Ibid. p. 6.
44 Ibid. p. 20.
45 Ibid. p. 20.
46 Ibid. p. 19.
47 P. Bacon, *An Economic Assessment of Recent House Price Developments* (Dublin, Stationery Office, 1998).
48 Ibid. p. 18.
49 Dublin Transport Office, *Transportation Review and Short Term Action Plan* (Dublin, DTO, 1998) p. 7.
50 Dublin Bus, *Investment Needs Review 2000–2006* (Dublin Bus, 1998, discussion paper sent to author) p. 1.
51 Ibid. p. 14.
52 Ibid. p. 2.
53 CIE Discussion Paper, *Bus/Suburban Rail: Investment Plans for the Greater Dublin Area 2000–2006*, May 1996, p 4.
54 Coras Iompair Eireann, *Group Annual Report and Financial Statement 1998* (Dublin, CIE, 1999) p. 11.
55 CIE, *Railway Safety Programme 1999–2003* (Dublin, CIE, 1999) p. 4.
56 Ibid. p. 3.
57 J. Curry, *Irish Social Services* (Dublin, Institute of Public Administration, 1998) p. 130
58 OECD, *Economic Survey: Ireland* (Paris, OECD, 1997) pp. 134–5.
59 Figures supplied to author by Voluntary Health Insurance.
60 F. Lynch, 'Health Funding and Expenditure in Ireland' in E. McAuliffe and L. Joyce, *A Healthier Future: Managing Health Care in Ireland* (Dublin, IPA, 1998) p. 105.
61 Alzheimer Society of Ireland, *Caring Without Limits?* (Dublin, Alzheimer Society of Ireland Policy Research Centre, no date) p. 116.
62 See ESRI, *National Investment Priorities for the Period 2000–2006* (Dublin, ESRI, 1999).

5
Where have all the unions gone?

Language does not construct our social world and while there are moral and political reasons for rejecting hate speech, the mere insistence that politically correct words are used does not change the realities of racism or sexism. Language, however, can be regarded as a marker that denotes traces of past social change. The widespread use of the term 'gay' today did not result from the activities of well-placed individuals who promoted 'verbal hygiene'.[1] It was in fact the product of a huge social movement that grew out of the revolts of the 1960s.[2]

These more general considerations are relevant as the ICTU engages in its own language reform project. 'There is no excuse for holding on to terms that are already past their sell-by-date and obstruct rather than facilitate effective communication', the ICTU has pronounced rather testily.[3] The particular items that have passed their sell-by-date are interesting. They include 'shop steward' and 'trade union movement' which are seen as barriers to communication. The word 'movement' seems particularly objectionable. 'Apart from its medical or musical connotation', the anonymous ICTU author asks a little facetiously, 'what is a movement?'. Moreover, is it not 'the most abstract and general word in the English language'?[4]

The ICTU's plea is remarkably telling. A simple term like movement with its connotation of solidarity and common struggle, of a march towards the goal of a better society has, it would seem, become 'abstract' for the union officialdom. A decade of sitting on partnership committees, of joint discussion papers, of common 'problem solving' with employers has generated its own contempt for 'the past' and there is a ceaseless advocacy of 'flexibility' and 'change' which are supposed to be inevitable in a high technology age. The ICTU's status has never been higher in official circles and it is consulted on almost every aspect of Government policy, yet the growth of its influence is in inverse proportion to the share that workers gain from the national economy.

This chapter looks at the specific nature of the union bureaucracy and how it has developed different interests from its rank and file. It examines the tendency for this bureaucracy to grow ever closer to the state machine and share its outlook. Finally, it discusses how the Celtic Tiger is also producing its own ironic effect – a revival of rank and file trade unionism.

Is a union bureaucracy inevitable?

The union bureaucracy is not a new phenomenon. When Sidney and Beatrice Webb wrote their classic *History of Trade Unionism* in 1894, they noted that the government of the unions rested in the hands of the salaried officials who they labelled the 'civil service' of the union world.[5] As Fabian socialists who wanted a tamer movement they welcomed this development, but described the psychology of the official very well

> Whilst the points at issue no longer affect his own earnings or conditions of employment, any disputes between his members and their employers increase his work and add to his worry. The former vivid sense of privations . . . gradually fades from his mind and he begins more and more to regard complaints as perverse and unreasonable.
>
> With this intellectual change may come a more invidious transformation. Nowadays the salaried official of a great union is courted and flattered by the middle class. He is asked to dine with them and will admire their well-appointed houses, their fine carpets, the ease and luxury of their lives . . .
>
> His manner to his members . . . undergoes a change . . . A great strike threatens to involve the Society (union) in desperate war. Unconsciously biased by distaste for the hard and unthankful work which a strike entails, he finds himself in small sympathy with the men's demands, and eventually arranges a compromise distasteful to a large section of his members.[6]

Robert Michels, who combined an unusual mixture of anarchism with support for the conservative sociologist Max Weber, noted a similar rise of bureaucracy in the German labour movement. He wrote that

> For a good many years now, the executive committees of the trade union federations have endeavoured to usurp the exclusive right to decide on behalf of the rank and file the rhythm of the movement for better wages, and consequently the right to decide whether strike is or is not 'legitimate'.
>
> When leaders claim that they alone have a right to decide in a matter of such importance . . . it is obvious the most essential democratic principles are gravely infringed. The leaders have openly converted themselves into an oligarchy, leaving to the masses who provide the funds no more than the duty of accepting the decisions of that oligarchy.[7]

Both these lengthy quotations summarise some of the dynamics of how union bureaucracies operate, but they do not explain why they emerge. All of this might lead one to suspect that the rise of a trade union bureaucracy is inevitable and this is certainly the point that Michels wanted to establish with his notion of an 'iron law of oligarchy'.[8] Much of the literature of industrial relations also sees an inevitable progress towards 'mature collective bargaining', where the unions and employers develop trustworthy relations and shared values.[9] However, this approach presents unions as static and outside the changing stream of history. Instead of examining how organisations operate in particular societies at particular times, it assumes that human beings can never control their own representatives and so bureaucracy is inevitable. In reality, the nature of union organisations is determined by whether they are shaped in a revolutionary period or are the outcome of 'normal' capitalist development.

During the early part of the twentieth century, for example, the main Irish union for unskilled workers effectively operated as a mass revolutionary organisation. James Connolly, the Marxist leader of the Irish Transport and General Workers Union (ITGWU) summed up its outlook when he wrote that

> no consideration of a contract with a section of the capitalist class absolved any section of us from the duty of taking instant action to protect other sections when said section were in danger from the capitalist enemy.
>
> Our attitude was that in the swiftness and unexpectedness of our action lay our chief hopes of temporary victory, and since permanent victory was an illusory hope until permanent victory was secured, temporary victories were all that need concern us.[10]

During this period there was little evidence of bureaucratisation. The union leaders did not regard strikes as problems. They did not put the needs of the union apparatus above a desire to respond immediately and swiftly to struggle. Neither Larkin or Connolly led a life that differed materially from their own membership. There was little attempt to abrogate to the leadership the sole decision on taking strike action. There was, in fact, a close organic link between the leadership and the rank and file.[11]

The modern union officialdom are the descendants of William O'Brien rather than Connolly and Larkin. O'Brien personified the aspirations of the officials, because he translated Connolly's revolutionary slogan of 'One Big Union' into an obsession with building an administrative apparatus. The playwright Sean O'Casey claimed that O'Brien had 'no look of a Labour leader about him, but rather that of a most respectable clerk at home in a sure job'. His 'clever, sharp, shrewd mind . . . was ever boring a silent way through all opposition to the regulation and control of the Irish labour movement'.[12] O'Brien became the pivotal figure in the ITGWU after 1923 when the labour movement's attitude to either revolution or accommodation with the existing order was finally resolved. Conscious attempts at increasing the power of the bureaucracy had begun in 1918, when a new rule book replaced part-time organisers with full-time organisers, specified that 75 percent of union dues had to be remitted to head office and gave the newly formed national executive the power to sanction or withhold approval of strikes.[13]

Yet bureaucratisation did not simply follow from the dictates of the rule book. The five years between 1918 and 1923 brought a host of general strikes and even the establishment of soviets.[14] It was only the defeat of these struggles and the launch of a savage assault by employers, who pressed for wage cuts, which undermined the revolutionary instinct of Irish unions. The process was only completed after the union split and its founder, Jim Larkin, broke away to form the Workers Union of Ireland.[15] Thereafter the outlook of the union leaders was to occupy a position on, what Peadar O'Donnell called, the 'prompter's stool' where they whispered advice and pleas to the incoming nationalist political elite.[16]

Modern union leaders sometimes argue that in Connolly's day the labour movement had to use its 'muscle', whereas today it uses its 'brain' – or more particularly the brains of the union hierarchy.[17] The suggestion is that an approach which relies on militant and direct rank and file activity belongs to the past. Yet the brains – muscle distinction is trite. Not a huge amount of 'brains' was displayed by union leaders who accepted wage increases that fell well below rises in the level of profits and, on the other hand, the co-ordination of solidarity action across industry cannot simply be described as a use of 'muscle'. Nor should the claim that revolutionary union activity only existed in the past be taken too seriously. When the Polish union *Solidarnosc* was founded in 1980, the members insisted that talks with the Government be broadcast over a tannoy system from a room with large windows so that workers on the outside could make their feelings apparent at every juncture.[18] Or consider the events in France during the general strike in December 1995, where 'general assemblies' of workers emerged as the rank and file discussed how to take on the Government. Here is one description of what occurred

> The small premises by the railway line became a humming beehive of activity where everything was debated – how to carry the movement forward, the preparation of demonstrations, providing daily meals, the organisation of the crèche for strikers' children .. and the making of links with other workers. The railway workers went to meet the postal workers, the hospital workers, the gas workers, the teachers, the council workers. And then everyone found themselves together in front of private factories with loudhailers, songs, red flags, leaflets with the call for the general strike in the public and private sectors.[19]

Even if we reject the argument that a bureaucracy is inevitable, there are other less satisfactory explanations of its origins, such as the notion that it grows with the size of a union. However, this fails to explain how small unions, which were originally founded through rank and file revolts,[20] also become bureaucratised. In the 1960s, a number of breakaway unions such as the National Busworkers Union and the Psychiatric Nurses Association were formed and remained small ever since, but there is no evidence that they sustained a model of trade unionism that differed from the larger unions. Similarly, explanations which focus on the politics of the union leaders are inadequate. It is sometimes claimed that if 'genuine' left wingers won a majority of the leadership positions, this could change the social role that the union officialdom plays. However, the remarkable thing about the modern Irish trade union movement is that, individually, many of the leaders come from Workers Party backgrounds and yet little has changed from the days when more conservative officials were in charge.

It is more useful to analyse the union officials as a distinct stratum in the labour movement with a set of interests that are at variance with their members. The roots of their power lies in the contradictory nature of trade unionism and its relationship to the wider society in 'normal' times. Trade unions represent both an opposition to capitalism and a component of it. They resist the unequal distribution of income within society, but accept the notion of wage labour itself. Their very existence implies a conflict of interest between capital and labour, yet it is a conflict they are incapable of permanently resolving. As Engels argued, the unions recognise 'that the supremacy of the bourgeoisie is based solely upon the competition of workers amongst themselves i.e. upon their want of cohesion' and by attacking this 'vital nerve of the present social order' they are potentially dangerous.[21] Nevertheless, they are also defensive organisations and their internal life is shaped by the wider capitalist society in which they operate.

The unions accept the contours of the capitalist labour market, with dockers being organised alongside dockers and teachers with teachers. The unions also mirror the status divisions that have been created by the market – between white-collar and blue collar, between craft and general, between employed and unemployed. As a result, they are sectional in their nature and, despite protestations to the contrary, it is often the officials who do most to insist on this sectionalism, because it limits the scope of the conflict with the employers. Even when workers are formally organised in large unions such as SIPTU, this still applies. The basic unit of SIPTU is the section committee, where workers are only supposed to discuss their own claims. In particular workplaces there are often two section committees, for manual and non-manual staff. Different grades of members from the same union in the same workplace are even encouraged to cross each others pickets.

Acceptance of capitalism also means that the unions separate politics from economics. The unions are primarily concerned with industrial relations issues, while politics is supposed to be dealt with by parliamentary representatives. This means that the unions are limited to either passing resolutions or engaging in correspondence with relevant ministers. This separation of politics and economics goes to the heart of liberal democracy. Theoretically, everyone is equal in deciding on the running of the country but only a few have a say in the companies which dominate our 'economic' lives. By accepting that legitimate union activity only focuses on 'industrial relations issues', the challenge of the working-class movement is blunted. The role of the bureaucracy is rooted in this narrow econ-omistic and sectional nature of trade unionism. The acceptance of capitalism in turn means that a division of labour develops between the mass of workers and a layer of people who engage full time in bargaining. The union official becomes the mediator between employers and workers and this implies not only the role of a mes-senger, but also a manager of discontent. A number of things follow from this.

First, as the Webbs indicated, union officials see the privations of workers only in an abstract way and so regard struggle as a nuisance and an inconvenience. They are removed from the shopfloor, with all its attendant dangers, dirt and stress and do not suffer the indig-nities or harassment meted out by managers or employers. Isolated from the fellowship of other workers, the officials develop a per-spective where they see the personnel manager as a fellow profes-sional. Despite the formal lines of division between themselves and management, their aim, as one official put it, is 'to get them to realise it is just business'.[22] There are no direct personal consequences for the officials from what they negotiate. If a plant is closed, the offi-cial who negotiates the redundancies will not get the sack. If a pro-ductivity concession is demanded in return for a pay rise, the official will not have to work harder. In brief, there is no direct experience of what lies beneath the benign jargon about 'flexibility' or 'team-working'.

Second, the officials put a premium on maintaining their negotiat-ing relationship with management, even if this is detrimental to the rank and file. They see their own skills in negotiating techniques as the key to bringing improvements for workers and so play down the importance of the rank and file taking the initiative. A stable nego-tiating relationship can only be forged when employers are con-vinced that the officials can hold workers to contractual obligations. Officials must therefore insist that workers stick to agreements, even if those agreements were made under unfavourable circumstances. As Gramsci put it

> the union bureaucrat conceives of industrial legality as a permanent state of affairs. He too defends it from the same viewpoint as the pro-prietor. He sees only chaos and wilfulness in everything that merges from the working class. He does not understand the workers act of

rebellion against capitalist discipline as a rebellion; he perceives only a physical act, which may in and for itself be trivial.[23]

It follows that the officials also see the expansion of the union apparatus as an end in itself. The livelihood and status of the official is derived from the finances of the union machine and so all legal threats to the union are to be avoided at all costs. The result is often a hyper-respect for laws, even if those laws directly hamper union activity.

Finally, the divergence of interests between the union officialdom and their rank and file is reflected in a more privileged lifestyle. Local union officials demand their salaries are on a par with the managers they negotiate with. Top officials compare themselves to higher executives or senior civil servants, with the three highest positions in SIPTU earning over £70,000 a year. On top of that officials are often entitled to generous expense accounts and a car. It is only recently that the expense accounts of SIPTU officials have been published for their own members. These living standards do not depend on the ups and downs of the market. There is no need for systematic overtime and there are no threats of lay-offs or short-time working. Increasingly, the union hierarchy uses its accumulated resources as a form of patronage to undermine militancy. The prospect of a full- or even part-time union position, for example, is held up as a reward for those who accept the line of head office.

None of this implies that the union officialdom belongs to a different social class or is equivalent to employers. The union officials' role and status depends on the existence of a union machine which has to give some expression to the conflict of interest with employers. The bureaucracy,

> Like the God Janus, it presents two faces: it balances between the employers and the workers. It holds back and controls workers' struggle but it has a vital interest not to push collaboration with the employers and the state to a point where it makes the union completely impotent . . .
>
> If the union bureaucracy strays too far into the bourgeois camp it will lose its base. The bureaucracy has an interest in preserving the union organisation which is the source of their income and their social status.[24]

Preserving the union apparatus while seeking closer relations with employers explains why the most conservative official can sometimes engage in militant rhetoric. Yet this rhetoric cannot disguise the fundamental role of the official, which is to vacillate between employers and workers.

The bureaucracy, the state and partnership

The divergent interests of the union bureaucracy and the rank and file help to explain the different responses to social partnership. Almost all union officials support partnership deals, but a considerable proportion of union members have rejected them. In the largest union, SIPTU, 42 percent of members voted against entering the Partnership 2000 deal. This was particularly high in view of the fact that opportunities to articulate an alternative viewpoint inside the official structures of the union was limited. The union newspaper only carried the pro-partnership standpoint; virtually all officials were mobilised to deliver a Yes vote; and even the ballot paper contained a recommendation to vote Yes. Nearly one third of SIPTU members voted against the subsequent Programme for Prosperity and Fairness. By contrast, the union leaders have seen partnership as the dawn of a new era where they can move from 'the clenched fist of confrontation to the open hand of co-operation'.[25]

This desire for a close collaborative relationship with the employers is presented as 'a radical break from the past'.[26] In many ways, however, it represents a continuation of one of the most traditional desires of the union leaders – to have a close relationship with the state in order to underpin a stable and safe relationship with the employers. The underdevelopment of Ireland helped lay the ground for an economic nationalist ideology which has assisted this process. Historically the union leaders have claimed that they had a role to play in promoting the Irish economy, rather than in just advancing the 'sectional' interests of workers. As far back as 1925, the labour leader Tom Johnson articulated the implications of breaking with Connolly's concept of class struggle trade unionism when he proclaimed, rather clumsily, that 'I am a community-ist, a nation-ist before I am a trade-unionist', and then argued that

> We must preach the gospel of faithful service – for the uplifting of the nation – materially and spiritually. We must insist on maintaining the rights won through suffering but the power to maintain our rights is increased ten fold when we also do our duty faithfully and fulfil our obligations.[27]

In the 1940s, the ITGWU leadership were so enthusiastic about this form of economic nationalism that they split the labour movement in an attempt to rid it of British-based unions. In the process they forged an informal but close alliance with Fianna Fail to promote national development.[28]

However, it was opening of the Irish economy to multi-nationals after 1958 which provided the stimulus for the development of more formal tripartite structures to incorporate the union leaders into an active economic nationalist agenda. Within the space of a few years, the unions were involved in the Irish National Productivity Committee, the Committee on Industrial Organisation and the National Industrial and Economic Council.[29] Ever since then, the Irish state has taken an active interest in restructuring the union movement itself so that it fits in with the needs of Irish capitalism. The dominant strategy has been to incorporate the union leaders so that they come to share the same general objectives as the employers and state officials. The political elite has long believed that the trade union movement was, quite literally, too important to be left to its own members. The former Fianna Fail leader, Sean Lemass, explained this approach well when he argued that

> In any free democratic society a strong well organised and competently administered trade union movement is essential for economic and social progress. The more highly developed a national economy, the more obvious does this become. All of us who are concerned with the preservation of our free democracy as well as our country's economic development have therefore a vested interest in the development, the efficiency and effectiveness of our trade union movement. It cannot be a concern of members alone – it is far too important for that.[30]

The nature of the state's interest in shaping the union movement is not hard to discern. After Ireland embarked on a strategy of attracting multi-nationals, guarantees about order and discipline in the workplaces were required and a close relationship with the union leaders was regarded as essential to this process. Irish industry also faced a major challenge to restructure and raise productivity. As this often involved considerable change in work practices, support from union leaders was again regarded as crucial. Finally, moderate wage expectations from workers were also deemed to be essential for both Irish companies and the multi-nationals. A strategy of offering a political exchange to the union leaders, whereby they got a voice in state policy in return for promoting low wage rises, was hit on at an early stage.[31] All of this depended on having a union leadership that was both ideologically committed to promoting Irish competitiveness rather than class politics and was also in a position to enforce its outlook on the union movement at large.

However, the degree to which the state and the union leaders can reach a close accommodation is not entirely dependent on themselves. It is only when the confidence of rank and file workers is sharply undermined that the union leaders have a greater autonomy to pursue their aspirations for stability. The employers' offensive which was launched in the midst of a recession in the 1980s created the conditions for precisely this. The signal for the offensive came from a Federated Union of Employers document in 1981, which called for a more 'hard-headed approach' to bargaining.[32] What followed was a concerted attempt to take on the unions at local level by insisting on industrial peace clauses, more flexibility and an end to the indexation of wage increases to prices. A number of well-organised factories soon suffered major defeats. In Rowntree Macintosh, management took on a militant workforce to make the use of the Labour Court obligatory for the resolution of disputes. In Packard, management used helicopters to fly out strike-bound produce and eventually forced workers to individually sign no-strike pledges In Semperit, workers accepted measures to increase productivity by 20 percent without any gains in pay. Against a background of a growing recession, union density fell and unofficial stoppages virtually ceased.

These defeats helped create the space for the union leaders to push through a major change in orientation. Against the background of the defeat of the British miners in 1985, a number of key union leaders argued that they had to reach a consensus with the Government to isolate the 'New Right' in Irish society. The 'New Right', which was deemed to include the Progressive Democrats and sections of Fianna Fail, was bent on privatisation and the introduction of Thatcherite policies. The ICTU believed that an accommodation could be reached with Charles Haughey to ward off these threats. Haughey had, in fact, written to assure them 'that Fianna Fail had no intention of privatising state bodies such as Aer Lingus, Bord Na Mona, CIE or any other commercial semi-state body'.[33] Simultaneously, the National Economic and Social Council was used to provide the ideological underpinning for a new

consensus-based trade unionism. The National Economic and
Social Council was the successor of the National Industrial and
Economic Council which had been founded with a tripartite structure designed to produce a consensus between unions, employers
and state officials. However, as one writer acknowledged 'consensus was rarely achieved by way of agreed reports' between 1973 and
1986.[34] Quite simply, the power and confidence of rank and file
workers prevented the union leaders following their instinct to
accommodate. The defeats of the 1980s, however, changed all that
and created a space for a '"new breed" of trade union leader who
accepted that the unions have a major role to play in tackling the
problems affecting national finances, a position their predecessors
in the 1970s were reluctant to accept'.[35]

This background is important because there is often a tendency
to explain social partnership as the outcome of a natural process of
maturity and as an adaptation to a high-technology age where 'flexibility' and 'consensus' are the only options. However, if as we have
argued, social partnership grew out of the greater autonomy
afforded to union officials as a result of defeats suffered by rank and
file militants in the 1980, it follows that it is not necessarily a permanent state of affairs. These defeats also enabled the state to
pursue its long-standing goal of radically restructuring the Irish
labour movement so that it fitted in better with the needs of capital.
Three major elements were involved in this restructuring process.

First, there was a shift in the nature of bargaining so that the
union leaders took on board the acute problems that Irish capitalism faced and accordingly enforced moderation on their members.
The first partnership agreement, the Programme for National
Recovery in 1987, set the tone. Not only did it accept low wage set-
tlements for three years, but it also acknowledged that the
Governments should be given a free hand to push through public
sector cuts. The agreement represented the pinnacle of Fianna Fail's
hopes for the unions, because it provided a framework whereby
'sectional interests' where subordinated to the national economy.
Even the Labour Party leader Dick Spring called the deal 'the con-
trick of the century' because the pay increases for the public sector
were to be financed from a loss of 20,000 jobs.[36] Nevertheless,
despite Spring's rhetorical denunciation, the Programme for
National Recovery set the model for future agreements. Even as the
Irish economy began to pick up, the union officials were determined

not to press too many claims, lest they rock the foundation of the 'national economy'.

Second, the Government and the union leaders agreed to 'rationalise' the union movement itself. The tight bureaucratic structure of Irish unions often meant that rank and file revolts were expressed in the formation of breakaway unions and so by 1970 there were ninety different unions, often with quite small memberships. The existence of rival unions often forced officials to respond more directly to rank and file pressures than otherwise they might have liked. As one union leader subsequently explained,

> The job of a trade union official is to see around the corner and to prepare the members to take appropriate evasive action. If a second union is in there shouting, 'sell-out' arguing that there is no need for the changes in question, it makes life impossible for anyone involved in negotiation. One's horizons are limited to the daily grind of not losing members. No one can take up a leadership position. Where an organisation is unified it is much easier to tell people the real facts of life. [37]

The simplest solution was to encourage the elimination of many of these small unions and state support was made available to encourage them to merge. In 1989, the Department of Labour paid out £290,000 in grants to facilitate union mergers. Prominent among these mergers was that between the Post Office Workers Union and the Irish Post Office Engineers Union to form the Communication Workers Union.[38] In 1990, the super union, the Services Industrial Professional Technical Union, was formed from the amalgamation of the old rivals, the ITGWU and the Federated Workers Union of Ireland. It received a grant of £700,000 from the Department of Labour and claimed a membership of 155,000 workers.[39] The sheer size of this union, comprising 40 percent of the union members, gave its leadership a huge influence on the direction of the official labour movement. Subsequently, the Government took further action to stop the formation of new breakaway unions by specifying that licenses could only be given to unions that had more that 1,000 members and were able to raise a substantial deposit.

The mergers also provided a further opportunity to shift the balance of power inside the unions towards the officialdom. In almost all the mergers, a pattern developed whereby the annual decision-making conferences of lay delegates was replaced by biennial conferences. Sometimes this was justified with a claim that sectoral conferences could be held in the intervening years. However, only the general conference held the power of decision making, whereas the sectoral conferences were primarily consultative. In addition, the number of delegates to the annual conferences was often reduced, so that only those union activists who had succeeded in moving up the hierarchy beyond the level of the workplace were able to be elected. Finally, in another gesture to the 'new realities', references in the union rule books to vaguely socialist aspirations were quietly removed and replaced with blander claims to service the membership.

Third, the Government introduced the Industrial Relations Act to restrict militancy further and also to strengthen the position of the union leadership. The Act outlawed strikes over an individual worker unless lengthy procedures were adhered to. This prevented immediate action being taking over the victimisation of union militants and the Minister for Labour made it clear that his target was 'wildcat action'.[40] It also made political strikes more difficult to organise, as immunities from losses suffered by companies were only guaranteed for trade disputes. Crucially, the Act insisted on a secret ballot of all workers who might possibly be involved in a strike and this helped to limit the scope of solidarity action. Even if the majority of workers voted for such action, their officials were not compelled to carry it out. Where workers voted to support the action of another union, their strike only became legal after 'the action has been sanctioned by the ICTU'.[41] Finally, the Act was ambiguous on the question of blacking, but according to one writer, 'the predominant view would appear to be that such action remains unlawful'.[42]

When introducing the bill in the Dail, Bertie Ahern, the Minister for Labour, went to great pains to insist that it had been discussed beforehand with the most senior officials of the ICTU and took great umbrage at the suggestion that the union movement was not involved in its formation. He stated that 'all I have to say is that if ever a Bill was discussed as much with the people concerned as this Bill has been, I would like to read the files on it'.[43] The scale of consultation was used by Ahern to escape from charges that he had invoked Thatcherite measures to restrict union activity. Nevertheless, it was a form of Thatcherism by stealth where, although there was no frontal assault on the unions, the thrust of the bill was to make effective industrial action more difficult to organise. In many ways the ambiguities in the bill about issues such as blacking only added to this effect. The degree of uncertainty about the 'immunities' that had been granted to the unions in the past allowed officials to shelter behind the claim that they could not advocate action, lest it was in breach of the law. The overall rationale of the act was to force workers to respect official procedures and look to their officials for guidance in negotiating the law. There was little doubting Ahern's sense of achievement when he noted that Department of Labour officials 'have spent about twenty three years working on this Bill'.[44]

Business unionism or rank and file trade unionism

Ever since the militant heyday of the 1930s, the majority of US labour leaders have opposed a link between trade unionism and socialist politics. Instead they pioneered the practice of business unionism, whereby there was supposedly no fundamental conflict of interest between workers and employers. What was good for American business was good for American trade unionism. In the 1950s the American Government went to considerable effort to export this model to undermine subversive influences in the European labour movement. They found a ready audience among Irish trade union leaders and a representative of the American embassy often spoke at the Congress of Irish Unions conferences to update delegates on the battle against communism and the benefits of America's productive economy. Trips were also organised to the USA for both the Congress of Irish Unions and their rivals in the Irish Trade Union Congress by the anti-communist Mutual Security Alliance to promote the US model of business unionism.[45] Yet despite the right-wing climate of the 1950s the concept never fully took off. The irony is that business unionism only conquered the official Irish labour movement after the end of the Cold War when it was embraced not only by the more traditional Catholic labour leaders, but also by most former left-wing officials.

Business unionism is one of the main reasons why workers have thus far watched the growing inequalities of the Celtic Tiger but have not found a ready-made vehicle to express their resentment. On one level, its growth may be explained by important ideological changes. One of the key political influences on many union officials in the 1980s was the Workers Party, which combined a strong class rhetoric with a belief that there had to be an Irish Industrial Revolution before politics could fully split on class lines. Alongside trenchant critiques of the banks and of the 'lazy' indigenous bourgeoisie, there was almost a messianic support for the role that multinationals played in promoting industrial development. This contradictory mix only began to unravel after the collapse of the Soviet Union, which had previously been held up as an example of 'actually existing socialism'. Many former Workers Party supporters gave up on the possibility of a viable alternative to the market and simply embraced the concept of industrial development as an end in itself.

However, important as these shifts were in re-uniting the union bureaucracy around an acceptance of a competitive economy, the primary reason why business unionism grew was because of the restructuring of the labour movement that occurred in the 1980s. The combination of working-class defeats and an intensified effort by the state to incorporate the labour leaders has underpinned a notion that Irish workers have common interests with their employers in promoting the Celtic Tiger economy.

The business union approach is evident in most official pronouncements from Irish labour. There is an almost obsessive concern with promoting Irish competitiveness against foreign rivals. Key union leaders sit on the National Competitiveness Council where they pour over detailed league tables to see how costs, including labour costs, can be reduced.[46] Discussions at EU level on proposals for tax harmonisation to prevent multi-nationals engaging in 'social dumping' have been marked by a strange silence from Irish union leaders who only want to set the tax on company profits marginally above the 12.5 percent rate. The concern with competitiveness often means that union leaders can increasingly sound like business leaders. A leader of a major civil service union, for example, argued that 'a pay explosion would mean inflation and problems for the economy, ultimately forcing prices back into the line'.[47] Prominent union officials have also extolled the virtues of financial stringency, with SIPTU's research officer Paul Sweeney claiming that 'the parties of the Irish left . . . and the trade unions did not believe that more public spending was the solution to problems unlike the Left in the UK and elsewhere'.[48]

The embrace of the market has led to a desire to establish 'high trust relations' with employers. Increasingly this involves a strategy of deepening partnership structures, so that they are embedded at workplace level and begin to encroach on the traditional adversarial structures of collective bargaining. A recent document from the ICTU argued that more time 'must be spent establishing trust and confidence, sometimes outside the normal bargaining arena and especially when there is no major crisis taking place. This is the responsibility of both progressive managers and progressive trade union representatives and it must be planned for'.[49] The focus on partnership arrangements at workplace level means that the union leaders often seem to share a similar outlook to human resource managers. Significantly, the unions distinguish between 'anti-union' firms such as Ryanair and 'non-union' firms such as the giant Intel plant, where Human Resource practices of 'employee empowerment' are used, and do not make a major attempt to unionise in the latter. The establishment of high trust relationships also mean that the union leaders support new work practices and 'atypical' forms of employment. Paul Sweeney argues that many workers 'to their surprise find they enjoy the change that being multi-skilled gives them or the flexibility of annualised hours'.[50]

Business unionism has also brought a new embrace of privatisation and a host of measures known as 'gain sharing'. Although it was originally argued that social partnership was necessary to ward off attempts at privatisation from the New Right, the union leaders now support privatisation provided workers are offered share options. The ICTU also promotes 'gain-sharing' such as schemes for performance-related pay, team-based incentives where 'teams operate as business units within a company', profit sharing and share option schemes.[51] All of these arrangements help reduce the pressure on unions to promote pay claims and so help to align the economic hopes of workers with those of their employers. They suggest that workers make gains by competing against fellow workers and by working closely with their companies.

Business unionism has a certain appeal in a booming economy when profits are rising and where the avenues of traditional trade unionism seem to be closed. However, it contains many dangers as was highlighted when one of the directors of the National Centre for Partnership, the former general secretary of a civil service union, John O'Dowd was asked to give an example of where partnership arrangements were working at local level. He chose Tara Mines.[52]

Yet a year after this pronouncement, the company demanded that workers take a major cut in their wage packets and agree to increase their production targets to compensate for a drop in world zinc prices. Despite the ethos of social partnership, the suggestions that the losses should be borne by a small fall in profits rather than cuts in wages was not even considered. The refusal of employers to act as partners in any real sense means that a different type of trade unionism is emerging from the base – and ironically, the Celtic Tiger may have played a major role in its birth.

Sometimes there is a mechanical understanding of the relationship between economic booms and slumps and working-class consciousness. An economic crisis is thought to be more favourable to a growth in left-wing ideas, because it exposes the underlying weakness of the market, while a boom supposedly pacifies workers, because the employers make more concessions. However, as we have seen, booms in late capitalism do not necessarily lead to major concessions to workers. Competition on a global arena and a greater sense of instability means employers feel compelled to intensify pressure on workers. Nevertheless, a boom can have effects in other ways.

The link between a boom and a revival of working-class confidence has played an important role in Marxist debate in the past. Writing in 1921, when capitalism seemed to be stabilising after its post-war crisis, the Russian revolutionary Trotsky argued for a more dialectical understanding of the relationship between economic booms and workers' consciousness. Contrary to a mechanical understanding which equated a slump with a growth in anti-capitalist consciousness, he claimed that an economic slump could devastate the worker's movement in particular circumstances. After the 1905 Revolution in Russia, for example, the economic slump of 1907 and 1909 added to a sense of defeat and helped to thoroughly demoralise the labour movement. An improvement in the economic situation was necessary before the labour movement revived. Commenting on the economic growth that occurred between 1910 and 1913, Trotsky noted that

> There was an improvement in our economic situation and a favourable conjuncture which acted to re-assemble the demoralised and devitalised workers who had lost courage. They realised how important they were in production and they passed over to an offensive, first in the economic field and later in the political field as well.[53]

He generalised from this experience by arguing that where workers enter a slump following a period of retreat and defeat, the slump can become a factor in adding to desperation and demoralisation. By contrast

> The industrial revival is bound first of all to raise the self confidence of the working class, undermined by failures and disunity in its own ranks; it is bound to fuse the working class together in the factories and plants and heighten a desire for unanimity in militant actions.[54]

There is some evidence that this pattern is occurring in the recent booms, albeit not quite on the scale that Trotsky envisaged. The Goldilocks economy of the USA has led to a small but significant revival of working-class militancy as auto and UPS workers engaged in major battles with their employers. The Irish boom also seems to have fed into a revival of sectional militancy, as workers become more acutely aware of the labour shortages and their own indispensability to their employers. One example of the new militancy has been the construction industry.

Bricklayers are among the most highly paid workers in construction and it is significant that the revival of militancy began with them. As labour shortages grew, bricklayers exerted their muscle in a host of strikes to establish an unofficial pay rate of between £16 and £18 an hour. In addition, a major campaign was launched to rid the building industry of sub-contracting. Sub-contracting is advantageous to employers as it does away with holiday pay, wet time money or social security. It had become the established pattern during the property boom of the late 1980s in Britain and union activists were determined to halt its advance in Ireland. By and large they have been successful and most construction sites employ direct labour. The activities of the bricklayers have also been an important stimulus to other groups in the construction industry. Crane drivers, scaffolders and general operatives have all staged short stoppages which sometimes involved attendance at city-wide mass meetings to press their claims. General labourers have also staged unofficial stoppages to protest at the accident and death rate on the sites.

The other sign of militancy has been the re-emergence of the unofficial picket. In May 1998, a major revolt of craft and general workers occurred in the health boards and local authorities after they rejected an offer which tied pay increases to substantial productivity concessions. The strike began in Waterford and then spread throughout Munster before finally reaching Dublin.[55] At its height, joint meetings of craft and general workers were held in Limerick which cut across union boundaries. In March 1999, an attempt to discipline a shop steward in the ESB Moneypoint station sparked an unofficial strike, which threatened national power supplies. After it finished it was followed by a further 'copycat' strike as the case of two other workers who had been disciplined was taken up.[56] Even the police seemed to pick up on the new pattern when two days of unofficial action, nicknamed the 'blue flu', won a significant wage increase from the Government. This revival of militancy has led to the re-appearance of small unofficial rank and file groups for the first time since the 1960s. The Busworkers Action Group called a one day stoppage over a company viability plan and successfully defied the Industrial Relations Act to bring Dublin to a standstill. The first small breakaway union has also been formed as a result of discontent with the wider union hierarchy. The Irish Locomotive Drivers Association has established the first small breakaway union in recent times and has staged stoppages to demand its own recognition from the company.

The revival of militancy is still at a low level and has not reached the levels that existed before the defeats of the 1980s. Nevertheless, it does indicate that a major conflict is opening at the heart of the labour movement. In the week after Ireland's latest social partnership agreement The Programme for Prosperity and Fairness was accepted, in March 2000 the country was convulsed by a national transport strike as Dublin bus drivers and rail maintenance workers demanded higher wage increases. It was a sharp reminder of the differences in approach that have now opened up in the unions. One option is the road of business unionism, which embraces the drive for competitiveness and seeks a closer relationship with the employers. The other promotes a form of rank and file activity which is driven by a recognition that workers have lost out under the Celtic Tiger. The rank and file activists reject social partnership, but their actions still outstrip their articulation of a political alternative to this approach. As a result, the lines of demarcation separating the two souls of the modern Irish labour movement have not yet been fully drawn. The union officialdom are sometimes forced to respond to the revival of militancy while the rank and file activists are also subject to an ideological offensive which argues there is no alternative to the logic of the market. Nevertheless, behind the shifting allegiances, conflict has re-emerged in Irish labour. How that conflict will be resolved will depend on political argument and the experience of struggle itself.

Notes

1 D. Cameron, *Verbal Hygiene* (London, Routledge, 1995).

2 See M. Holborow, *The Politics of English* (London, Sage, 1999) for a Marxist account of language and society.

3 Irish Congress of Trade Union, *Challenges Facing Unions: Irish Society in the Millennium* (Dublin, ICTU, 1999) p. 22.

4 Ibid.

5 S. Webb and B. Webb, *A History of Trade Unionism* (London, Longman, 1907) pp. 456–7.

6 Ibid. p. 453.

7 R. Michels, *Political Parties* (Glencoe, The Free Press, 1958) pp. 153–4.

8 Ibid. pp. 393–409.

9 R. Lester, *As the Union Matures* (Princeton, Princeton University Press, 1958) pp. 160–7.

10 O. D. Edwards and B. Ranson (eds), *James Connolly: Selected Writings* (London, Jonathan Cape, 1973) p. 313.

11 See C. D. Greaves, *The Irish Transport and General Workers Union: The Formative Years: 1909–1919* (Dublin, Gill and Macmillan, 1982).

12 Quoted in A. Mitchell, 'William O'Brien, 1881–1968 and the Irish Labour Movement', *Studies* (Autumn-Winter 1971) pp. 311–31.

13 Interview with Frank Robbins, ITGWU Official, in K. Allen, An Approach to the Study of Shop Stewards in Irish Trade Unions. M.A. Thesis, University College Galway, 1977.

14 See E. O'Connor, *Syndicalism in Ireland 1917–1923* (Cork, Cork University Press, 1988).

15 C. Kostick, *Revolution in Ireland: Popular Militancy 1917–1923* (London, Pluto, 1996) pp. 193–8.

16 P. O'Donnell, *There Will Be Another Day* (Dublin, Dolmen Press, 1963) p. 17.

17 See M. Riordan, *The Voice of a Thinking Intelligent Movement: James Larkin Junior and the Ideological Modernisation of Irish Trade Unionism* (Dublin, Irish Labour History Society, 1995).

18 C. Baker and K. Weber, *Solidarnosc: From Gdansk to Military Repression* (London, International Socialism, 1982) p. 15.

19 C. Harman, 'France's Hot December', *International Socialism Journal*, no 70 (1996) p. 69.

20 C. McCarthy, *Decade of Upheaval* (Dublin, IPA, 1973) Ch. 2.

21 Quoted in R. Hyman, *Marxism and the Sociology of Trade Unionism* (London, Pluto Press, 1971) p. 6.

22 'IRN Interview: Tony Walshe, SIPTU', in *Industrial Relations News* (8 October 1998).

23 A. Gramsci, 'Soviets in Italy', in *New Left Review*, 51 (September-October 1968).

24 T. Cliff and D. Gluckstein, *Marxism and Trade Union Struggle: The General Strike of 1926* (London, Bookmarks, 1986) p. 27.

25 ICTU, *Challenges Facing Unions*, p. 14.

26 Ibid. p. 15.

27 Johnson to ITUC Executive, 5 July 1925, Tom Johnson collection National Library of Ireland, Ms 17230.

28 K. Allen, 'Forging the Links: Fianna Fail, the Trade Unions and the Emergency' *Saothar*, no. 16 (1991).

29 W. Roche, 'State Strategies and the Politics of Industrial Relations' in T. Murphy (ed.) *Industrial Relations in Ireland: Contemporary Issues and Developments* (Dublin: Department of Industrial Relations, UCD, 1987) p. 5.

30 Irish Transport and General Workers Union, *Annual Report and Conference Proceedings* (Dublin, ITGWU, 1963) pp. 119–20.

31 Roche, 'State Strategies and Politics of Industrial Relations', p. 7.

32 M. Fogarty, D. Egan and W. Ryan, *Pay Policy for the 1980s* (Dublin, Federated Union of Employers, 1981) p. 72.

33 ICTU, *Annual Report and Conference Proceedings* (Dublin, ICTU, 1987) p. 209.

34 B. Sheehan, 'NESC's Role in Underpinning National Agreements Since 1987', *Industrial Relations News* (12 November 1998) p. 17.

35 Ibid.

36 D. Spring, 'The Programme for National Recovery', *Irish Times* (17 October 1987).

37 'IRN Interview: Shay Cody, Deputy General Secretary, IMPACT', *Industrial Relations News* (23 April 1998).

38 Department of Labour, *Annual Report 1989* (Dublin, Stationery Office, 1990) p. 12.

39 Department of Labour, *Annual Report 1990* (Dublin, Stationery Office, 1991) p. 54.

40 A. Kerr, 'Collective Labour Law' in T. Murphy and W. Roche (eds) *Irish Industrial Relations in Practice* (Dublin, Oak Tree Press, 1994) p. 369.

41 Ibid. p. 372.

42 Ibid. p. 370.

43 Dail Debates, 15 March 1990, vol. 397, col. 377.

44 Ibid., col. 366.

45 K. Allen, *Fianna Fail and Irish Labour: 1926 to the Present* (London, Pluto, 1997) p. 100.

46 National Competitiveness Council, *Annual Competitiveness Report 1999* (Dublin, Forfas, 1999).

47 'Interview: Blair Horan, General Secretary, CPSU', *Industrial Relations News* (25 March 1999).

48 P. Sweeney, *The Celtic Tiger: Ireland's Economic Miracle Explained* (Dublin, Oak Tree Press, 1998) p. 95.

49 ICTU, *Managing Change: Report of Review Group on Union Involvement in Company Re-structuring* (Dublin, ICTU, 1995) p. 23.

50 Sweeney, *Celtic Tiger*, p. 106.

51 'Text of ICTU Guidelines on Gain-sharing, Profit sharing and ESOPs', *Industrial Relations News* (22 April 1999).

52 'IRN Interview: John O'Dowd, Joint Director, National Centre for Partnership, *Industrial Relations News* (20 August 1998).

53 L. Trotsky, 'The Interaction Between Booms and Slumps', *International Socialism Journal*, no. 20 (1983) p. 135.

54 Ibid. p. 139.

55 'Wildcat Action a Cause for Alarm as Key Union Advises Rejection of Pay Offer', *Industrial Relations News* (21 May 1998).

56 'The ESB Dispute – Weakness in Partnership Exposed at Plant Level', *Industrial Relations News* (18 March 1999).

6

Crony capitalism

On the outskirts of most towns in Ireland, there is a Dunnes Stores with its advertising slogan 'Better value beats them all'. The stores sell everything from cheap clothing manufactured in Burma to its own foodstuffs which are made to order from a stream of suppliers. Today the stores have a slightly dated feel, but in the past they symbolised the boom of the 1960s when mass shopping emerged to challenge the staid respectability of stores like Clerys. They had been founded by Bernard Dunne who ran them personally up to 1963. Being a canny businessman who disliked the very concept of taxes, he transferred the entire business into the Dunnes Settlement Trust because 'a trust would avoid a massive inheritance tax bill for his children when he died, but more importantly, it would make it much more difficult for the children to sell the company and it should ensure that Dunnes Stores remained a family business'.[1]

After he departed, Dunne Senior left two legacies – the St Bernard brand name in all his stores, and his children locked into a close commercial relationship with each other. The whole enterprise worked famously and in the ten years after Bernard Dunne's death, the turnover grew from £300 million a year to £850 million in 1993.[2] Yet few families are free of conflicts and the Dunnes were no exception. In 1992, Ben Junior, the key figure in expanding the stores, was charged in a Florida court with possession of cocaine. If he had been black and poor he might have received a long sentence, but being Irish, white and rich he got away with spending a month in a rehabilitation clinic. The scandal, however, provoked a major split in the Dunne family and Ben Dunne was removed as executive director of the company.

If the split had not occurred, the Irish people might not have learnt about the unofficial networks that dominate the country. For much of the time, the ruling elite manages a subtle practice of internalising the official values of democracy, where all are equal before the state, while operating the informal mechanisms which provide real power for the wealthy. A unity of purpose and a sense of delicacy about these arrangements are enough to keep them concealed. Yet the bitterness in the boardroom of Dunnes overrode all this and the other Dunnes' family members commissioned the auditors Price Waterhouse to investigate their brother Ben, who had until then sole and complete control of the financial side of the business.

It transpired Ben Dunne made very large donations to politicians. He paid out approximately £395,000 for refurbishment work on the house of the Fine Gael Minister Michael Lowry and put a number of bonus payments for work done by Lowry's company into accounts in the Isle of Man. According to the McCracken Tribunal 'these accounts were opened and moneys paid in this way . . . to assist him in evading tax'.[3] Dunne also paid out over £2 million to Charles Haughey while he was Taoiseach. The payments had begun when Haughey's friend, Des Traynor, contacted a half a dozen wealthy businessmen to help pay off Haughey's debts. Ben Dunne, however, took full responsibility for paying off the debt saying 'I think Haughey is making a huge mistake trying to get six or seven people together . . . Christ picked twelve apostles and one of them crucified him'.[4]

These were the two unusual payments that led to the formation of the McCracken Tribunals. However, there were also a host of 'ordinary political donations' which McCracken found perfectly legitimate and did not pay much attention to. They included a series of payments which totalled £180,000 to the Fine Gael party between 1989 and 1993, £15,000 to the Labour Party's campaign to elect Mary Robinson as President and a host of smaller donations of between £1,000 and £5,000 to ten TDs in all. The TDs came from the two main right-wing parties, Fine Gael and Fianna Fail, and it would appear that Ben Dunne was quite flexible in his political allegiances.

Why do wealthy businessmen make such large payments to politicians? No satisfactory answer has been provided by the various tribunals which have investigated a series of scandals in the Celtic Tiger. The McCracken Tribunal offered two suggestions for Dunne's behaviour. One was that Ben Dunne was 'an impetuously generous person'.[5] This, however, seems a little far fetched, as there is no evidence that this generosity extended to his own staff who have staged strikes to fight over additional payments for Sunday working. The other explanation deserves quotation,

> It is no part of the function of the Tribunal to conduct a psychological study of Ben Dunne. However, it does appear to the Tribunal that a possible motive for the actions of Ben Dunne, in the absence of any ulterior political motive, was simply to buy friendship, or at least the acquaintance of a person in a very powerful position. Mr Ben Dunne appears to have had many friends in the business community, but few if any, in the political community.[6]

This is a wonderful sentence which is hedged with qualifications. Yet the report effectively discards the point about 'any ulterior political motive' when it concluded that neither Haughey or Lowry engaged in any 'political impropriety' or 'intervened in any way for the benefit of Dunnes Stores'.[7] If Dunne had no 'ulterior political motive', we are then left wondering why he needed this friendship. Why did a sharp-headed businessman who used the slogan 'Better value beats them all' never consider the value of his own political donations? The delicate suggestion from Justice McCracken is that there was a craving for friendship from people in power. This may have resulted from insecurity, or a desire for social company but it is no part of the tribunal's brief to examine this 'psychological' craving. This is as far as official Irish society can go in offering an explanation for why one of the richest businessmen wanted to buy politicians.

State and capital

In order to grasp the real link between big business and politics, we need to move beyond the dominant ideology. Officially, every modern society is a democracy, where the majority of citizens direct their state. Individual greed may exist in civil society but the state transcends this to become the collective expression of a national will. The state expresses the common good and even gives embodiment to the national character. Where this breaks down and vested interests distort politics for their own ends, the term 'corruption' is used. However, the dominant ideology regards this as the exception in modern democracies.

The term 'crony capitalism' illustrates this. Up to 1997, the success of the Asian Tigers was sometimes explained by their particular value systems which apparently stressed discipline and collective effort over individual aspiration. After they collapsed, however, these very same virtues reappeared as vices. The links between the state and business, the suppression of individual freedoms in the marketplace were seen as the cause of the collapse. So, for example, the 'chaebol' system in South Korea, where giant conglomerates developed close ties to the state bureaucracy, was denounced as a form of crony capitalism where the state and the business elite were too intermeshed. This in turn resulted from a failure to develop a proper civil society which was normally associated with a more mature market system. The point of the argument was that the calamitous collapse of the economies of south east Asia was the result of exceptional factors that were not intrinsic to the nature of capitalism itself, but rather to a non-European value system. The proper norm was that business and the state maintained an arm's length relationship which was functional for both.

This ideology has deep roots. Adam Smith argued that the state had to perform the role of a night-watchman and avoid any interference in the economy. It needed only to patrol the perimeter and ensure that security and the law were maintained. Milton Friedman made a similar argument when he asserted that capitalism, rather than working-class struggle gave rise to democracy. He argued that 'the kind of economic organisation that provides economic freedom directly, namely, competitive capitalism, also promotes political freedom, because it separates economic power from political power and in this way enables the one to offset the other'.[8] Unlike feudalism, where there is a concentration between political and economic power, the market apparently allows individuals to generate wealth independently of the state and so creates space for a change of government and a voting system based on individual preference.

Yet there is ample evidence to suggest that this is an idealised model of capitalism and that crony capitalism is in fact the norm. In the USA, although Etzioni argues that 'the separation of private from public power is essential for democratic government', he also concedes that the US Congress is 'corrupt to the core' because it is dominated by Political Action Committees who channel funds to representatives from big business.[9] In Japan, the factions in the ruling Liberal Party are structured around a set of magnates who have close ties to the main companies. The Italian political system has been variously described as 'partitocrazi' or even 'cleptocracy' where the state was run by political figures for their own profit.[10]

Real existing capitalism works quite differently from the idealised model of classical economics. Nation states arose out of the developing capitalist organisation of production, but then fed back into the development of that capital to leave their imprint on its tempo and character of development. The state and capital are intertwined, with each feeding off the other. The state attempts to regulate the supply of labour to companies, to remove obstacles to the sale of their products, to create an infrastructure to fit their requirements, to establish rules so that companies can both compete and co-operate within the national territory, as well as acting as the 'night-watchman' by providing a security service to protect property both from domestic and external threats. The state in turn looks to capital to provide a viable economy from which it can derive its taxes and uphold the lifestyle of a state bureaucracy.[11]

All of this means there is a structural interdependence between the state and capital and this is expressed in the intermingling of their personnel. Far from companies acting as individual atoms engaging in blind competition, they cement alliances with each other and with political figures through marriage, socialising and networking. This circulation of elites between business and industry has been noted by many writers. Miliband's early study of the state in capitalist society produced an instrumental view, where the state appeared to be tied to the capitalist class mainly because its leading personnel were drawn from the same milieu as the owners of private capital.[12] From a non-Marxist viewpoint, Hill has shown how non-executive directors on company boards often focus on making political contacts. The directors of the largest companies, he surveyed, expected access to senior members of the Cabinet, including the Prime Minister on a regular basis.[13] These networks explain why corporate headquarters tend to be located in particular cities close to the orbits of political power. Despite the growth of sunbelt industry in America, for example, only 12 percent of company head offices were in the southern states.[14]

None of this, however, implies there is a smooth relationship between the state and capital. Inside individual countries, there are different forms of capital based on finance or production, which have different interests. Sections of the state bureaucracy in turn can transform themselves into 'political capitalists' who seek to promote state industry or industrial development within a country. Because the ruling class operates like a band of 'hostile brothers', these varying sectors conflict and co-operate. Thus a former political capitalist like Tony O'Reilly, who once chaired the Irish state Sugar Board, transformed himself into a private sector capitalist and then railed against intrusions of the state into industry. Nevertheless, as Harman argues

> Each element branches out on its own, like nerves in a human body, but still cannot escape its dependence upon huge ganglions where it intertwines with all other. These ganglions, knots where the mass of different capitals are entangled with the state bureaucracy they sustain and depend upon, are the national capitalist economies.[15]

Nigel Harris has argued that the process whereby the state and capital merge has broken down because of globalisation and claims that a form of world capital is breaking free from the parasitic nation state.[16] Yet this does not tally with the recent experience of the Irish economy, or other economies for that matter. As global competition increased, companies sought an ever closer relationship with their state in order to guarantee access to export credit insurance, or to a share of cheap loans or an influence in law making at EU level. If anything, the growth of a global market has meant that the boundaries between state and capital became blurred. Companies wanted ever closer personal ties and access to the state on a more regular basis. The state bureaucracy in turn increasingly concerned itself with the welfare of major firms.

If the dominant ideology presents an idealised picture of a state, its picture of business organisations can often almost resemble a fairy story. The pressure on a company to develop strong relations with the state also means a pressure to cut others out and gain advantage over its rivals. Often the methods used are secretive, underhand and border between legality and illegality. This is hardly surprising as the culture of every capitalist firm is to breach rules, to cut through 'red tape' so that its demand for profits are fulfilled. As Dalton argued in his study of managers, the weak are seen as those who are rule-bound, the 'do it by the book types' who are handicapped by their own rigidity, while the strong see that rules are 'not sacred guides but working tools to be revised, ignored, dropped . . .'.[17] The result of this drive is invariably a form of 'double think and double act'[18] where companies maintain an adherence to the public values of separating business and politics, but engage in strategies of bribery and financial inducement to achieve their means.

Legalised corruption is built into the nature of all modern capitalist societies and is increasing as competitive pressures became more intense. Reisman's study of commercial bribery noted that companies operate a 'myth system' whereby they express support for the democratic system and its values but then adopt an 'operational code' which is covered in secrecy and is concerned with how things are actually done.[19] In brief, there is a private and unacknowledged culture which tolerates extraordinary payments as the normal way of doing business. Etzioni's study of legalised corruption in America is of relevance to the recent scandals in the Celtic Tiger.

Etizoni's argues that instead of focusing on individual bad apples, it is better to look at the structure of the barrel which causes the apples to rot. One of the main elements of that structure is that illegality and corruption are endemic in big business. He cites a study of insider trading which found that of the 172 mergers in the USA, unusual stock run ups occurred in 172 cases![20] Another study of the Fortune 500 leading US industrial corporations in the period 1975–84, which looked only at recorded incidents of corruption, found that 62 percent were involved in one or more incidents of significant illegal activity.[21] If private business has this record of illegality, it can have little compunction about seeking to influence political representatives, by whatever means necessary. Two main methods are employed according to Etizoni. One is the 'retail method', where private money is made available to gain specific favours. The other is the 'wholesale method' where massive funds are used to elect representatives who will be co-operative with big business. The latter method is seen as more effective because, as Harold Scroggins, an oil-industry lobbyist, put it, 'We came to a decision some time ago that the only way we could change the political fortunes of the petroleum industry was to change Congress'.[22]

Whichever the chosen method, a distinctive pattern emerges. First, the law is circumvented through deals between lobbyist and political representatives which are 'implicit, rather than fully spelled out, but nevertheless specific, relating to clear outcomes'.[23] If a donation, for example, arrives before a particular request is made, there is no need to explicitly state that the money was a bribe, but politicians are more than capable of tacit understandings. Second, this form of legalised corruption is often rationalised as simply a means of getting access to the ear of the lawmaker but as Justin Dart, a California industrialist, put it somewhat sarcastically, 'With a little money, they hear you better'.[24] Third, the focus of much of this lobbying is the winning of tax loopholes and the allocation of credit to particular industries. Rather like the Irish tax code, loopholes in US tax laws have spiralled since the Reagan era. In 1974, tax breaks amounted to $82 billion but this had jumped by 299 percent to $327.5 billion in 1984.[25] Similarly, credits to industry in the form of cheap loans, distress relief and trade adjustment grants have also escalated and are the focus of rival efforts by different companies to win their share against others.

All of this carries important lessons for the Irish experience. It would seem, for example, that the methodology of the tribunals in seeking a one-to-one relationship between a donation and a specific measure pushed by an individual politician is misplaced. In America, where there is a highly developed lobby system which works through individual representatives who speak openly in Congress, this is an inadequate measure of legalised corruption. In Ireland, where the main recipients of donations have been Cabinet members who take decisions in secret and who can get others to propose measures, it makes even less sense. The failure to look at the broader context in which legalised corruption takes place has forced the judges back onto slightly bizarre psychological explanations. Yet accepting any other approach would challenge the ideology which governs this society itself.

Crony capitalism in the Celtic Tiger

If by Etzioni's 'wholesale' method, we understand a structure of financial dependency such that politicians feel beholden to their benefactors, then the chief subjects of the McCracken Tribunal provide two interesting cases.

Michael Lowry began working as an apprentice engineer for Butler Refrigeration and rose to become its sales manager. One of the company's major contracts was to service the refrigeration of Dunnes Stores. Two years after Lowry was elected to the Dail in 1987, he was called to Ben Dunne's office in Dublin and offered the contract to service refrigeration at Dunnes in place of his own employers, Butler Refrigeration. He established his own company Streamline Enterprises, which was in effect a wholly owned subsidiary of Dunnes although Lowry could and did masquerade to others as an independent contractor. Dunne promised him that if he achieved savings for Dunnes Stores, he would make him a wealthy man. However, as Sam Smyth points out, 'It did not come cheap. The ambitious young TD for Tipperary North's political fate and his financial future was now in the gift of the country's wealthiest and most successful businessman'.[26]

Lowry's apparent financial success and business acumen marked him out as a key financial organiser for Fine Gael and when he offered to help reduce the party's debt, his assistance was immediately accepted. It was Lowry who arranged for the party leader, John Bruton, to call to Dunne's house to collect a major donation. Significantly, when a leadership contest seemed to be in the offing in 1993, Lowry was also the pivotal figure who organised substantial individual donations to defray election expenses for Michael Noonan and Ivan Yates, two potential contenders for the leadership of the party. Some months later, Lowry had become the Director of Party Finances and soon reduced the party's substantial debt, thanks again to a major donation from Ben Dunne. Throughout all this process Lowry had grown to become one of the Fine Gael leader John Bruton's 'most trusted confidants'[27] and was charged alongside Bruton's brother Richard with negotiating the formation of a coalition government with the Labour Party in 1994. Smyth's summary of what happened is to the point, 'Ben Dunne's money had bought Michael Lowry a lot of influence at the highest levels of Fine Gael'.[28]

Michael Lowry and Charles Haughey shared two things in common: they both had effective control of their parties' finances and they were both beholden to Ben Dunne. Haughey's dependence on substantial personal donations from wealthy figures was however much more extensive. Haughey's day-to-day personal finances were organised through Des Traynor, a personal friend and board member at various times of some of Ireland's largest companies. Although Haughey seems to have spent lavishly, he claimed to have no knowledge of where much of the money came from.[29] Between 1 August 1988 and 31 January 1991, for example, Haughey was paid £708,850 in personal expenses which amounted to £23,603 a month or £5,500 a week.[30] Ben Dunne was one of the contributors, but there were also others who used the Ansbacher account to simultaneously avoid tax and make donations to fund Mr Haughey's lifestyle.

We can postulate two specific reasons why businessmen might have been willing to pay so highly for winning the goodwill of these two prominent politicians. First, both Lowry and Haughey were highly committed to a strong pro-business policy. They favoured the tax cutting neo-liberal agenda which reduced Corporation Taxes and cut public spending. They also served in Cabinets that turned a blind eye to wide-scale tax evasion through the use of non-resident accounts.[31] Indeed their own individual willingness to use offshore accounts indicated they were positively in favour of this sort of facility.

Second, the 'goodwill' of the state is often essential to the specific arrangements of individual companies. Dunnes Stores, for example, had a unique tax arrangement, whereby ownership was vested in a Dunnes Settlement Trust which minimised tax. This Trust had been set up in March 1964 for a period of twenty-one years and when the Trust came to a close in 1985, the Revenue Commissioners ruled that the Dunnes family were liable for a £30 million tax bill for capital gains, as its value was deemed to have been disposed among the beneficiaries. However, a ruling from the Revenue Appeal Commissioners overturned this tax bill and the Revenue Commissioners decided not to pursue an appeal to the Circuit Court.[32]

Formally the Revenue Commissioners and the organs of Government maintain a strict separation. Yet the Appeals Commissioners are nominated by politicians and, in the case of Dunnes Sores, political representations were made on the issue. The McCracken Tribunal found that 'the only request for special favours' that Ben Dunne made of Charles Haughey was 'a request for a personal meeting with the chairman of the Revenue Commissioners'.[33] It was 'satisfied that it was merely a routine meeting, at which nothing specific was requested by Ben Dunne'.[34] However the then chairman of the Revenue Commissioners, Mr Philip Curran, told the Tribunal of being called into Mr Haughey's office in 1988 and being told by him that 'business was booming and Ben and the family were making an awful lot of money but that there was some problem they had about, I think it was the family trust and the question of capital acquisitions tax'.[35] He also stated that when he eventually met Ben Dunne he had spoken about 'accumulating tax in trust'.[36] Whether or not

Mr Dunne made a 'specific request' is therefore hardly the issue. The fact remains that the Taoiseach and the chair of the Revenue Commissioners were made aware of the tax difficulties that Dunnes Stores faced. Moreover the demand for a £30 million tax bill was withdrawn and the Dunnes Settlement Trust had its life extended for a further twenty-one years.

If the 'wholesale' method of business influence on politicians is seen to reap benefits, it is also possible to examine the outcomes of specific decisions and correlate them with specific donations. None of this need suggest that a political decision was taken because of a transaction. The norm, as Etizoni has pointed out, is for business-men to get greater access to politicians and, presumably, receive an opportunity to state their case more strongly than would otherwise be the case. As this form of regular, open access is denied to poorer groupings, it would appear that, quite literally, money talks. We may categorise the benefits that ensued for crony capitalism in a number of specific ways.

Export credit
Export credit insurance is an important subsidy which many firms seek, because it allows them to preserve an image of being risk-takers while ensuring that the state provides a safety net if they fall. Export credit insurance is particularly important in a high-risk market where there is both a prospect of large profits and a threat of sudden non-payment from customers.

No market was more risky than the Iraqi meat market in the late 1980s when it was at war with Iran. Yet it had one unspoken advantage. Although Western arms dealers were content to supply both sides, there was a tilt in US foreign policy towards Iraq near the end of the war when it appeared that Iran might win. The US export credit agency Eximbank was pressurised by its government to provide $4,200 million additional credit facilities to Iraq and a host of other Western powers followed suit. By the end of 1987, it is esti-mated that £7.3 billion was due from Iraq to credit agencies world-wide.[37] The rationale behind these subsidies was that the Western rulers had a vital interest in stopping the spread of the Islamic rev-olution in Iran and in preventing the emergence of a strong Middle Eastern country that might affect oil supplies. The Irish Government supported the Western intervention by agreeing to supply large amounts of beef to the Iraqi army.

This helps to explain the extraordinary decision of Albert Reynolds to raise the export credit insurance to Iraq to £150 million in September 1987 even though the overall limit for export credit remained at £300 million world-wide. As one opposition spokesperson pointed out, this meant that 'Irish exports to markets other than Iraq were to be denied cover because so much was concentrated on Iraq, a market in which the risk of non-payment was exceptionally high'.[38] This decision, however, needs to be seen in a context where political imperatives temporally outrode economic ones because Ireland was playing an auxiliary role in a policy that was led by the USA.

Only a small number of companies benefited from the decision to underwrite the meat exports and all had strong links with Fianna Fáil. One of these companies was Hibernia Meats, one of whose owners had contributed £50,000 to Fianna Fáil funds in 1987.[39] The major beneficiary however was the Goodman organisation, which had even closer links with Fianna Fáil. It contributed £50,000 to Fianna Fáil in 1987 and there was a Fianna Fáil TD, Liam Lawlor, on the board of one of its subsidiaries.[40] Goodman was able to visit Charles Haughey at his personal home on a number of occasions.

This particular case is an interesting example of how the dynamics of crony capitalism work. It would be facile to suggest that political donations were the *cause* of the Government's behaviour. As Fintan O'Toole has argued the overall rationale for increasing export insurance was 'not economic at all, but political: Charles Haughey's determination to ensure that Iraq was not defeated in the Iran–Iraq war'.[41] Moreover, as the Goodman organisation was the country's largest beef exporter and had been selected by the Industrial Development Agency in its 'pick a winner' strategy of promoting one or two major Irish firms to compete on world markets, it was inevitable that it should be chosen. However, the scale of the export credit subsidy and the exclusion of rival meat companies from the scheme was influenced by the 'goodwill' that Fianna Fáil ministers clearly had for one of the party benefactors. Put briefly, it seems that political donations are a factor not so much in shaping wider state policy, but in tilting the state in one direction rather than another to meet the needs of particular firms.

Tax loopholes

Business has long pressed for relief from taxation and lobbying for tax loopholes, as we have seen, is focused on an annual Finance Act which follows the main budget speech each year. A well-structured system of 'making representations' has been established to allow different industrial groups and companies press their case. The loopholes are typically established through a change in a small number of words or clauses in the Finance Act. Often the wording is highly complex and is open to interpretations that may not at first seem obvious. This, however, creates an opportunity for highly specialised accountants who can interpret the changes to bring major benefits to their wealthy clients. Much of this form of decision making – or sometimes non-decision making – takes place outside the public gaze.

One of the major beneficiaries of these tax breaks is the Irish bloodstock industry as income from Irish stallions is tax-free. This occurred as a result of a legislative change introduced by Charles Haughey when he was Finance Minister in 1969 and has remained in place ever since. There is little doubt that this measure, which was not subject to much debate, has generated considerable wealth for Ireland's largest bloodstock firm, Coolmore Stud and has allowed it to develop a major global business. Coolmore Stud leases many of its stallions to Australia and is able to use Irish law to avoid tax liability. According to Australia's former Prime Minister, Bob Hawke, the company 'took £35 million a year in stallion fees out of Australia to its home based tax haven'.[42] The owner of the Coolmore Stud, John Magnier, is described as one of Ireland's 'spectacularly wealthy and successful business people'.[43]

Magnier is also a prominent supporter of Fianna Fail and has donated to both the party and individuals connected with the party. Five of Mr Haughey's horses have visited Coolmore Stud between 1985 and 1997 and Magnier was also appointed by Mr Haughey to the Senate in 1987. During the McCracken Tribunal, it was revealed that a cheque from Magnier for £10,000 made its way to Celtic Helicopters, the firm owned by Ciaran Haughey, the son of the former Fianna Fail leader. Mr Magnier stated that he had no idea how the cheque ended up in this firm. However, as the *Irish Times* noted, 'It was therefore another remarkable co-incidence that it ended up financing the helicopter firm of the then Taoiseach, to whom he was personally close'.[44]

Another interesting tax loophole is Section 19 of the 1994 Finance Act which has given considerable relief to the property developer and art collector, Ken Rohan. In 1993, he faced a major benefit-in-kind tax bill from the Revenue Commissioners. However, he and his friends lobbied the Minister for Finance for a specific piece of legislation, which they wrote themselves and submitted for his consideration. The officials of the Department of Finance and the Revenue Commissioners advised against the proposed change. Yet Bertie Ahern, the then Minister for Finance, overruled his officials and insisted on giving the legislation retrospective effect for twelve years, thereby rendering any tax claim against Rohan redundant. Rather coincidentally, Rohan had also made political donations to Fianna Fail and had hosted a dinner in his Wicklow estate in early 1994, at which Ahern, the then Taoiseach Albert Reynolds and the Fianna Fail fundraiser were present.[45]

Sometimes even more direct evidence becomes available on how the lobbying system for tax loopholes works. When the Irish Distillers was put up for sale, National City Brokers (NCB) assisted Pernod Ricard to acquire it. A confidential letter was written by owner of NCB, Dermot Desmond to the head of Pernod Ricard which subsequently came into public view. It stated that 'we orchestrated entirely the successful campaign to get a positive tax opinion from the Revenue Commissioners, which involved using personal contacts at the highest level'.[46] Further on the letter explained, 'We used up a large proportion of favours we can call upon from our political contacts – and no doubt we will pay a price on the other side'.[47] It was a rare glimpse of how the 'operational code' as against the 'myth system' worked.

State contracts and state property

Historically Fianna Fail took a pragmatic line on the development of the state sector, establishing publicly owned industries in areas where private capital proved unable to operate. In this way the necessary infrastructure was established so that private industry could expand. Ireland's relatively large public sector was deemed to be at the service of, rather than acting as a rival to, private capital. This also meant that it was viewed as another resource for business to draw on to expand its profits. A steady contract to supply services to a hospital or a college could offer better prospects of long-term profit than relying solely on the market. The selling and buying of state property or commitments by the state to rent particular office blocks also provided lucrative opportunities. A number of examples have emerged of how contracts were awarded in the Celtic Tiger in an unusual manner.

In 1987, for example, G-Tech, a company run by Guy Snowden, was rewarded the contract to install and operate the online system for Lotto by the state-run postal service. The £multi-million contract was renewed in 1993, just months after Guy Snowden invested £67,000 in Celtic Helicopters, the firm owned by Charles Haughey's son, Ciaran. Coincidentally, G-Tech was also accused of 'improper' lobbying and giving gifts in relation to the Texas lottery in 1997.[48]

General Automotive and the bus building company Bombardier set up a joint venture in Shannon in the early 1980s to build buses for CIE. General Automotive ultimately took over the entire project. According to the *Irish Times*, 'it is estimated that CIE spent over £50 million on Bombardier buses, even though they cost more than buses built elsewhere, were unreliable and are all now being replaced'.[49] The chairperson of General Automotive was Cruise Moss who had taken out a shareholding in Celtic Helicopters, the firm owned by Mr Haughey's son.

In recent years, the wealthy have also developed a particular interest in the sale of state assets or state contracts to rent offices from property developers. Carysfort College was a former teacher training college which was purchased by Pino Harris, a long-standing Fianna Fail supporter, in 1990 for £6.25 million. Shortly afterwards, the property was sold onto University College Dublin (UCD) for £8 million. According to the *Irish Times*, UCD 'was in effect force-fed with money available through the Department of Education to buy the site'.[50] It later transpired that Charles Haughey had several meetings with college officials.

Glen Ding Wood in County Wicklow contained valuable sand and gravel deposits and was owned by the state until it was sold to Cement Roadstone for £1.25 million in 1992. A subsequent parliamentary inquiry into why the sale had been organised through a private rather than a public tender did not find the official explanation credible.[51] It subsequently emerged that a company controlled by Cement Roadstone made payments of £18,150 to a company controlled by Conor Haughey and Eimear Haughey.[52] The chairman of Cement Roadstone at the time when the sale was conducted was Des Traynor, who also organised Charles Haughey's personal expenses. Most of the directors of Cement Roadstone had also invested in the Ansbacher account which made donations to Haughey. The Blessington Heritage Trust, which has sought a further inquiry into the affair, has estimated that the 147 acres of land were worth more than £50 million.[53]

In 1991, the site of the former Johnson, Mooney and O'Brien bakery was sold to Bord Telecom, the state-run telephone service. The ownership of the site passed through a circuitous route of several different companies before the purchase was made and a number of the shareholders gained considerably. Michael Smurfit, the chairman of Bord Telecom, which was purchasing the site, had a financial interest in one of the companies, Bacchantes Ltd, which owned the site.[54] After the scandal broke, Mr Smurfit had a 'confidential meeting' with the leader of the Progressive Democrats, Desmond O'Malley, Minister for Industry and Commerce, who appointed a special inspector to investigate the issue.[55] It later transpired that a donation of £30,000 had come to the Progressive Democrats from the Smurfit group with an enclosed letter which stated that 'Michael will prove to be an extremely good supporter of the party and I cannot tell how appreciative he was of our confidential meeting in January'.[56]

Another key investor who gained from the sale of the Johnson, Mooney and O'Brien site to Bord Telecom was Mr Dermot Desmond. Mr Desmond had considerable financial dealings with the Haughey family and had acted as an advisor to Mr Haughey when he established the International Financial Services Centre.[57] His firm, NCB received ten major semi-state contracts from eight separate public bodies between 1987 and 1992, while its four major stock-broking rivals received a total of just nine contracts.[58] One of its first major state assignments was the sale of the Government's stake in Tara Mines, for which it was paid a large commission which was estimated to be three times the going rate.[59] By 1991, after only ten years in business, NCB had become the country's second largest stockbroker, accounting for a quarter of all Irish broking business. Interestingly in the same year, Mr Desmond found himself at the centre of a mystery concerning how documentation relating to the main rival of Celtic Helicopters – the state-run Aer Lingus subsidiary Irish Helicopters – got into the hands of Celtic Helicopters. The documentation had apparently been leaked from his company NCB.[60]

An important source of revenue for property developers are state tenants who rent offices on a long-term basis. One beneficiary of these rents is the Carlisle Trust, which is owned by John Byrne, who is one of the wealthiest property developers in the state.[61] According to Frank McDonald, Byrne never encountered any problem in filling his office blocks with state tenants, at least until 1978 when he acquired a building on St Stephen's Green in Dublin. McDonald notes that 'what happened was that all proposals to lease the building were vetoed by George Colley, then Minister for Finance, because he was convinced that Haughey, who was Minister for Health at the time, had a share in it'.[62] At the time Colley and Haughey led to the two main rival factions in Fianna Fail and there was considerable animosity between them. The reasons for Colley's suspicions are not hard to detect, as Des Traynor, who had full control of all of Haughey's personal accounts, had been on the Carlisle Trust for thirty years.[63] At the end of the 1980s, some of Byrne's other companies benefited from the Urban Renewal Tax Incentive scheme. Most unusually, the Mount Brandon in Tralee was unexpectedly included in an urban renewal area even though the local council had not sought a designation for this site.[64]

Planning

Planning regulation by its very nature is an interference in the free market. It is an attempt to impose restrictions on where builders and property developers can expand. For this very reason, business often seeks a close link with the planners in order to circumvent particular restrictions or to make full commercial use of their land they possess. Planning regulations are formally determined by elected local representatives who listen to representations and decide on the best interest of their city or town. However, in reality planning is often driven through by either full-time local authority officials or by a ring of local politicians who manage to swing party machines behind particular decisions. The unelected city officials play a major role, as their advice can be quite crucial in establishing the framework through which decisions are made. Considerable evidence has emerged that it is not unusual to seek political influence in order to achieve a favourable hearing for planning applications. Again, political donations seem to play a key role in this.

One of the more interesting cases of political influence being used to affect planning decisions was the offer that the builder Michael Bailey made to Joseph Murphy Structural Engineers (JMSE) regarding the rezoning of land in north Dublin. Bailey was a long-standing Fianna Fail activist and was close to Ray Burke, Fianna Fail Minister from the area. In 1989, Bailey wrote to JMSE to state that he would have to be offered a 50 percent stake in the land in exchange for, among other things, the 'procurement of a majority vote of a full council meeting'.[65] A few days after sending this letter, Joseph Gogarty who was an executive of JMSE went to the house of Ray Burke in the company of Michael Bailey and, according to Mr Burke, handed him an unsolicited donation of £30,000 from JMSE.[66]

In another major case, the builder Tom Gilmartin stated that he ran into some difficulties when he tried to purchase the Quaryvale site in west Dublin and get planning permission to turn it into a major shopping centre. He claimed he rang Bertie Ahern, the current Fianna Fail leader, in May 1989 to explain his difficulties and the following month gave the Environment Minister Padraigh Flynn a cheque for £50,000, which was intended as a donation to Fianna Fail. After his talks with Ahern, a Fianna Fail councillor undertook to sort out Gilmartin's problems.[67] Subsequently one lobbyist, Frank Dunlop, admitted giving £112,000 to fifteen Dublin councillors.

The Flood Tribunal which investigated any improprieties in the allocation of planning has established that Dublin's Assistant County and City Manager, George Redmond, had put away £660,000 in various accounts in the 1980s. At the time his salary from the local authority amounted to £29,000 a year. Redmond explained this discrepancy by claiming that he gave 'advice' to various builders who sought planning permission and that he accumulated such a large sum because he was a heavy saver. While Redmond has admitted that the payments were inappropriate, others have gone much further and claimed that he was paid for services he rendered to the big builders.[68]

Passports

One of the more bizarre ways in which crony capitalism has operated has been through the sale of Irish passports. While the concept of nationality is sometimes mystified with references to an exclusive birthright, Irish passports have been made available to those who were wealthy enough to invest money in the country. This investment often provided a form of cheap capital for companies and so was much sought after. Here again the nexus between particular politicians and business interests influenced which firms received the investment.

Up to 1992, applications from foreigners who wished to obtain an Irish passport were brought to the Taoiseach, Charles Haughey and some unusual decisions were made.[69] One Palestinian businessman who obtained an Irish passport for his wife and son invested

£1.1 million in C & D Foods, the company which the Fianna Fail Minister and subsequent Taoiseach, Albert Reynolds, had a 41 percent shareholding.[70] Sheikh Khalid bin Mahfouz obtained eleven passports for his extended family after committing himself to investing £20 million in Irish industry. Mahfouz was under investigation in the United States in connection with the BCCI affair, which was one of the biggest financial frauds in recent banking history.[71] One of the companies he invested in was Leisure Holdings, whose main shareholder was John Magnier, the owner of the Coolmore Stud, and a close associate of Charles Haughey.[72] Another investor who obtained an Irish passport made a £10,500 interest-free loan to Fianna Fail.[73] For many years the passports for sale scheme was kept secret and when details emerged it took on an air of scandal. The scheme was discontinued in 1998.

One law for the rich

All of the above revelations have caused a major difficulty for Ireland's political establishment because they provided a rare opportunity for people to gain an insight into the real links between business and politics. They raise major questions about the nature and scope of democracy in the Celtic Tiger. According to the dominant ideology, each citizen is equal before the law and at the ballot box the majority rule. Ultimately the direction a country takes is supposed to be decided by a sovereign people who cast their votes for parties which represent their viewpoints. Yet it would appear that this theory ignores the awesome power which money bestows on a small number of individuals. Quite literally, a tiny minority of very rich people can subvert the wishes of the majority either by purchasing politicians wholesale or through the retail method of using specific donations to influence specific outcomes. Sometimes it is not even a case of persuading politicians to make a decision. A non-decision, or an acceptance of past inertia, can be enough to safeguard a valuable tax loophole or a steady contract for state rent. The consequence in terms of the actual resources which are removed from schools or hospitals barely enters the picture.

A recent historical study of European business noted that the withdrawal of business people from direct personal involvement in political life is a long-standing trend, 'top businessmen's personal involvement in parliamentary politics waned with the advance of

the twentieth century. The increased professional demands, combined with the decline of Parliament as a decisive instrument of
policy-making, accelerated a trend well under way before 1914'.[74]
However, as direct personal involvement in Parliament declined,
business people sought access to the more central instruments of
policy making. The more they withdrew from public life, the more
they demanded direct access to the areas where the many unre-
corded decisions or decisions not to act were taken by a state
bureaucracy outside the formal debates in Parliament. The main
reason why this access was granted was simply because of the power
that money bestowed.

Catch-all consensus politics has strengthened the links between
business and politics. Political parties today rely on huge amounts
of money rather than a committed cadre to get their politics across.
The very blandness of their message means they require more
expensive advertising to 'package' their message. As the membership of political parties declines, business donations become
increasingly important and with that has come even more open use
of 'influence'. As politicians facilitate the process whereby key decisions are taken outside the public gaze, legalised corruption has
flourished. Sometimes this legalised corruption assumes the form of
'normal donations to uphold the democratic system'. On other
occasions it is, as they say, more up front and personal. In both
instances, however, the key thing is the outcomes which are favourable for business, not the specific mechanisms used to achieve them.

All this explains why no serious charges of bribery or corruption
have been levelled against any business person or politician in the
Celtic Tiger and instead a series of tribunals have been established
to unearth the truth. However, the methodology behind these tribunals has ensured there is little challenge to the official 'myth system'.
Typically, the tribunals have sought to find an explicit correlation
between a donation and a favour and the donors have easily circumvented this by rationalising their actions in terms of seeking 'access'
to key politicians. The tribunals have also been limited by terms of
reference which seem designed to protect the most sensitive aspects
of how our rulers operate. Thus, the Dail voted to exclude any investigation of the Ansbacher accounts from the tribunals because the
account holders included some of the key business people in the
country. Similarly, the involvement of the Irish state in supporting
Iraq's war effort was also deemed a sensitive matter which was

hardly aired publicly.[75] The tribunals have also faced a series of intricate legal battles which have hampered their investigation. Both Haughey and the Fianna Fail TD Liam Lawlor have won legal challenges which, in the former case, indefinitely postponed a criminal charge of obstructing a tribunal and in the latter case have hampered detailed questioning of Lawlor's involvement in various companies. More fundamentally, the judges who preside over the tribunals are drawn from the same elite who have much to lose from a full disclosure of how the top echelons of the system really work. The contradiction between the elite investigating another section of the elite came to the fore when it was revealed that Justice Moriarty, the chair of one of the tribunals, had £500,000 of shares in Cement Roadstone, the company that was chaired by Des Traynor, the close confidant of Charles Haughey and linked with the Ansbacher account.[76]

All of this brings into quite sharp focus the nature of the law in Ireland and the experience of who gets punished. Paul O'Mahoney summarised the outstanding characteristics of the prison population as follows,

> they tend to be young, urban, under-educated males from the lower socio-economic classes and the so-called under class, who have been convicted predominantly for relatively petty crimes against property without violence. Very few offenders are imprisoned for white-collar crime. As in many other countries large number of prisoners are dependent on alcohol or opiate drugs and many have psychiatric problems and disturbed family backgrounds.[77]

Sometimes it is assumed that this occurs because of an 'unfair' application of the law or because the law is distorted. Yet the essence of the law is the protection of private property and in capitalist society that means protecting the ability to acquire more property to stay ahead of rivals. These elementary facts help to explain why the discretion of the law is more likely to work to the advantage of the wealthy rather than the poor.

Nevertheless the scale of the hypocrisy can be astounding. In May 1999, a labourer was brought before the Mallow District Court for working while receiving unemployment assistance. When he explained to the Judge, Michael Patwell, that he was in dire circumstances and needed money to pay for his son's confirmation, the Judge sentenced him to prison and told his court that 'He (the defendant) was going to cheat and defraud and tell lies because a child was getting a sacrament of the church. It's a bit of a contradiction isn't it?'.[78] Indeed, but not half as much of a contradiction, as the fact that those who defraud social welfare are imprisoned but those who engage in tax evasion and bribery are pillars of society.

Notes

1 S. Smyth, *Thanks a Million Big Fella* (Dublin, Blackwater, 1997) p. 5.
2 *Report of the Tribunal of Inquiry (Dunnes Payments) McCracken Tribunal* (Dublin, Stationery Office, 1997) p. 6.
3 Ibid. p. 69.
4 Smyth, *Thanks a Million Big Fella*, p. 62.
5 McCracken Tribunal, p. 50.
6 Ibid. p. 51.
7 Ibid. pp. 70 and 73.
8 M. Friedman, *Capitalism and Freedom* (London, University of Chicago Press, 1962) p. 9.
9 A. Etzioni, *Capital Corruption: The New Attack on American Democracy* (New Brunswick, Transaction Books, 1988) p. 162.
10 M. Gilbert, *The Italian Revolution: The End of Politics, Italian Style* (Boulder, Westview Press, 1995) p. 5.
11 C. Harman, 'State and Capitalism Today', *International Socialism Journal*, no. 51 (1991) pp. 3–57.
12 R. Miliband, *The State in Capitalist Society* (London, Weidenfeld and Nicholson, 1969).
13 S. Hill, 'The Social Organisation of Boards of Directors', *British Journal of Sociology*, 46:2 (June 1995) pp. 245–78.
14 D. Clark, *Post Industrial America: A Geographical Perspective* (London, Methuen, 1984) p. 93.
15 Harman, 'State and Capitalism Today', p. 19.
16 N. Harris, *Of Bread and Guns* (Harmondsworth, Penguin, 1983) Ch. 4.
17 M. Dalton, *Men Who Manage* (New York, John Wiley, 1959) p. 218.
18 M. Punch, *Dirty Business: Exploring Corporate Misconduct* (London, Sage, 1996) p. 218.
19 M. Reisman, *Folded Lies* (New York, Free Press, 1979).
20 Etzioni, *Capital Corruption*, pp. xx.
21 Ibid.
22 Ibid. p. 25.
23 Ibid. p. 57.
24 Ibid. p. 69.
25 Ibid. p. 86.

26 Smyth, *Thanks a Million Big Fella*, p. 68.
27 Ibid. p. 78.
28 Ibid.
29 *McCracken Tribunal*, p. 57.
30 Ibid. p. 48.
31 See the *Report of Investigation into the Administration of Deposit Interest Retention Tax and Related Matters During the Period 1st January 1986 to 1st December 1998 (Comptroller General's Report)* (Dublin, Stationery Office, 1999).
32 C. Keena, 'Dunnes Won Appeal Against £30m Tax Bill From Revenue', *Irish Times* (5 February 1999).
33 *McCracken Tribunal*, p. 51.
34 Ibid.
35 Keena, 'Dunnes won appeal, 5 February 1999.
36 Ibid.
37 F. O'Toole, *Meanwhile Back at the Ranch* (London, Vintage, 1995) p. 140.
38 M. Noonan, 'Meat Exporters and Insurance', *Magill* (October 1997).
39 O'Toole, *Meanwhile Back at the Ranch*, pp. 152–3.
40 Ibid. p. 69.
41 Ibid. p. 212.
42 U. Halligan, 'The Senator and the Taoiseach: The Wealth and Connections of John Magnier', *Magill* (March 1998).
43 Ibid.
44 'Tangled Web All Benefited From Haughey Connection', *Irish Times* (6 March 1999).
45 'Editorial: Time for Some Answers', *Sunday Tribune* (29 August 1999).
46 S. MacCarthaigh, 'Haughey Link With Desmond Long-standing', *Irish Times* (9 January 1998).
47 Ibid.
48 'Tangled Web All Benefited From Haughey Connection', 6 March 1999.
49 Ibid.
50 F. O'Toole, 'Questions for Former Colleagues', *Irish Times* (19 July 1997).
51 *Committee of Public Accounts, Report on Special Report of the Comptroller and Auditor General on Sale of State Lands at Glen Ding, County Wicklow* (Dublin, Stationery Office, 1999) p. 1.
52 R. Balls, 'CRH Subsidiary Paid Firm Owned by Haugheys', *Irish Times* (2 February 1998).
53 Ibid.
54 *Chestvale Properties Ltd, Hoddle Investments Ltd, Final Report of John A. Glacken, Inspector Appointed by the Minister of Industry and Commerce* (Dublin, Stationery Office, 1992) Appendix.

55 G. Kennedy, 'Harney to Initiate Investigation', *Irish Times* (15 December 1997).
56 Ibid.
57 'Desmond Reveals His Dealings With Haugheys', *Irish Times* (12 January 1998) and MacCarthaigh, 'Haughey link with Desmond long-standing', 9 January 1998.
58 U. Halligan, 'The Kaiser and the Boss', *Magill* (January 1998).
59 Ibid.
60 'Tangled Web All Benefited From Haughey Connection', 6 March 1999.
61 C. Keena, 'Carlisle Trust Contacted by Tribunal', *Irish Times* (18 December 1998).
62 F. McDonald, 'Haughey's Rise From Santry 'Semi' to Abbeville', *Irish Times* (18 July 1997).
63 Ibid.
64 Ibid.
65 J. Ryan, 'The Procurement of Planning Permission', *Magill* (October 1997).
66 Ibid.
67 E. O'Reilly and L. Walsh, 'The Life and Prosperous Times of George Redmond', *Magill* (March 1999).
68 H. McGee, 'The Cost of Exposing Villainy', *Sunday Tribune* (26 September 1999).
69 J. Maher, 'Investment for Passports Cash Funded Tennis Clubs', *Irish Times* (9 August 1997).
70 Ibid.
71 'Sale Concluded', *Irish Times* (22 April 1998).
72 J. Maher, 'Investment for passports', 9 August 1977.
73 C. Taylor and M. Muire-Tynan, 'Government, ICC to Re-check FF Bank Account', *Irish Times* (22 February 1999).
74 Y. Cassis, *Big Business: The European Experience in the Twentieth Century* (Oxford, Oxford University Press, 1997) p. 222.
75 O'Toole, *Meanwhile Back at the Ranch*, p. 53.
76 C. Keena, 'Party Leaders Cannot Recall Shareholding', *Irish Times* (2 July 1999).
77 P. O'Mahoney, 'Punishing Poverty and Personal Adversity' in I. Bacik and M. O'Connell (eds) *Crime and Poverty in Ireland* (Dublin, Round Hall, 1998) p. 54.
78 'Judge Jails Three Men for Breach of Social Welfare Regulations', *The Corkman* (28 May 1999).

7

What's changing in Ireland?

James Connolly, Ireland's leading Marxist of the early twentieth century, bequeathed an ominous prediction to his followers when he claimed that a partitioned Ireland would lead to a 'carnival of reaction'. The division of Ireland between a Protestant-dominated North and a Catholic-dominated South would 'help the Home Rule and Orange capitalists to keep their rallying cries before the public as the political watch words of the day' and so drown out any form of class politics.[1]

Connolly's prediction was confirmed for most of the twentieth century. In Northern Ireland, the state was indeed built around the exclusion of Catholics, with local authorities and Orange employers engaging in extensive discrimination. Basil Brooke, a future Prime Minister, set the tone when he told fellow landowners that 'he had not a Roman Catholic about his own place..[they] were endeavoring to get in everywhere and were out in force and might destroy Ulster . . . he appealed to Unionists everywhere to employ good Protestant lads and lassies'.[2] In order to deal with a disgruntled minority of Catholics, internment was introduced regularly and an auxiliary police force of B Specials was recruited from local Orange halls.[3] Until a decade ago, Catholics were effectively forbidden to hold marches in the centre of Belfast.

By and large, the Protestant working class supported this state of affairs and the votes of Protestant workers ensured that a one-party Unionist regime was established. In the fifty years between the foundation of the state and the fall of Stormont in 1972, only one opposition bill was ever passed – the Wild Bird Conservation Act. In the early part of the twentieth century, approximately 60 percent of Protestant men were members of the Orange Order and while there was a slow decline, the Order still held the allegiance of many Protestant workers until recently.[4] The main challenger to Unionism inside the Protestant working class, the Northern Ireland Labour Party (NILP), adapted to this sectarianism. Speeches in favour of the Orange Order were made from its platforms and leading members displayed their Orange sashes.[5] The NILP failed to condemn internment or massacres such as Bloody Sunday and even refused to back measures which called for 'one man, one vote' when thousands of both Catholics and Protestants marched for this in 1968.[6] The unions were also contaminated by the atmosphere of sectarianism. One union, the Boilermakers Union, which organised skilled Protestant workers, was actually found guilty of practising discrimination in membership applications.[7] Protestant workers accepted the argument that the slightest fissure in the Unionist community would open the way to the Southern Government to impose a United Ireland and Rome Rule on loyal Ulster.

Across the border, the South was a mirror image of the Northern regime as Fianna Fail and the Unionist Parties fed off and reinforced each other. Fianna Fail claimed to pursue two goals: the reunification of Ireland and the restoration of the Irish language. The third aim – the building of a Catholic state for a Catholic people – was left implicit, but there was little doubt where it stood in the order of priorities. The 1937 Constitution recognised 'the special position of the Holy Catholic and Apostolic and Roman Church'[8] and this was by no means empty rhetoric. From 1932 to 1973, when Fianna Fail was only out of office for eight years, divorce and even information on contraception was banned. Control of the hospitals and the schools was vested in the hands of the Church. Many books by leading Irish writers were banned and laws were passed which gave the state the right to exclude married women from the workplace. And again Southern workers, by and large, supported this set-up.

Fianna Fail prided itself on being a party of workers and small farmers. The close links between Fianna Fail and some union leaders was symbolised when Charles Haughey became Taoiseach in 1981. He was heralded into the Fianna Fail conference by the ITGWU band playing 'A Nation Once Again'. Just as in the North, the Labour Party was marginalised and forced to conform to the ethos set by Fianna Fail. The Labour Party leader of the 1960s, when its left-wing rhetoric was at its height, was Brendan Corish, who had once proclaimed that 'I am an Irishman second, I am a Catholic first

. . . If the hierarchy gives me any direction with regard to Catholic social teaching or Catholic moral teaching, I accept without qualification. . .'.[9] The party never reaped any rewards from this adaptation to Catholic domination and received one of the lowest votes of any Labour Party in Europe. Throughout the 1980s, for example, the average left vote in the Republic of Ireland stood at 12.8 percent, compared to a Western European average of 37 percent.[10]

The carnival of reaction in the South was founded on the twin pillars of Fianna Fail and the Catholic Church. Yet in the space of a short decade, the base of both institutions has been undermined, so that the old Ireland appears as 'another country'.[11] These changes coincided with the Celtic Tiger and means that the discontent which is growing may take unpredictable forms. Let us look at how each of the pillars of the conservative apparatus has been weakened.

Fianna Fail: from a national movement to a mere political party

The Fianna Fail Party used to be an awesome phenomenon. Not only did it dominate the Government of Ireland for decades, almost as a one-party state, but its tentacles were everywhere, because it had a relatively large and active membership. Although there are some difficulties with its figures, the party claimed a membership of nearly 100,000 people until the early 1980s.[12] This was extraordinarily high for a state that numbered just over 3.5 million adults and children. Everywhere one looked the influence of the party was to be found. The major sporting body, the Gaelic Athletic Association, was often organised at local level by Fianna Fail activists. The political nominee of the primary teachers union in the Senate was a Fianna Fail member. If you wanted a job or a local authority house, you often had to approach the local Fianna Fail councillor. The party drew its votes from right across the class spectrum and, until recently, never got less than 40 percent of the votes of the skilled and unskilled manual working class. While its local leadership has traditionally been drawn from small business people who run pubs, taxis or auctioneering firms, there have also been a fair proportion of workers who have been members. As late as 1986, it could still organise a major conference for its trade union members and supporters.

Many commentators seem to be mystified by how the party won its base. One of the first books to be written about the party came from the *Irish Times* journalist Dick Walsh, who claimed that at the heart of the party was 'a blazing mystique [which had] no social content'.[13] Academic writers have fared little better. J. P. O'Carroll has written extensively on the party's founder, Eamon de Valera, and has argued that the strength of his politics 'lay in the fact that it drew on much that was beyond the rational'.[14] Similarly, Jeffrey Praeger has argued that Fianna Fail represented a form of Gaelic romanticism and, after it first took office in 1932, 'hot politics' became the order of the day.[15]

However, there is little need to resort to this mystification. Fianna Fail originally grew out of the republican resistance to British colonial rule and many of its leading figures were able to use the credibility won in that struggle to build an electoral base. Irish workers traditionally vacillated between republicanism and a class militancy that discarded all politics. As Trotsky put it, 'the Irish working class was formed in an atmosphere saturated with heroic memories of national rebellion and coming into conflict with the egotistically narrow and imperially arrogant trade unionism in Britain, has wavered between nationalism and syndicalism'.[16] The high point of workers' struggles coincided with upsurges of rebellion against the British Empire and the greatest expansion of the Irish trade unions occurred during the War of Independence. Not surprisingly then, a party which argued for continuing opposition to British colonialism was bound to get support among workers.

This was all the more so because, when the Irish Free State was established, it was very much a neo-colony of the British Empire. Sovereignty was limited not only by partition but by the office of a Governor General and the presence of British naval bases. When de Valera founded Fianna Fail in 1926, he described the Irish economy as 'an out-garden of Britain'.[17] It was quite an accurate remark. Some 97 percent of exports went to Britain and these were overwhelmingly agricultural. A full 18 percent of the value of these exports was derived from live animals and another 40 percent was composed of food and drink.[18] Fianna Fail's early success derived from the fact that its nationalist rhetoric seemed to pose a solution to the problem of underdevelopment. Increasingly it was the project of economic nationalism and its promise to build up Irish society that guaranteed its base. Officially the party decried partition and demanded the unification of Ireland, but its actual practice showed that this was entirely rhetorical. It used internment and even execution against the republican dissidents with the same enthusiasm as the Unionist Party. Partition was used as a symbol of a national wrong to smother class divisions and impose a Catholic culture in the South. The real focus of Fianna Fail's politics was the establishment of full national sovereignty and economic development in the South.[19]

The nearest parallel to Fianna Fail in the 1920s and 1930s was the populist movements in Latin America. Like Varga in Brazil, Cardenas in Mexico and Perón in Argentina, de Valera created a pro-industrial bloc which united workers and small capital in a fight against neo-colonial structures which limited Irish development to supplying agricultural goods to the old empire. The analogy is not perfect, because there was not the same intensity of conflict with the *latifundia* owners who dominated many parts of Latin America and, accordingly, Fianna Fail did not need to establish as tight an alliance with the workers' movement as, for example, the Peronist movement. However, some of the same dynamics were at work. Fianna Fail was also greatly helped by the failure of the Labour Party to offer any real alternative. Working within the limits of a relatively backward form of capitalism, the Labour Party had extremely moderate horizons and, ironically, Fianna Fail delighted in exposing them on this score. Lemass's jibe at Labour expressed Fianna Fail's contempt for their weakness, 'I have already said that the outstanding characteristic of the Labour Party is that it is the most respectable party in the state . . . So long as they cannot be accused of being pale pink in politics they seem to think they have fulfilled their function towards the Irish people'.[20]

The success of Fianna Fail, however, ultimately rested on the fact that it was able to dismantle Southern Ireland's neo-colonial status and deliver on national development. This occurred in two main periods. In the 1930s, the protectionist policy laid the basis for the expansion of native capital and this in turn led to some material improvements for workers. In the 1960s, the party switched to a strategy of inviting in the multi-nationals in order to expand the economy through an export programme. This was by no means a 'betrayal' or retreat from its ideals, because it offered the only realistic and viable way for native capitalism to grow. This in turn also seemed to deliver some benefits to workers. Social spending increased, paid for mainly by the taxes of a growing number of employed workers, and Fianna Fail was seen to deliver the rudiments of a Welfare State, free secondary schooling and better access to hospitals.

Capitalism, Marx remarked, creates its own gravedigger in the shape of the working class and the very success of Fianna Fail's project eventually began to undermine its own political base. The Irish society which Fianna Fail helped to create is now a mainly urban, working-class society. In 1951, 38 percent of the Irish labour force worked on farms, but by 1999 the figure had declined to 8 percent. By contrast, the working class has grown in both manufacturing and services, making a mockery of claims that there is a 'post-industrial' society. Moreover, a very high proportion of the population identify themselves as workers. One study, for example, showed that some 42 percent of the Irish population regard themselves as working class, a figure that is only slightly below the British figure.[21] The growth of the working class has been accompanied by a major increase in trade union density. Between 1945 and 1984, the number of trade unionists practically trebled,[22] giving the Republic of Ireland one of the highest levels of trade union density in Europe outside the Scandinavian countries. All of this lay the basis for an increased class conflict and an awareness of class division. As in other countries, the tempo of that conflict can vary and workers are still recovering from the defeats of the 1980s. Nevertheless, the growth of these class divisions has begun to undermine Fianna Fail's notion of a united society pulling together for the good of the country.

Fianna Fail has also created a stronger indigenous bourgeoisie who feel they have little need to disguise their wealth. In the past, a prominent Fianna Fail supporter, Todd Andrews, could title his book *A Man of No Property* and claim that 'none of us ever got grandiose notions about ourselves or about our families, and since we had no income apart from our salaries, none of us ever became rich and were thus relieved of the temptation to indulge in any kind of ostentation'.[23] However, by the 1960s a new 'mohair-suited' politician had arrived who had no qualms about flaunting their wealth. The first public sign of this was the formation of Taca, a two hundred strong businessmen's organisation which raised funds for Fianna Fail. The suspicion that this grouping received certain privileges from the state were by no means allayed when the Education Minister, Donough O'Malley, answered these charges by saying that 'of course we look after our own'.[24] This, however, was only a rudimentary public celebration of the power of wealth and as Fianna Fail's business backers grew, the old republican ideology of sacrifice and high moral principles was completely brushed aside. When Charles Haughey assumed the leadership of Fianna Fail in 1981, it was the final confirmation that wealth was to be openly celebrated. Ultimately, these developments found their fullest expression in the crony capitalism we discussed in Chapter 6 and led to a profound disillusionment.

The signs of Fianna Fail decline as a 'national movement' that could transcend class division are already visible. At the sixtieth anniversary of the party in 1993, the general secretary claimed it had 30,000 members, a third of the numbers it had at the height of its power.[25] More interesting is the fall in its annual Church gate collection. The party raised £496,000 in its 1983 collection, but in 1991 it raised only £345,000 despite the fact that inflation has increased by 47 percent in the intervening period.[26] The newspaper which was once the party's unofficial organ, the *Irish Press*, has disappeared. The typical Fianna Fail trade unionist who combined a fierce sectional loyalty to an individual group of workers with support for the wider party is more difficult to find. Most crucially, the share of the party's vote has declined and an absolute majority now appears as a chimera. In 1992, the party's vote fell below 40 percent of the electorate, its lowest share since 1928, and it has not recovered significantly since.

There are, however, a number of factors which have helped to stabilise its position. One was the extraordinary decision of the Labour Party to join with it in coalition in 1992. Although it was the main beneficiary of the anger with Fianna Fail, it offered the party a rescuing hand and even accepted some of its schemes, such as giving the wealthy a tax amnesty. Labour's own record in government has also disillusioned many and led to a cynical disregard of all politicians. Despite the growing number of scandals, the party has not been able to distance itself from the establishment and pose a strong radical electoral alternative. The defeat of the 'country and western faction' around Albert Reynolds and his replacement with the popular Dublin politician Bertie Ahern has also helped. The party has also been seen to preside over the growth of the Celtic Tiger and the creation of extra jobs. However, it is doubtful if any of these factors can prevent its long-term decline.

The Church

'You are the most Catholic country in the world', the Vatican official Montini told the Irish ambassador Joseph Walshe in 1949.[27] It was no exaggeration. Up to 1981, 93 percent of the population declared themselves to be Catholic and until the early 1970s 91 percent of these attended mass every Sunday.[28] At its high point in the 1940s and 1950s, there were over 20,000 members of religious orders.[29] Few aspects of Irish life have not been touched by the power of the Catholic Church. One writer summarised the atmosphere which was set in the 1930s, but continued up to the 1960s,

> In 1931 we got a new parish priest. He condemned dancing in every form, even the kitchen dances were sinful and against the wishes of our church. Boys and girls should not be on the roads after dark. The Curate was sent out to patrol the roads and anybody found or seen on the roads had to give their names. The people who allowed boys and girls into their homes to dance were committing a grave mortal sin . . . Dancing was the devil's work .. So was company keeping.[30]

The labour movement was by no means immune from the influence of the Catholic Church. In 1951, one of the two Irish trade union congresses sent a telegram to the Pope claiming that their affiliated unions were 'humbly prostrate at the feet of his Holiness'.[31] Trade union officials often received their first training in Catholic adult education centres which preached the virtues of anti-communism. Conferences of the ITGWU were regularly addressed by the right-wing Bishop of Galway, who denounced proposals for a Welfare State as producing a 'slave plantation mentality'.[32] However, this was only one indication of the Church's general endorsement of practices which led to great inequality. In 1963, for example, less than 30 percent of national school leavers had a Primary Certificate, the lowest certificate for education.[33] Gene Kerrigan explains from his own personal experience why this occurred,

> The education set-up, over which the network of parish priests and bishops had presided since the nineteenth century, didn't care very much about such matters. The families of kids from the appropriate class would have sufficient resources to pay for secondary education (clerically controlled) and those destined to run the country, the professions, business and the civil service would go on to university. For the rest of us, minimal education standards would suffice for the emigration boat or the grinding dead-end jobs for which we were destined.[34]

The Catholic Church owed its unique power to a combination of factors. It was seen by many as a badge of identification that was opposed to colonial rule in Ireland. In the distant past, the penal laws had discriminated against Catholicism and this gave it an image of an oppressed Church. The image was not, of course, entirely consistent with the truth, as British rulers recognised after the French Revolution that it had an important role to play in stemming revolutionary movements. Almost every militant challenge to the Empire faced the wrath of the Church. The Bishop of Kerry, for example, said of the Fenians that 'hell was not hot enough nor eternity long enough to punish such miscreants'.[35] Despite such pronouncements, however, it was not the Church of the oppressor and this conveyed certain unforeseen advantages. It never became a powerful landowner to the extent it had in Spain and thus avoided coming into conflict with the peasantry. Moreover, while condemning the militants in the anti-colonial movement, it was able to maintain links with the moderate forces. One of the early leaders of Sinn Fein was a priest and when Terence McSwiney, the Lord Mayor of Cork, died on hunger strike in protest at British rule, his funeral mass was celebrated by a number of bishops and priests.

The other factor was the rural roots of the Church. Prior to the great famine of 1847, the Catholic Church had a relatively loose institutional structure. In 1840 the ratio of priests to people was only 1:3,023 and there were few public places of worship.[36] It is estimated that in 1842 only 40 percent of the population could have attended mass on any given Sunday [37] but the transformation of the Irish land structure after the famine changed that. Tens of thousands of agricultural labourers and cottiers who often owned between five and ten acres were driven from the land and in their place a class of more secure farm owners emerged. The clergy were drawn from the wealthier sections of this new property-owning peasantry. The slow accumulation of wealth on the land gave rise to a Catholic middle class in the cities from the end of the nineteenth century. The more secure farmers sent their sons to the cities as lawyers, publicans, civil servants, and priests. The number of priests rose by 150 percent between 1861 and 1911, despite the overall decline of the population[38] and by 1911 there was one priest for every 210 Catholics.[39]

The particularly repressive sexual morality that is so distinctive of Irish Catholicism fitted in well with the needs of the new farm-owning class. For them marriage and sexuality were intimately connected with the ownership of land. The farming classes dreaded anything that might lead to the break-up of their moderately sized farms and illegitimate birth was regarded as a major threat. Marriage was postponed until land became available to the eldest sons and many of the remaining offspring were condemned either to a life of celibacy or emigration. In 1926, for example, 84 percent of what the Irish CSO classified as males aged 45–54 who were 'relatives assisting' on farms never married.[40] This sexual repression was encouraged by a Marian Cult where the Virgin Mary was held up as a role model for Irish women. The morality may have been propagated by priests who came from the 'better farming stock', but it got a hearing from the majority of the population who saw religion as a solace in a poverty-stricken life. The tight institutional control that the Church won over schools and hospitals grew out of this culture, but also reinforced it in the most repressive of ways.

Despite all this power, however, the edifice began to crumble in the space of a decade. The institutional Church has declined to such an extent that it has difficulty replenishing itself as the numbers joining the priesthood have dried to a trickle and the age profile of surviving clerics has risen dramatically. In 1970 there were 750 entrants to the clergy, but by 1998 this had declined to only 92.[41] The drop was even more pronounced in the urban areas and the Dublin Diocese had no new seminarian in 1997 and only three in 1996.[42] As a result, the overall number of clerics has declined from 33,092 in 1970 to 19,996 in 1980s and the age profile has risen dramatically with 59 percent of diocesan priests now aged over 65 years.[43] The diocese of Cork and Ross estimates, that by 2010 there will be no priest under the age of 30 and there will be very few under the age of 40.[44] The religious orders who controlled the schools have retreated into holding the managerial positions and leaving the lay vice-principal in charge of the day-to-day running of the schools. Orders such as the Christian Brothers have effectively withdrawn from teaching to look after their ageing congregations. The declining number of entrants to the clergy has forced the Church to sell off some of its land simply to make provision for the care of aged priests and nuns. The shrinking of the full-time cadre of the Church has been accompanied by a sharp fall in morale. One delegate to the National Priests Conference of Ireland in 1998 stated that 'wearing a Roman Collar in public can evoke a wide variety of reactions, most of them unpleasant'. The journalist who covered the event summed up the prevailing mood when he wrote that 'Rarely can it have been so difficult to be a priest in Ireland. It may have been argued that it was worse in the penal days but that was when the priest was a hero among Catholic Ireland'.[45]

There has been a decline in religious practice. Weekly attendance at Mass has dropped from 77 percent of Catholics in 1994 to 55 percent of Catholics in 1998 while in Dublin, the figure is lower again at 38 percent.[46] This level of attendance is still comparatively high in Europe, but the pace and speed of the fall is much quicker than elsewhere. Practices like attendance at Confession have also fallen off and 40 percent of Catholics now say that they rarely or never go to confession and only 1 percent say they go every two or three weeks.[47] Irish Catholics have also adopted a more Protestant approach to their religion, as individual conscience now appears to count far more than the teachings of the Church. An *Irish Times*/MRBI opinion poll found that only 21 percent of Catholics were guided by the teaching of the Church when contemplating serious moral decisions and 78 percent said they followed their own conscience. More than 50 percent disagreed to varying extents with the Church's attitude to divorce, contraception, priestly celibacy and women priests.[48] Far from provoking anger, pronouncements by Church leaders often elucidate scorn.

Why did the Church decline?

How can we account for this extraordinary level of change? One approach is to assume that a shift to a liberal and secular society is an inevitable accompaniment to the process of modernisation. There is an important element of truth in this view, but it can also lead to a tendency to believe that progress and enlightenment emerge smoothly from on high. Another approach is to assume that any organisation such as the Catholic Church which attempts to promote a defined world view cannot survive in a post-modern age. A variant of this argument has been made by Fintan O'Toole who claims that Irish Catholicism embodied an absolutist utopia in a world where all utopian and big projects were 'domesticated' by conventional politics. The Church faced a crisis because it had not developed the 'complex lay culture which the Catholic Church had in other countries'.[49] As a result there was 'no genuinely Catholic intelligentsia and no Catholic society' to manage the transition to a post-modern world.[50] Others argue that the key to the change lay in Ireland's involvement with the EU. Thus, Dillon argues that 'the extension of women's right in Ireland owes more to Irish judicial review and equality directives from the European Commission than to the lobbying efforts of organised women'.[51]

All of these views, however, play down the capacity of people to struggle and win change for themselves. They assume there is some process that proceeds behind the backs of people who remain relatively passive. However, the very success of Irish capitalism posed new contradictions for the Catholic Church and these were not resolved by the elite in either Ireland or Europe. At first the ruling elite sought to make huge concessions to fundamentalist Catholics who wanted to maintain the power of the Church. This was demonstrated by the all-party support given for the 'Pro-Life' amendment which was inserted into the Irish Constitution in 1983 and the subsequent acceptance by the EU of a special Protocol which guaranteed that abortion could never be introduced in Ireland as a result of European law. The contradictions posed by the modernisation of Irish society were in fact partially resolved by decisive popular mobilisation. If it were not for huge demonstrations and protests against the power of the Church, the changes which eventually occurred would have been far more limited. However, it is still necessary to highlight the partial nature of the outcomes because, far from the 'liberal agenda' being completed, there still is a long way to go before it is delivered to the wider working class.

The root cause of many of the changes lay in the slow, imperceptible developments that occurred at a molecular level in Irish society. For decades the Catholic Church promoted a role model of either virgin or mother for women and it was the mother's decision to stay at home to devote herself to a large family that was the linchpin of the Catholic Church's 'moral monopoly'.[52] As late as 1961, only 5 percent of married women were in paid employment and this extremely low figure was the principal reason why Ireland had the second lowest overall rate of female participation in the labour force in the EU, behind Greece. The pattern was, however, broken by rapid industrialisation. Many of the new jobs were in the electronics industry where the US multi-nationals traditionally tended to employ women workers and there was also an expansion in services, which again tended to employ women. Between 1971 and 1996, the number of women at work grew by 212,000, compared to a growth

in male employment of just 23,000.[53] These changes accelerated as
the millennium approached, so that the female participation rate
jumped from 31 percent of the labour force in 1986 to 39 percent in
1997 and 43.7 in 1999.[54] The principal reason for the change is that
women no longer regard marriage as a reason to withdraw from paid
employment. The most dramatic shift has been among younger
married women in the age group of 25–44, where the participation
rate has risen to match the EU average. Table 7.1 indicate the scale
of the changes that occurred among married women since 1987.

Table 7.1   Labour force participation rates of married women 1987–99

	\multicolumn{9}{c}{Age group}
	15–19	20–24	25–34	35–44	45–54	55–59	60–64	65+	Total
1987	32.0	46.0	35.8	22.0	19.9	13.1	8.5	2.1	22.9
1999	–	56.0	64.6	56.5	44.7	28.7	16.9	3.1	43.7

Source: CSO, *Labour Force Survey 1987* (Dublin Stationery Office, 1987)
and *Quarterly National Household Survey First Quarter 1999* (Dublin
Stationery Office, 1999).

The growth in the numbers of women, and particularly married
women working led to a clash with Catholic morality. The timing
and spacing of children could no longer be left to the gift of God and
the very idea of a large family, which fitted with a more rural society
as a hedge against old age, soon became an anathema to many. Up
to the 1950s Ireland had a unique pattern of family life in Europe
because, on one hand, late marriages were common but, on the
other hand, the average family size was very large. Today however
this has changed dramatically, with the fertility rate halving from
2.96 in 1982 to 1.93 in 1998 and it is now below the level at which
the population replaces itself.[55] Irish women are having their first
child at a later age and are limiting the size of their families. In 1980,
the average age of a married woman when she had her first child
was 26, but by 1998 this had risen to 29.[56] Contraception is widely
used and the '"natural" family planning' which the Church had promoted in the 1970s has declined. A survey of women conducted in
1993 showed that 22 percent used the pill, 22 percent used condoms
and 14 percent used 'natural' methods.[57]

All of this has brought about a sexual revolution. Issues like premarital sex have ceased to be a matter of serious debate and are simply practised on large scale. Marriage is no longer a necessary condition for sexual activity, nor is sex a sufficient reason to get married. In 1973, a survey of Catholic respondents showed that 71 percent thought that sex before marriage was always wrong, yet by 1997 another survey found that 21–24 year olds had on average thirteen different sexual partners.[58] Similarly, even when women have children, marriage was no longer considered a necessity. In 1980, one in twenty births took place outside marriage but by 1996 this had risen to one in four and that was the fastest growth in births outside marriage in the EU.[59] Despite the absolute strictures on abortion, thousands of Irish women also travelled to Britain to have an abortion. In almost every area, a different sexual morality has developed to challenge the deeply held beliefs of Irish Catholicism. The core of that new morality revolves around a notion of choice and the right of people to control their own bodies. It asserts that neither the state nor the bishops should dictate how people conduct their sex lives.

The very strength of the Catholic Church made it more difficult to adapt to these changes because Irish Catholicism had pioneered a successful model for giving the bishops a high degree of influence in a democratic country. The Church hierarchy had considerable influence in fascist regimes such as Salazer's Portugal and Franco's Spain, but they were also identified only with a limited section of society and needed the dictatorship to maintain their power. Ireland was unique because the power was underpinned by overwhelming public support, so that it appeared the terms Irish and Catholic were almost synonymous. A close knit informal network had been established around the pivotal figures of Eamon de Valera and John Charles McQuaid, so that the bishops became an informal auxiliary wing of the state itself. Irish Catholicism brimmed with confidence in its own right to rule. Its lay activists in a host of professional associations from the Knights of Columbanus to the Irish Catholic Guild of Doctors believed that Ireland had a mission to offer an example to a heathen world. They drew solace from the manifest authority the Church could exercise with a few quiet words in the ears of the political elite.

All of this however meant that it was singularly ill equipped to deal with the challenges that grew with every new factory and office that was opened. So when the first visible signs of the change surfaced with the debates over contraception, the response was extreme. Family planning clinics were picketed, prayer vigils were organised outside their premises, and all manner of ruses were tried to legally entrap them. By the late 1970s a wide range of fundamentalist lay Catholic organisations had emerged to oppose liberal change. They were determined to hold onto the culture and structures that had been formed over decades. Far from the Catholic Church lacking an organised laity, as Fintan O'Toole suggested, these groupings were determined to fight as Church militants.

By 1980, they hit on the idea of a preventive strike against liberalism by inserting a Pro-Life amendment into the Constitution, even though the only other country in the world to have such an article was Pinochet's Chile.[60] The base of the original 'Pro-Life' groupings lay in the professional medical establishment which had worked closely with the Church ever since the defeat of the Mother and Child Scheme in 1951, because it had promised free medical care. The Pro-Life Amendment Campaign numbering no less than five medical professors and most of the leading gynaecologists among its sponsors.[61] The respectability that came with these positions gave them a ready access to political leaders who had been trained to respect such authority and they quickly agreed to the proposal for a referendum. The victory of the anti-abortion amendment to the constitution in 1983 and the subsequent confirmation of the ban on divorce in a referendum in 1986 produced two major effects. On the one hand, it emboldened the right wing to try to stop the tide of liberalism through strictures from on high and this revived authoritarianism was soon evident in many arenas. Dublin public libraries banned books such as *Our Bodies, Our Selves* because it contained information on abortion.[62] Irish newspaper distributors refused to distribute the *Guardian* when it contained an advertisement for the Marie Stopes clinic.[63] Students unions which gave out information on abortion were brought before the courts and fined heavily. As the fundamentalists believed that most forms of contraception were 'abortifacients', the confrontation on abortion became a convenient way to attack all forms of birth control. On the other hand, however, the right wing also paid a major price for their victories as they drove a significant minority into an open rebellion against the Catholic Church for the first time. In the two referenda on abortion and divorce, one-third of the population voted against the bishops and many of them were very angry with the results. No longer could the terms Irish and Catholic be equated; instead as one writer put it a 'second partition' had occurred.[64]

The clash between these opposing forces came to a head during the 'X' case in 1992 when an injunction was taken out by the Attorney General, Harry Whelehan, against a 14 year-old-girl who had been raped, to prevent her travelling to Britain for an abortion. Whelehan was a Fianna Fail supporter who had worked as a part-time counselor with the Catholic Marriage Advisory Bureau and was said to hold outspoken views on moral issues.[65] The High Court judge who ruled that the young girl should be prevented from travelling to Britain was Declan Costello. When he was the Attorney-General in 1973 he tried to take out an injunction against the Irish Family Planning Association for distributing the booklet *Family Planning for Parents and Prospective Parents.*[66] The reaction of thousands of people to the Court's decision was one of intense anger. It was one thing to vote for the 'right to life' in the abstract – it was quite another to force a young rape victim to go ahead with her pregnancy. Wendy Holden describes what happened,

> Dublin's traffic police had to escort march after march down O'Connell St. Thousands took part in a silent, candlelit march to Leinster House, the parliament buildings, and festooned the railings with white ribbons on behalf of the girl and her family. A group of several hundred stood outside the gates of the parliamentary debating chamber, chanting the telephone number of an abortion information line in between cries of 'Not the Church, Not the State. Women must decide their fate' . . . In Waterford in the south, thirty seven girls at the Sacred Heart of Mary's Convent walked out of class to join fellow students from the city's Mercy Convent in a demonstration. They said they had 'made their stance for freedom of choice' because of their profound sympathy for the girl. Their disobedience led to mass suspension.[67]

That was only the immediate response. Within a few days many more were demonstrating to demand the Supreme Court reverse the judgment of the High Court. So intense was the pressure that the Supreme Court made a bizarre re-interpretation of the Pro-Life clause which had been inserted into the Constitution in 1983. They argued that the 'Pro-Life article' which had assigned an equal right to life to the mother and the foetus in fact allowed abortion in the case when a woman was suicidal. It is, of course, possible to isolate any set of words from their immediate context and lend it surprising meanings but it is doubtful, however, if this particularly unusual interpretation, resulted solely from abstract logic. It was, in fact, forced on the judges by the huge numbers who mobilised. Many felt that if the Supreme Court had not allowed the girl to travel, there would have been riots on the streets.

In many of the accounts of Modern Ireland there is a fleeting reference to the 1992 mobilisation, but there is little recognition that these protests forced the state to move out of the grip of the Catholic Church. The belief that change comes from on high, though the action of enlightened and progressive men is a deeply held prejudice that is encouraged by our society. The fact the tens of thousands mobilise suddenly and then disappear as quickly gives rise to an unspoken assumption that struggle plays only a side role in the process of social change. Recognising the importance of 'people power' or even the threat of force can often be uncomfortable for those who see history marching slowly towards its destiny of a moderate, civil society. Yet as Marxists have argued, slow, molecular changes in quantitative relations can at some point transform into decisive qualitative changes, so that the past does indeed look like another country. Historically, the midwife for these enormous transformations has been struggle and mobilisation. These struggles sometimes stop short and often simply force our rulers to reorder the manner of their rule, but they are nonetheless the decisive conjunctures on which historical changes pivot.

One of the main concerns of the fundamentalist groups in the 1980s was that the slightest concession to liberalism could 'cause the floodgates to open'. The slogan may have been emotional and designed to mobilise their supporters but it recognised an important truth. The experience after the 'X' case protests proved them right because within a year, the Fianna Fail dominated Government had embarked on an extensive programme of reform. In 1993, laws were passed decriminalising suicide and providing for the extensive availability of condoms. The Department of Health's AIDS awareness programme included reference to the use of condoms and notices to this effect appeared in public toilets. One of the key indicators of the degree of change was the issue of homosexuality. At the time, Britain was in the last years of a Conservative Government and legal discrimination against gay people was at a height. The infamous Clause 28 prohibited the promotion of homosexuality by Education Authorities and the age of consent was set at 18. Yet the intense radicalisation that had occurred in the traditionally more conservative Ireland produced very different results. When the Irish

Government was required to legalise homosexuality after an EU court case, it proposed a far more liberal regime, with an equal age of consent for heterosexuality and homosexuality being set at 17. Family Solidarity, the organisation which successfully defeated divorce in 1986, argued that 'the proposal to legalise buggery for 17 year olds is repulsive and grossly irresponsible and parents will not buy it'.[68] Yet an opinion poll in Dublin showed that two-thirds of the population supported an equal age of consent.[69] Later when a Government minister from the Labour Party was found cruising in a gay area of the Phoenix Park, sections of the police leaked the story to the press in the hope of provoking a backlash. However, not only did he hold on to his Cabinet position, with the Government acknowledging that it was a personal matter, but he retained his seat at the following election. That more that anything summarised the huge changes that occurred in the aftermath of the 'X' case protests.

The changed political atmosphere that occurred after the 'X' case also provided the backdrop for a host of revelations about clerical child abuse and sexual hypocrisy. At first, the torrent of revelations began accidentally when the Bishop of Galway's former mistress wrote a book to reveal how he fathered a son. It was also discovered that Michael Clery, the priest who helped to found the militant anti-abortion group Youth Defence, had two sons who he did not acknowledge. Crucially, however, it was the scandals about child abuse which destroyed the moral authority of the Church. In the past, many were aware that priests abused their power to interfere with children and it was almost a common folklore that certain priests should be avoided. However, the changed atmosphere after the 'X' case gave confidence to hundreds of people to speak out about this side of the hidden Ireland.

For all that, however, it would be wrong to conclude that the liberal agenda has been completed. The conflicts over abortion and divorce polarised Irish society to such an extent that that no political party which based itself on a purely electoral considerations dared to carry through on the changes for fear of losing some of its voters. As a result, the Supreme Court judgment of 1992 still has not been carried through into Irish law. Moreover, the breakthrough that occurred during the 'X' case was not sustained by a broader ideological offensive against the Church and instead the dominant idea which emerged was that Ireland had reached a synthesis between the old world and the new so, that it could now be regarded as a 'more humane and less fragmented' society than Britain or the USA.[70] The effort to rebuild a consensus led to a more 'even-handed' outlook where both sides were asked to compromise. Fintan O'Toole expressed this plea for a new consensus when he argued that 'if you want to see an open, pluralistic society emerging on this island, then it is vital that the Catholic Church should be confident about its place in the world and not embattled to the point of being incommunicado. . .'.[71] From a different perspective, John Waters put the matter more sharply when he claimed that 'the backlash against the Church . . . has been driven by the agenda of the neurotic middle classes rather than a popular movement'.[72] Yet the irony is that the failure to carry through on the liberal agenda has meant the poorer sections of society have not benefited from some of the changes. The liberal agenda may have begun in Dublin Four but it had the potential to reach beyond it. The failure to do so means that there have been many legal changes, but the deeper social structures that underpinned Church control in the past have not been overthrown. As always when there are only legal changes, the main beneficiaries are the upper middle classes rather than the poor. This can be illustrated in a number of ways.

First, the failure to legalise abortion directly discriminates against the poor. Wealthier women can take advantage of the right to travel and information and have abortions relatively easily. For many working-class women, the requirement of travelling to Britain rather than having the operation performed in their own country represents a considerable expense. A report which was commissioned by the Department of Health noted that there was

> considerable financial cost for women both in terms of travel and accommodation and because they attend the abortion clinic as private patients. The typical cost of an abortion includes an initial £45 consultation fee plus £320 for a abortion up to 14 weeks with an overnight stay in the clinic which is obligatory for non-UK residents; £430 for an abortion over 14 weeks and up; £510 for an abortion over 20 and up to 24 weeks. Travel and accommodation would generally cost women another £200 as well as the cost of travel and accommodation for a companion if they are being accompanied.[73]

In addition, to these not inconsiderable costs, Irish clinics are not permitted to directly refer women to British clinics. This means that medical records are not easily transmitted, a factor of some relevance as more women have later abortions because of the difficulty in raising money.

Second, the domination of the Church over education has not been broken and this works to the disadvantage of the poorer sections of society. In order to sustain the concept of denominational education, primary and secondary schools receive a mixture of state funding and voluntary local contributions from parents. This means that schools in wealthier areas can raise a higher local contribution and, accordingly, provide better equipment for learning, while children in working-class areas make do with the less provision. In addition the managerial structural of schools is not geared to progressive forms of education which seek to compensate for class disadvantages, but is selected on the basis of promoting a denominational ethos. The chairperson of the Board of Management in most primary schools is a parish priest and the majority of these boards are appointed by the local bishop on the basis of loyalty to the Catholic Church rather than because of any expertise in education. In 1985, the Catholic Primary Schools Managers' Association issued guidelines to the effect that principals should be exemplary in the observance of their religious duties and teachers should be practising Catholics committed to handing on the faith.[74]

On top of this resources that might be devoted to core parts of the curriculum are diverted onto the promotion of a religious outlook. Religious instruction can take up considerable time in the curriculum, with key classes in primary schools such as First class and Sixth class devoting a large amount of time to preparation for communion and confirmation. One result is that no foreign language is taught in primary schools and the time devoted to science is extremely limited. The wealthier sections of society compensate for this by organising extra-curricular classes, but the poor cannot afford this. Subjects in the primary school curriculum also have to be taught in such a way as to convey religious values, even though this may be of little intrinsic use in education. The Rules for National Schools assert that

> Of all parts of a school curriculum, Religious Instruction is by far the most important, as its subject matter, God's honour and service, includes the proper use of man's faculties, and affords the most powerful inducements to their proper use. Religious instruction is, therefore a fundamental part of the school course, and a religious spirit should inform and vivify the whole school's work.[75]

As there is no state provision for primary education, this means that the vast majority of students are forced to accept this form of education. However, even in state-controlled sectors of second level and third level, the churches receive public money to pay chaplains to propagate their beliefs. No such privilege is offered to any other viewpoint in society and this money could be spent on educational materials for those who rely exclusively on the public system.

Third, Church control of the voluntary hospital sector has been a major factor inhibiting the development of a comprehensive and free national health service. Twenty-six of the sixty-three hospitals in the Republic are Catholic voluntary hospitals.[76] In almost all of these hospitals, and indeed in some state hospitals, an Ethics Committee ensures that the ethos of the Church is maintained. Procedures such as sterilisation and artificial fertilisation are not available and amniocentesis tests to detect deformities in the foetus are banned, because it is felt there is little use in prior knowledge when the abortion option has been foreclosed. Some of these procedures are available in hospitals run by the Regional Health Boards, but the bans imposed in the Church-run hospitals has increased the delays. The wealthy can circumvent this by paying privately or by travelling to Britain. On top of this, patients in voluntary hospitals, whatever their own views, are forced to accept various manifestations of Catholic control. These include, in some hospitals, the daily broadcasting of mass from televisions sets which cannot be turned off. For many Protestants, for example, 'their fears have more to do with holy pictures and devotional objects. They have not been brought up with them and feel uncomfortable with them. Many would worry about the prospect of dying before a picture of the Sacred Heart'.[77]

The influence of the Catholic Church is still evident in hierarchical institutions, such as the Medical Council and in many of the medical teaching colleges, where the moral and philosophical justification for the Church ethos is conveyed. In the past the bishops opposed a fully free medical service on the basis of a 'principle of subsidiarity' where the state should not interfere in roles that were more naturally allotted to the family. This position is more rarely articulated today, but there has been no criticism from the Catholic Church of Ireland's two-tier medical system, whereby private patients get quicker access and often more direct contact with consultants than poorer patients. Indeed, one of Ireland's top private hospitals, the Mater private hospital is run by the Sisters of Mercy.

The continuing conflict about the role of the Church in modern Irish society can no longer simply be defined in liberal terms. By its very nature, liberalism tends to challenge only so far and to shrink from more radical conclusions. It contents itself with legal changes when far wider social changes are required. Yet, as we have seen, the benefits of the liberal agenda are unevenly distributed in class terms. Carrying the changes through so that a secular health and education service is available will demand new struggles. Most likely these struggles will be linked to a wider movement for change which benefits the working class as a whole. However, before discussing the prospects for this, it is necessary to look at some of the continuing strengths of Irish conservatism.

The new conservatism

The continued institutional power of the Catholic Church and the existence of a substantial minority of fundamentalist Catholics who are deeply alienated by the liberal changes mean there is still scope for conservative policies. Moreover, as many people do not feel the Celtic Tiger is delivering, frustration can be deflected in this direction. There are some indications that this dynamic is already at work, albeit at a relatively low level. In the last General Election in 1997, independent candidates scored more than 10 percent of the vote and those who were elected on the basis of highly localised grievances tended to be conservative in their outlook. The independent TD for Donegal, Harry Blaney, has argued against the provision of a vasectomy clinic in Letterkenny and all three independent TDs who supported the Government demanded another Pro-Life referendum. Similarly, the 1999 Euro elections in Connaught-West returned Dana, Rosemary Brown, who combined an anti-abortion campaign with a rhetoric about exclusion from the Celtic Tiger.

The main theme of the embattled conservative forces remains the issue of abortion, as it is implicitly acknowledged that the battles over divorce and contraception have been lost. The abortion issue also allows the fundamentalists to link up with right-wing American groups who have long campaigned to shut down clinics. Groupings such as Human Life International are now heavily funded from the USA and there is a regular interchange of visitors to discuss tactics for rolling back the liberal agenda. The result is a combination of the most traditional attitudes with the most modern methods of US advertising techniques. The anti-abortion movement has also drawn considerable sustenance from the fact that no government has dared to legislate to implement the decisions of the Supreme Court. Despite the use of street tactics by groupings such as Youth Defence, the main approach has been to use positions of authority to stigmatise any moves to liberalise abortion. It is still extremely rare, for example, to hear an Irish doctor advocate a woman's right to choose, because pro-choice doctors are more likely to stay silent when control of promotion and access to consultancy positions lie in the hands of a medical establishment which shares a conservative Catholic ethos.

However, if abortion remains the centrepiece of the battle over sexual freedom, there is also a more defuse discourse, which stresses how Ireland is losing its morality and becoming a more consumerist and therefore it is claimed, a more maladjusted society. Liberalism is being held to account for many modern evils such as the dramatic rise in male suicide. Yet the conservative analysis is not as sure-footed on this score as it might first appear. Using a standard interpretation derived from Durkheim, it is sometimes claimed that the rise in suicide is linked to the lack of integration in society and that this in turn is associated with the weakening of a strong moral bond.[78] If this argument were correct, it should follow that the rate of suicide should be far less in rural areas, which maintained more traditional values, than in areas which embraced the liberal agenda. Yet, while the main rise in suicide has occurred in Dublin, the most traditional areas of the country have also seen a rise in suicide. Outside of Dublin and Cork city, the highest figures for suicide come from Cork County, Galway County, Kerry and Donegal, where some of the highest votes against abortion and divorce were recorded. Other factors may therefore be at work and the rise in suicide cannot simply be attributed to the weakening of traditional values. The decriminalisation of suicide may have led to a growth in the official figures. The commercialisation of rural life, which has seen a new consolidation of land, is destroying the economic role once assigned to elder sons of small farmers. The constant talk of boom in a society where many young men find themselves in dead-end jobs could also contribute. In brief, a return to Catholic morality is not the only solution to the terrible pressures that grow when capitalism is in full throttle.

The other major theme for the new conservatism is racism. Traditionally the Irish elite has had a keen eye to the political advantages to be gained from emigration and one politician expressed this succinctly when he claimed 'High emigration, granted a population excess, releases social tensions which would otherwise explode and makes possible a stability of manners and customs which would otherwise be the subject of radical change'[79]. During the 1980s, when Ireland was in the grip of an economic recession, the Irish Government encouraged their 'surplus' population to go to the USA. There they were welcomed by right-wing politicians who had won concessions on European immigrant quotas because of a 'diversity programme' that cut back on the numbers of blacks and Hispanics entering the country.[80] When the tide of liberalism was flowing strongly in the mid-1990s, it seemed that the historical memory of emigration led to a more caring attitude to the small number of refugees who had arrived in Ireland. When the Refuge Bill was introduced in 1995, the Minister who was responsible explained that its purpose was to ensure that 'immigration officials will not have any discretion to refuse entry to asylum seekers and accordingly the general rule will be that such applicants will be given free entry into the country'.[81] Despite this tenor however, there were some difficulties with the Bill and it was none other than the Fianna Fail opposition spokesperson, John O'Donoghue who attacked provisions which prevented refugees taking up employment and which did not give them free legal aid to process their claims.[82]

This tolerant climate however changed dramatically during the General Election campaign of 1997 after a mini-riot of refugees, who had been forced to queue for hours in a social welfare office, hit the news. Lurid stories began to appear in the media about 'trafficking gangs' using the Internet to get information on Ireland's welfare system and about hordes of 'professional beggars' taking advantage of the country's well-known generosity. Right-wing politicians also found that refugees could be used as a useful scapegoat to divert attention from the failures of the Celtic Tiger.[83] The shortage of local authority housing or the growing queues in hospitals were no longer the responsibility of politicians who cut taxes, but the refugees who were taking scarce resources. On the eve of polling the Justice Minister, Nora Owen, effectively abolished the common travel area between Ireland, Northern Ireland and Britain and gave immigration officials extra powers to detain people to examine their papers. In practice it was an invitation to pick out black faces who were entering Ireland in order to subject them to special scrutiny. The more liberal Refugee Act was also effectively suspended and a new policy of deportations was begun.

Today Government policy is caught between two contradictory imperatives. Sections of business see immigration as a means to deal with the growing labour shortages in the Celtic Tiger and, alongside anti-racist organisations, have pressed for immigrants to be given the right to work. However, others, particularly in Fianna Fail, see an anti-immigrant rhetoric as useful means for diverting attention away from the failings of the Celtic Tiger. As the party came under considerable attack during a spate of scandals to do with corruption, some of its spokespersons have been anxious not to throw away the race card. The result has been that refugees have been given a very limited right to work and their status is very much dependent on the goodwill of the employer.

In conclusion, the growth of Irish capitalism has produced considerable contradictions and the two main pillars of conservatism in Fianna Fail and the Catholic Church have been undermined. However, this did not happen as part of an inevitable process of modernisation. Rather, the lives of tens of thousands changed in slow imperceptible ways at first and as the contradictions between their experience and Catholic morality emerged, Irish society became more polarised. It was only the outbreak of struggle on a major scale around the 'X' case which broke the log jam and created the conditions whereby the Irish state was forced to withdraw from its close relationship with the Catholic bishops. However, while the struggle was sudden and dramatic, it was not sustained and the full political and ideological implications were not drawn. Instead a new consensus emerged which presented Ireland as a satisfactory combination of old traditions and new liberal values. This consensus, though, has hidden how the continued institutional power of the Church has disadvantaged the working class. It has also left the fundamentalist forces with considerable reserves to draw on to create a backlash when frustration with the Celtic Tiger emerges. However, this is only one possible alternative for the future, because the revival of working-class confidence is also creating the base for the emergence of stronger socialist forces.

Notes

1 Forward 21 March 1914.
2 G. Bell, *The Protestants of Ulster* (London, Pluto, 1976) p. 40.
3 See M. Farrell, *Arming the Protestants* (London, Pluto, 1983) for how the auxiliary forces were formed on sectarian lines.
4 M. Goldring, *Belfast: From Loyalty to Rebellion* (London, Lawrence and Wishart, 1991) p. 123.
5 P. Devlin, *Straight Left: An Autobiography* (Belfast, Blackstaff, 1993) p. 79.
6 Ibid. p. 132.
7 A. Boyd, *Have the Trade Unions Failed the North* (Cork, Mercier, 1984) p. 72.
8 J. H. Whyte, *Church and State in Modern Ireland 1923–1979* (Dublin, Gill and Macmillan, 1980) p. 54.
9 M. Gallagher, *The Irish Labour Party in Transition 1957–82* (Manchester, Manchester University Press, 1982) p. 42.
10 P. Mair, 'Explaining the Absence of Class Politics in Ireland' in J. Goldthorpe and C. Whelan, *The Development of Industrial Society in Ireland* (Oxford, Oxford University Press, 1992) p. 386.
11 G. Kerrigan, *Another Country: Growing Up in 50s Ireland* (Dublin, Gill and Macmillan, 1998).
12 P. Mair, *The Changing Party System: Organisation, Ideology and Electoral Competition* (London, Pinther, 1987) p. 103.
13 D. Walsh, *The Party: Inside Fianna Fail* (Dublin: Gill and Macmillan, 1986) p. 32.
14 J. P. O'Carroll, 'Eamon de Valera, Charisma and Political Development' in J. P. O'Carroll and J. A. Murphy (eds) *de Valera and His Times* (Cork, Cork University Press, 1983) p. 33.
15 J. Praeger, *Building Democracy in Ireland: Political Order and Cultural Integration in a Newly Independent Nation* (Cambridge, Cambridge University Press, 1983) p. 208.
16 L. Trotsky, 'Lesson of the Events in Dublin' in J. Riddell (ed.) *Lenin's Struggle for a Revolutionary International 1907–1916* (New York, Monad, 1984) p. 373.
17 Dail Debates, vol. 25, col. 478, 12 July 1928.
18 Department of Industry and Commerce, *Trade and Shipping Statistics 1926*, vol. 111, no 4, p. vi.
19 K. Allen, *Fianna Fail and Irish Labour* (London, Pluto, 1997).
20 Dail Debates, vol. 34, col. 318, 2 April 1930.
21 J. Goldthorpe and C. Whelan, *The Development of Industrial Society in Ireland* (Oxford, Oxford University Press, 1992) p. 389.
22 W. Roche and J. Larragy, 'The Trend of Unionisation in the Irish Republic' in UCD Department of Industrial Relations (ed.) *Industrial*

Relations in Ireland (Dublin, UCD Department of Industrial Relations, 1987) p. 21.

23 Quoted in F. O'Toole, *Black Hole, Green Card* (Dublin, New Island Books, 1994) p. 178.

24 T. P. Coogan, *Disillusioned Decades* (Dublin, Gill and Macmillan, 1987) p. 18.

25 F. Mockler, 'Organisation Changes in Fianna Fail and Fine Gael', *Irish Political Studies*, vol. 9 (1994) pp. 165–71.

26 Ibid. p. 166.

27 D. Keogh, *Ireland and the Vatican: The Politics and Diplomacy of Church-State Relations* (Cork, Cork University Press, 1995) p. 358.

28 M. Nic Ghiolla Phadraig, 'The Power of the Catholic Church in the Republic of Ireland' in P. Clancy, S. Drudy, K. Lynch and L. O'Dowd (eds) *Irish Society: Sociological Perspectives* (Dublin, Institute of Public Administration, 1995) pp. 593–4.

29 Conference of Major Religious Superiors, *Profile of Religious in Ireland* (Dublin, Conference of Major Religious Superiors, 1990) p. 94.

30 Quoted in J. H. Whyte, *Church and State in Modern Ireland*, pp. 29–30.

31 Minutes of Central Council of Congress of Irish Unions, 30 March 1951.

32 Congress of Irish Unions, *Annual Report 1951*, pp. 37–8.

33 G. Kerrigan, *Another Country*, p. 49.

34 Ibid. p. 49–50.

35 Quoted in J. Connolly, *Labour, Nationality and Religion* (Dublin, New Books, 1972) p. 10.

36 M. Nic Ghiolla Phadraigh, 'Religious Practice and Secularisation' in P. Clancy, S. Drudy, K. Lynch and L. O'Dowd, *Ireland: A Sociological Profile* (Dublin, Institute of Public Administration, 1986) p. 147.

37 Ibid.

38 E. Strauss, *Irish Nationalism and British Democracy* (London, Methuen, 1951) p. 104.

39 Ibid.

40 R. Breen, D. Hannon, D. Rottman and C. Whelan, *Understanding Contemporary Ireland: State, Class and Development in the Republic of Ireland* (Dublin, Gill and Macmillan, 1990) p. 104.

41 Figures supplied by Council for Research and Development, St. Patrick's College Maynooth.

42 F. McNally, 'Sharp Drop in Number of Priests in Dublin', *Irish Times* (24 January 1998).

43 Figures supplied by Council for Research and Development, St. Patrick's College Maynooth.

44 D. Hogan, 'Article Warns of Church Vocation Crisis', *Irish Times* (5 May 1999).

45 P. McGarry, 'Priests Feeling Alienation From People', *Irish Times* (9 October 1998).

46 MRBI Public Opinion Poll (4621/98) prepared for RTE. Figures supplied to author by Market Research Bureau of Ireland.

47 Ibid.

48 J. Waters, *An Intelligent Person's Guide to Modern Ireland* (Dublin, Duckworth, 1998) p. 64.

49 F. O'Toole, *Black Hole, Green Card* (Dublin, New Island Books, 1994) p. 129.

50 Ibid.

51 M. Dillon, *Debating Divorce: Moral Conflict in Ireland* (Lexington, University Press of Kentucky, 1993) p. 27.

52 T. Inglis, *Moral Monopoly: The Rise and Fall of the Catholic Church in Modern Ireland* (Dublin, UCD Press, 1998).

53 CSO, *Women in the Workforce* (Dublin, CSO, 1997) p. 1.

54 CSO, *Quarterly National Household Survey First Quarter 1999* (Dublin, Stationery Office, 1999).

55 CSO, *Vital Statistics: Fourth Quarter and Yearly Summary 1998* (Dublin, Stationery Office, 1999) p. 99.

56 Ibid. p. 101.

57 M. Wiley, *Women and Health Care in Ireland: Knowledge, Attitudes and Behaviour* (Dublin, Oak Tree/ESRI 1996) p. 59.

58 T. Inglis, *Lessons in Irish Sexual Morality* (Dublin, UCD Press, 1998) p. 10.

59 Ibid. p. 12.

60 E. O'Reilly, *Masterminds of the Right* (Dublin, Attic Press, no date) p. 98.

61 P. Brennan, 'Backlash and Blackmail', *Magill* (July 1982).

62 A. Smyth, 'The Politics of Abortion in a Police State' in A. Smyth (ed.) *The Abortion Papers* (Dublin, Attic Press, 1992) p. 140.

63 Ibid. pp. 140–1.

64 T. Hesketh, *The Second Partitioning of Ireland: The Abortion Referendum of 1983* (Dublin, Brandsma, 1990).

65 W. Holden, *Unlawful Carnal Knowledge: The True Story of the Irish 'X' Case* (London, Harper Collins, 1994) pp. 29–30.

66 O'Reilly, *Masterminds of the Right*, p. 32.

67 Holden, *Unlawful Carnal Knowledge*, p. 80.

68 K. Rose, *Diverse Communities: The Evolution of Lesbian and Gay Politics in Ireland* (Cork, Cork University Press, 1994) p. 56.

69 Ibid.

70 C. Coulter, 'Hello Divorce, Goodbye Daddy: Women, Gender and the Divorce Debate' in A. Bradley and M. G. Valiulis (eds) *Gender and Sexuality in Modern Ireland* (Amherst, University of Massachusetts Press, 1997) p. 277.

71 O'Toole, *Black Hole, Green Card*, p. 147.

72 Waters, *An Intelligent Person's Guide*, p. 75.

73 E. Mahon, C. Conlon and L. Dillon, *Women and Crisis Pregnancy* (Dublin, Stationery Office, 1998) p. 29.

74 Irish National Teachers Organisation, *The Place of Religious Education in the National Schools System* (Dublin, INTO, 1992) p. 16.

75 Ibid. p. 16.

76 T. Inglis, *Moral Monopoly*, p. 226.

77 W. Fitzgerald, 'Bibles and Bedside Manners', *Magill* (March 1990).

78 E. Durkheim, *Suicide: A Study in Sociology* (New York, Free Press, 1966).

79 Quoted in J. Lee, *Ireland 1912–1985: Politics and Society* (Cambridge, Cambridge University Press, 1989) p. 381.

80 E. Luibhead, 'Irish Immigrants in the United States Racial System' in J. MacLaughlin (ed.) *Location and Dislocation in Contemporary Irish Society* (Cork, Cork University Press, 1997) p. 265.

81 Dail Debates, volume 457, col. 715, 19 October 1995.

82 Dail Debates, volume 462, col. 874, 28 February 1996.

83 K. Allen, 'Immigration and the Celtic Tiger: A Land of a Thousand Welcomes' in M. Cole and G. Dale (eds) *The European Union and Migrant Labour* (London, Berg, 1999) pp. 91–113.

8
Alternatives

When Marx wrote the Communist Manifesto in 1848 there was still a sense of awe about the achievements of capitalism. His description of the dynamism of a system where 'all fixed, fast frozen relations . . . are swept away' and where 'all that is solid melts into air' contains more than a hint of admiration.[1] He saw capitalism as a necessary stage in human development and, while there had often been people who dreamed of a more equal world, their tragedy was to have lived when the economic foundations did not exist to underpin that ideal. Groupings like the Diggers and the Agitators who sprung up during the English Civil War and demanded that land be held as a 'common treasury for all' expressed the sentiment of many socialists ever since.[2] However, society had not arrived at a point where it was possible to *both* promote equality and also raise human productivity so that the majority did not have to engage in back-breaking toil. Marx's central critique of capitalism was that it produced immense possibilities, but simultaneously withdrew them from our grasp. In previous societies, human beings starved or died at a young age because there were insufficient resources to allow them to survive. Capitalism, however, is the only society where this is not necessary; the causes are now primarily rooted in a form of class rule that has outlived its usefulness.

These quite general considerations are of some relevance to the Celtic Tiger. One of the benefits of the recent economic boom is that it has demonstrated that mass unemployment and emigration are not inevitable parts of the Irish experience. Through a series of fortuitous circumstances, significant economic development has taken place. Derelict land has been cleared; factories have worked at full tilt; workers have felt needed. Most crucially, the old excuse that 'the country cannot afford it' has been eliminated. Yet even as the boom was in full swing, new problems and contradictions were thrown up. Even though tens of thousands of building workers are employed, cheap and accessible houses cannot be provided for them. Home ownership has moved beyond the reach of many and others are burdened with ever-higher debt repayments. The country has a £multi-million Government surplus, but it cannot provide a public transport service that guarantees comfort, frequency and reliability. Instead workers now face a longer working day as they spend hours in traffic in gridlocked cities or rise earlier to battle for places on overcrowded buses. Most crucially, in a society where so much wealth has been created, one might expect that those who spoke constantly about 'partnership' might share at least some of it. Yet the Tiger economy has led to greater class inequality than ever before.

Ireland had never experienced such a sustained boom and so the opportunities for a major reform programme were great. In the past, economic booms were supposed to bring in a tide that lifted all boats. British workers could, for example, point to the National Health Service as a lasting legacy of the post-war reconstruction. During the 1950s and 1960s, mass consumption grew in the USA and each new generation expected to do a little better than the preceding one. However, in modern capitalism, the tide only lifts the yachts. When the Celtic Tiger runs out, Irish workers will not be able to look back and point to many substantial gains.

Of course the very idea that the boom could end abruptly has barely been countenanced by the economic planners. The ESRI has predicted that growth rates of around 5 percent will continue to 2005 and, after that, slightly lower rates will sustain the boom until 2010. They also argue that 'over the next 15 years Ireland may achieve a standard of living among the highest in Europe'.[3] Moreover, in a huge note of optimism, they forecast that inflation would stay close to only 2 percent until 2003.[4] The leadership of the labour movement seems to have even more exaggerated hopes. Paul Sweeney, the SIPTU research officer who is the author of a highly optimistic account of the Celtic Tiger, has argued that the 'Irish miracle' is built on a solid edifice that can last and that it has the potential to become 'one of the world's leading economies'.[5]

However, there are many good reasons to doubt this facile optimism and to make the contrary assumption: that the Celtic Tiger will not last. One reason for being sceptical is that the optimists of today were precisely the pessimists of yesteryear who failed to predict the boom. The confidence of the ESRI, for example, stands in stark contrast to their consistent pattern of underestimating growth before this. As late as 1994, ESRI economists were still highlighting Ireland's economic woes, pointing to among other items, the weakness of indigenous industry, the low levels of private investment and a appalling infrastructure.[6] The introduction to the 1997 Medium Term Review contains an admission that 'even if Ireland were truly a tiger, we would be the last to see it'.[7] However, they explain that the reason they 'nearly always erred on the side of pessimism', by claiming they were victims of 'the poor self image in Ireland'.[8] This is rather a spurious explanation, as few non-Irish economists, who escaped the national inferiority complex, predicted the boom either.

A more likely explanation for the ESRI's failure is that conventional economics is singularly inept at predicting booms and slumps because it fails to recognise any inherent contradiction in the market system. Few economists predicted the demise of the Asian Tigers and until recently many were hailing the 'Goldilocks' economy of the USA as a 'new paradigm' where the business cycle had finally been suppressed. Economics cannot simply be regarded as an objective science, because it contains a large element of advocacy for the free market. This explains why sometimes the more prestigious the economist, the greater the mistakes they make about the boom-slump cycle. In 1970, for example, Paul Samuelson, the author of a best-selling textbook on economics, wrote that 'the National Bureau of Economic Research has worked itself out of one of its first jobs, namely business cycles'.[9] Three years later a major global recession occurred which shook the Western economies. More bizarrely, on the day before the stock market crash of 1929, one of the leading economists, Professor Irving Fischer, predicted that the market would 'return eventually to further steady increases'.[10] It would appear that confident predications about lasting booms from prestigious economists should carry a health warning.

The lack of planning and co-ordination in capitalism means that many factors can emerge to choke a boom. Business traditionally tries to reduce public-spending programmes, but then screams that the ports, airports and road network are inadequate to cope with an economy growing at full speed. The increasingly shrill references to 'an infrastructural deficit' in the Celtic Tiger highlight the fact that previous policies of cutting taxes have produced bottlenecks which increase costs. In the past, individual employers did not take on apprentices in order to reduce costs and stay ahead of rivals, but then found they were confronted with skilled labour shortages in the boom. The frenetic rush to make profits also means that individual companies adopt measures which work to the detriment of the economy as a whole. The boom, for example, has attracted more foreign banks to enter the Irish market, and this in turn has led Irish banks to expand their loans to clients with limited security in order to shore up profits. However, by increasing demand for mortgages, house prices continue to rise and this in turn feeds back into demands for higher wages. In brief, the boom brings its own chaos which is exacerbated by the lack of planning that is endemic in capitalism.

All of this takes place against the background of an unstable global economy. The ESRI's prediction of a decade-long boom was first made in 1997 and was premised on an assumption of world growth. However, soon after their predications were published, the Asian Tigers collapsed setting off a chain reaction which spread outright panic in the world financial system as the Long Term Credit Management hedge fund went bankrupt and another Wall Street crash was feared. Alan Greenspan and the Federal Reserve managed a rescue plan, but economists were not quite sure why it worked. As Paul Krugman argued, 'In retrospect, Greenspan seemed to be like a general who rides out in front of his demoralised army, waves his sword and shouts encouragement, and somehow turns the tide of battle: well done, but not something you would want to count on working next time'.[11] In such an unstable world, the ESRI's prediction of a sustained boom until 2010 seems positively foolhardy.

There are, however, even more specific reasons to be concerned. As we have seen, the levels of private investment in the Celtic Tiger are surprisingly low and much of the stimulus for growth came from an injection of outside capital. It is estimated that EU structural funds contributed around 2.5 percent to GNP and helped to prevent even more serious underfunding of the infrastructure.[12] However, as the major EU economies enter a period of low growth, it is doubtful if these funds can continue for much longer. More seriously, Ireland has become dependent on an influx of US capital to sustain its manufacturing base and it was the surge in US investment seeking a location inside the EU which helped create the Tiger economy. However, there are in fact deep structural problems in the US economy. Much of the growth has been financed by massive borrowings by both companies and households. These borrowings are in turn sustained by an extraordinary inflation of share prices which bear little relationship to the growth in the real economy. Between 1987 and 1997, the US stock market tripled in value and in a slightly shorter period the financial net worth of the US stocks mushroomed by over $5.5 trillion.[13] This represents the equivalent of the total amount of savings which US households had accumulated over the previous twenty years.[14] If this was based on a huge growth in profitability and productivity, it would be extremely impressive. However, while there have been modest gains in the real economy, the spectacular increase in share prices presages major difficulties for the future. In brief, there are good reasons for thinking that the close ties to the US economy which worked well in the past may not continue to do so indefinitely.

As many feel that the Celtic Tiger is a temporary rather than a permanent state of affairs, it is no wonder that workers seek to recover their share of the boom while it lasts. No other section of society has shown any particular restraint. Landlords have pushed up rents, banks have increased profits, companies have paid out more dividends; yet the only item which is controlled is wages. As wage earners sense they have lost out, pressure has grown for higher pay rises. Sometimes the increased pay is sought as a means to maintain 'relativities' – traditional links with other groups who gained pay rises – or, on other occasions, as a 'special case' to compensate for increased skills or productivity. However, the sectional form in which the demands are presented merely reflects the institutional game of industrial relations and it does not preclude solidarity between the various groups. What is really at stake is whether workers can reverse a pattern where the share of the national economy going to profits, dividends and rent has risen dramatically, while the corresponding share granted in income to working people has declined.

Every attempt by workers to increase their pay beyond set limits is met with an ideological offensive from the employers, the state and conventional economists. It is argued that wage increases will lead to a rise in inflation and cause the Celtic Tiger to collapse.

Yet the demand for more pay is often a response to inflationary pressures that have already taken place. Although the CPI may not measure items such as rising house prices or child care, workers have felt their pay packages diminish because of higher mortgage payments or crèche fees. Moreover, in an open economy such as Ireland, domestic wages cannot be regarded as the sole cause of inflation. Despite more than a decade of wage restraint, Irish inflation rose substantially and by 2000 it was the highest in the European Union. The rising prices soon wiped out the pay increases that were due under the Programme for Prosperity and Fairness.

Ideologies often work by combining elements of people's experience and reconfiguring them in ways that suits ruling groups. Irish people have been haunted by the fears of unemployment and mass emigration and the threat of a return to this state of affairs can provide a powerful weapon in the hands of our rulers. Instead of telling people that 'the country cannot afford it', they threaten workers who demand more that they could bring the Celtic Tiger crashing down. There is, however, a deep irony in this discourse. The market, we are sometimes told, is a wondrous mechanism that conforms only to its own laws and no form of intervention can buck its insistence that supply and demand automatically come into harmony. Yet when workers respond to growing labour shortages with demands which reflect their increased bargaining power, calamity is threatened. Everything else in the market is presented as beyond human control, but arguments rage over whether or not workers should seek higher wages, while the rises in bank profits, or accountancy fees or brokerage costs are supposed to simply reflect the market itself.

The decade of social partnership has brought major restrictions on union activity and the unions have appeared to many workers only as an insurance deduction on their wage packets. Employees were not allowed to collectively formulate their own claims, but were forced to leave matters in the hands of the union hierarchy. Many union activists found that much of their time was spent on 'case work', where they processed individual grievances through many stages of the lengthy procedures they had been locked into. All of this means that the union organisation on the shopfloor level can atrophy. If this leads to a major weakness today, it will become even more serious if workers have to confront an employer class which drops all pretence at partnership. During the last major recession in the 1980s, this is precisely what occurred, as the employers launched a major offensive. The Celtic Tiger provides no evidence that employers took the notion of partnership seriously when it came to sharing out the wealth. They viewed it only as a mechanism for incorporating union leaders and controlling their members. If the economy slumped, redundancies and mass unemployment would obviate the need to collaborate closely with union leaders and provide the whip to discipline their members.

The struggle for higher pay during the boom can, however, revive workers' organisations and make them ready for resistance during a slump. This form of active trade unionism helps to transfer power away from the head offices and restore confidence to the shopfloor. It encourages workers to pin their hopes in collective organisation rather than seeking individual avenues for playing the market. All of these factors can become crucial when employers try to transfer the costs of the recession onto workers with the same determination they denied them their share of the boom. A revival of working-class militancy can set the stage for more active and political resistance to the wasteful chaos that accompanies a slump. A continued belief in social partnership, though, can only disarm workers politically and economically.

Myths of globalisation

Whichever strategy Irish workers adopt, they operate on the terrain of one of the most open economies in the world. Today more goods are produced in US owned manufacturing plants than in all the equivalent Irish companies combined. Most of these goods are exported and so the economy is influenced both by international flows of capital and by the state of markets elsewhere. Despite the country's history of nationalist politics, few are unaware that their economic fate is tied up with the global economy.

Living in a global economy is one thing – accepting the myths of globalisation, however, is quite another. Globalisation myths systematically disempower people. As Bourdieu has argued globalisation is an idea that has social force and 'it is in the name of this model that flexible working, another magic word of neo-liberalism, is imposed meaning night work, weekend work, irregular working hours, things which have always been part of employer's dreams'.[15] The myth assumes that multi-nationals can move about the world at will and subject every population to their insatiable demands. Ties to nation states are supposed to be broken and the multi-nationals operate as free agents which can move to where labour is cheapest and so thwart any union ambitions. The myth of globalisation provides a powerful alibi for those who want to discourage resistance and militancy. When General Motors demanded that their Irish employees in Packard Electric work two hours longer a week for no extra pay, they threatened closure if the workers did not accept. The union leaders urged acceptance on the basis that there was no alternative because of globalisation. After strong initial worker resistance, they convinced their members to accept this advice. Yet tragically the factory closed shortly afterwards anyway. Resistance might have had least left workers with some pride and confidence, not to mention an extra two hours for themselves.

The globalisation myth paints an idealised picture of capitalism as the neo-liberal economists might like it to appear. It is a world composed of a large uniform market, where companies are operated like isolated atoms that have no relationship to each other or to nation states. Real existing capitalism, however, works very differently. Far from capital flowing evenly across the world, it is concentrated in particular advanced zones of the system. 'Triadization'[16] would be a more accurate description of the process, as capital predominantly flows to Japan plus south east Asia, Europe and North America. Whole parts of the world which offer an abundance of cheap labour have effectively been abandoned by the multi-nationals. The share of foreign direct investment going to Africa, for example, has never exceeded 1.5 percent of global investment in the past twenty years.[17]

Companies also need a home base that is provided by nation states to gain extra leverage and security. States provide lucrative contracts, tax subsidies and grants, mechanisms for negotiation over changes proposed by international bodies such as the EU. Many of the world's leading firms would not be in existence today if their local state had not organised rescue plans when they neared bankruptcy. Chrysler, Daewoo or the AIB were all shored up by their respective states in America, South Korea and Ireland. Companies also look to the power of states to impose their particular vision of what constitutes economic normality. The extraordinary concept of intellectual property rights means that software is not technically sold but licensed to customers, who are prevented from passing on their product to associates. Only the enormous power of the US Government could impose such a practice on global markets on behalf of firms. All of this means that far from multi-nationals being free-floating agents, they are tied to particular states and as a result can be subject to some pressure from these states.

Nor is it true that multi-national firms can move their factories around the world at will. Machinery and equipment can, of course, be moved, but it is an arduous process that carries many costs. New staff have to be recruited; they have to be sufficiently trained in the required skills; there has to be an adequate infrastructure in the new location. Instead of sudden moves in response to political or industrial pressure, multi-nationals are more likely to plan to relocate well in advance to minimise these costs. In addition, the modern factory is not normally a self-contained unit, but depends upon a surrounding network of other firms which contract to provide parts and services. These sub-supplier firms are usually locked into long-term franchises to supply items on favourable terms. Ruigock and van Tulder have coined the term 'industrial complexes' to describe the elaborate network into which modern factories are inserted.[18] The concept serves to emphasise why multi-nationals are not foot-loose entities that can hop up and leave at the slightest sign of an Oliver Twist asking for more. One writer has provided a more realistic assessment of the constraints on multi-nationals

> While there is some evidence of production switching to offset strike bound plants . . . the feasibility of production relocation appears to be much lower . . . It is important to distinguish actual, from threatened, production relocation. Cases of production relocation by MNCs are fairly rare . . . The threat of plant closure is a little more frequent. . . . Clearly there are constraints on the ability of MNCs to switch production, certainly in the short term. Not only are transference, set up and production costs likely to be substantial, but where the MNC operates a global strategy production relocation may have global restructuring repercussions. This type of consideration is likely to discourage the relocation of production in the event of industrial troubles or the opportunity of lower cost labour. A more likely strategy for the MNC would concern the placement of new investment, not the switching of existing facilities.[19]

If multi-nationals are not free agents who can transverse the world at will, then workers need not be their victims, but can also impose demands on them. In fact, the very integration of production lines may actually increase the potential bargaining power of workers. Relatively small groups of workers located in one country can bring a whole company to a halt by denying other plants vital parts. This occurred at the General Motors plant in Dayton when workers who struck against compulsory overtime brought the company's American plants to a close very quickly. It also occurred in 1988 when Ford workers in Britain struck and brought the whole of Ford Europe to a halt within three or four days. Modern management techniques can also have the unintended effect of making companies extremely vulnerable. A common practice has been to establish Just-in-Time systems, where storage costs are decreased by using information technology to ensure that parts and supplies arrive at the production line just before they are to be used. However, the low level of inventories means that companies are ill prepared for sudden outbursts of direct industrial action.

All of these considerations are of particular relevance in the Celtic Tiger. Ideologists who support the present division of wealth often play on Ireland's colonial past to suggest that an entirely subservient attitude to foreign multi-nationals is required. Every possible demand for environmental controls, for union rights or claims for decent pay is met with a response that the multi-nationals can 'up and leave' if people are too pushy. Yet the pattern of agglomeration whereby a large proportion of US investment in electronics and pharmaceuticals is located in Ireland actually gives Irish workers enormous potential power. Far from being able to relocate instantly in response to workers seeking the right to join a union, a stoppage in one of the world's largest chip manufacturing plants or many of the computer plants would exert considerable pressure on leading US firms. The problem is often not the power bestowed on multi-nationals because of globalisation; it is rather that union leaders share a common perspective with Ireland's elite that these plants should not be pressed too hard. This helps to explain why, to date, little attempt has been made to unionise many recent US multi-national plants.

Strategies

The neo-liberal revival of the 1980s has lost much its shine. Behind the benign language of flexibility and competitiveness, too many have experienced the scars of stress, overwork and low pay.

Traditional aspirations for decent pensions or a health service that treats all equally, regardless of money, have not gone away. The market also stands condemned in the eyes of a new generation for its destruction of the Third World. Today the interest payments on debt from poorer countries are greater than all the aid sent by industrialised countries. In Zambia, for example, nearly ten times as much is spent on debt repayments than is spent on primary education.[20] In a world where $40 billion can be put together in an instant to fight a supposedly humanitarian war in Serbia and Kosovo, there is an almost complete paralysis when it comes to offering relief to the millions of children who die because they do not have clean water. For many the issue is no longer, is radical change desirable but how can it come about?

Throughout Europe this has led to a revival of social democracy. Contrary to past predictions, centrist parties have not displaced parties which have links to labour movements and at the end of the millennium every country in the EU, bar Ireland and Spain, had a social democratic party in government. This shift is also reflected at the level of the intelligentsia. In the past, post-modernism successfully argued for a retreat from politics lest any attempt to produce a 'grand narrative' led to tyranny. Ultimately support for such intellectual currents came from the elite of the 1968 generation which had moved on to occupy professional, managerial and administrative positions and enjoyed the benefits that accrued to the new middle class.[21] By the mid-1990s, however, the poverty, pain and chaos caused by neo-liberal economics could no longer be ignored. The 150th anniversary of the Communist Manifesto has seen a revival of interest in Marx with even the *Financial Times* columnist, Edward Mortimer noting that 'Marx and Engels described a world economy more like that of 1998 than of 1848'.[22] This has coincided with a host of new biographies and discussion of Marx's ideas.[23] After the Seattle protests against the World Trade Organisation a new anti-capitalist movement has emerged.

The French sociologist Pierre Bourdieu offers an important point of discussion for the debates that have developed with this new shift to the left. Not only has he documented at close hand some of the realities that lay behind modern capitalism, but he has also proposed a new engagement to change them. He supported the magnificent 1995 general strike in France; he is a founder of the popular ATTAC movement (Action pour une Taxe Tobin d'Aide aux

Citoyens) in France which campaigns for new taxes on global finance; he helped to organise a public declaration of French intellectuals against the Balkans War. The core of Bourdieu's outlook is a reassertion of 'old Labour' values – he wants the state to impose itself on and control the forces of global capital. He writes,

> At the present time, the critical efforts of intellectuals, trade unions or associations should be applied as a matter of priority against the withering away of the state. The national states are undermined from outside by these financial forces, and they are undermined from inside by those who act as the accomplices of the financial forces, in other words, the financiers, bankers and finance ministry officials. I think that the dominated groups in society have an interest in defending the state, particularly in its social aspect. This defence of the state is not inspired by nationalism. While one can fight against the national state, one has to defend the 'universal function' it fulfils, which can be fulfilled as well, or better, by a supranational state.[24]

However, while one can admire the ferocity of Bourdieu's attack on neo-liberalism, it raises many questions about strategy. Who, for example, is to carry through this project? The shifting nature of modern capitalism has also impacted on the leaders of social democracy, so that even when they win government positions, they offer little resistance to the dictates of capital. In 1992, the Irish Labour Party became the touchstone for popular anger against the corruption and arrogance of a Golden Circle that linked business and politics. Yet after receiving their largest vote in seventy years, they not only joined Fianna Fail in coalition, but they agreed to a tax amnesty for the wealthy elite they had rhetorically attacked. As one journalist put it, 'That Labour, after all the passion and eloquence with which it had denounced the old system, agreed to and defended an amnesty which benefited, in the words of Dick Spring's adviser, Fergus Finlay, in his book *Snakes and Ladders*, "every sleazebag in the country" seemed at the time inexplicable'.[25]

Despite its impressive economic boom, it might be argued that Ireland is a relatively insignificant country in terms of political developments in Europe. However, events in Germany, in the heartland of European social democracy, only confirm the argument. Here the Social Democratic Party swept to power in 1998 in a wave of enthusiasm and Oskar Lafontaine, who urged interventionist Keynesian measures, was appointed Finance Minister. Yet when he proposed increasing taxes for big companies, the Government was threatened with the closure of whole enterprises and a cutback of investment. Instead of facing down this threat, Lafontaine was forced to resign amidst open celebration by the rich who saw their share prices rise at speeds which set a post-war record. After Lafontaine's resignation, Corporation Tax was cut from 40 percent to 25 percent, while the budget for pensions and unemployment was reduced.

Social democratic parties have always been contradictory phenomena, with a foot in the camp of both major classes. The leaders of these parties typically adhere to the values of the business elite and constantly demonstrate their loyalty to their demands. Yet rank and file supporters expect these parties to deliver on their traditional aspirations for decent health, welfare and education. In the past, this contradiction was overcome when a more stable form of capitalism allowed these aspirations to be met while simultaneously ensuring that profit levels remained high. Today, the instability and ferocity of the system means that the demands of the wealthy are insatiable and there is little room for substantial reforms that costs money. If 'Red Oskar', as he was known, could last less than a hundred days as a Finance Minister, there is little hope that social democracy could ever muster the means to tame international capital.

The other problem with Bourdieu's argument is that while the state may appear to have 'universal functions', it is structured in such a way as to serve the very sectional interests of capital. Democracy in a society where so much wealth is centralised is necessarily limited. There is no mechanism to allow electors to control their representatives or nothing to stop TDs breaking electoral promises. Even the parliamentary representatives do not control the Cabinet, but rather the Cabinet controls the TDs through a mixture of patronage and pressure. Parliament itself is only the front stage for a wider state apparatus of undemocratic institutions. In the police, the army, state industry, national television, the civil service and the Revenue Commissioners, the principle of administration is the same: authoritarian appointment from above of people who have displayed their loyalty to the system. Crucially, the Government foregoes any control over the most decisive area of society, namely the economy, which remains in the hands of big business.

The experience of the Celtic Tiger illustrates that this is an ideal structure for capital. Far from the state imposing any 'universal functions' on the wealthy, they can use the state to impose their sectional interests on the rest of society. Aside from the normal practices of giving state hand-outs to business, wholesale illegality on a massive scale has been condoned. The very rich were allowed to open offshore accounts through an illegal Ansbacher bank while the moderately 'well-off' lied about their 'non-resident status' to evade tax. Politicians at the highest level were bought 'wholesale', while the 'retail' method of making donations for specific favours was used in a host of incidents. Even when Tribunals were established as an outlet for public anger, nothing was done to punish the guilty, and in one instance, the judge who presided over one Tribunal was a major shareholder in one of the most prominent companies involved in the Ansbacher accounts. Yet all of these facts were known beforehand in the state circles that exist beyond the public gaze. Few of the decisions which led to this state of affairs were ever debated in Parliament. The framework of public political debate was, of course, set by capital's insistence on measures to increase competitiveness, but the detailed decision or non-decision making was left to the unelected state.

If the present state is not the vehicle for imposing the aspirations of the majority on the economy, a different approach is needed. Here a return to some of the beliefs of the first major Irish Marxist, James Connolly, is required. Connolly was highly critical of assigning a central role to the state and instead advocated a form of 'socialism from below', which relied on the capacity of workers to emancipate themselves. He wrote

> Socialism implies above all things the co-operative control by workers of the machinery of production; without this co-operative control the public ownership by the State is not socialism – it is only state capitalism.
>
> To the cry of the middle class reformers, 'make this or that the property of the government' we reply, 'Yes, in proportion as the workers are ready to make the government their property'.[26]

A focus on workers' own activity in freeing themselves is a necessity if genuine liberation is to be achieved rather than a spurious freedom that is handed down from on high. It is also vital because it is only in the course of wide-scale class struggle that, what Marx called, 'the muck of ages' can be removed. Racist and sexist ideas will always receive support in a class society that promotes divisions and need to be countered and it is only when people fight together as black and white, or male and female workers against a common enemy that petty notions of superiority or bigotry can be fully uprooted.

Today such an immense power has been concentrated in the hands of business that many see either political adaptation to that power or a form of ironic withdrawal into personal lifestyles as the only realistic options. What is required are practical methods of winning change. Yet the most practical way of defeating capital is by mobilising against it a power that is of equal, or greater, strength to it. Such power will not be found in speeches in Parliament or in guerrilla movements that look to the gun. It can only be found in the collective strength that workers have when they mobilise together. Despite the myths about post-industrial society, workers, both blue collar and white-collar, make up the vast majority of modern society. They are also highly productive and capable by their actions of bringing an economy to a halt. This latent power is the only force that terrifies big business. The denunciations of workers who ask for more are themselves tribute to that fear.

All of this requires politics. The sheer anarchy of capitalism as it shifts from booms to slumps can weaken particular groups who appeared strong at one time. Moreover, the employers rarely fight alone, but increasingly bring the power of the state to bear on workers who defy their rule. All of this implies a need to move from economic struggles to a revolutionary challenge to the system as a whole. What is required is a political movement that starts from the struggles of today, but links them to strategy for overall change. Ironically, the Celtic Tiger has laid a new basis for this politics to emerge. The constant talk of economic advance has whetted workers' appetites for more and has helped to restore their economic strength. After the Irish rich have so blatantly vandalised the public services to avoid taxes, the legitimacy that was once accorded to the traditional political institutions has declined. In this situation, the prospects for a socialist movement which stands well to the left of Labour are very good.

Notes

1 K. Marx and F. Engels, *Manifesto of the Communist Party in Selected Works*, vol. 1 (Moscow, Progress, 1977) p. 111.

2 C. Hill, *The World Turned Upside Down* (Harmondsworth, Penguin, 1991).
3 ESRI, *Medium Term Review 1997–2003* (Dublin, ESRI, 1997) p. 109.
4 Ibid. p. 110.
5 P. Sweeney, *The Celtic Tiger: Ireland's Economic Miracle Explained* (Dublin, Oak Tree, 1998) p. 15.
6 P. Honohan and P. O'Connell, 'The National Development Plan in the Context of Irish Economic Problems in ESRI', *Economic Perspectives for the Medium Term* (Dublin, ESRI, 1994) pp. 63–77.
7 ESRI, *Medium Term Review*, p. 3.
8 Ibid.
9 Quoted in C. Harman, 'The Crisis of Economics', in *International Socialism Journal*, no. 71 (Summer 1996) p. 3.
10 Quoted in L. Corey, *The Decline of American Capitalism* (New York, Covici-friede, 1934) p. 21.
11 P. Krugman, *The Return of Depression Economics* (London, Allen Lane, 1999) p. 135–6.
12 OECD, *Economic Surveys Ireland 1998–1999* (Paris, OECD, 1999) p. 44.
13 R. Brenner, *The Economics of Global Turbulence* (London, New Left Review, 1999) p. 246.
14 Ibid.
15 P. Bourdieu, *Acts of Resistance: Against the New Myths of Our Time* (Cambridge, Polity, 1998) p. 34.
16 R. Petrella, 'Globalization and Internationalization' in R. Boyer and D. Drache *States Against Markets* (London, Routledge, 1996) p. 77.
17 P. Hirst and G. Thompson, *Globalization in Question* (Cambridge, Polity, 1996) p. 67.
18 Quoted in C. Harman, 'Globalisation: A Critique of the New Othrodoxy', *International Socialism Journal*, no. 73 (1996) p. 15.
19 P. Enderwick quoted in P. Dicken, *Global Shift: The Internationalization of Economic Activity* (London, Paul Chapman, 1992) p. 406.
20 F. M. Lappe, J. Collins and P. Rosset, *World Hunger: 12 Myths* (London, Earthscan, 1998) p. 145.
21 See A. Callinicos, *Against Post-Modernism: A Marxist Critique* (Cambridge, Polity, 1998) Ch. 5.
22 E. Mortimer, 'Global Gloom', *Financial Times* (25 March 1998).
23 J. Derrida, *Spectres of Marx* (London, Routledge, 1994); T. Eagleton, *Marx* (London, Phoenix, 1997); F. Wheen, *Karl Marx* (London, Fourth Estate, 1999).
24 P. Bourdieu, *Acts of Resistance*, p. 41.
25 F. O'Toole, '1993 Tax Amnesty Rewarded the Cheats', *Irish Times* (8 October 1999).
26 J. Connolly, *The New Evangel* (Dublin, New Books, 1972) pp. 27–8.

Select bibliography

Adams, G., *The Politics of Irish Freedom* (Dingle, Brandon, 1986).

Adonis, A., and S. Pollard, *A Class Act: The Myth of Britain's Classless Society* (London, Penguin Books, 1997).

Allen, K., 'Forging the Links: Fianna Fail, the Trade Unions and the Emergency', *Saothar*, no. 16 (1991) pp. 48–56.

Allen, K., *Fianna Fail and Irish Labour: 1926 to the Present* (London, Pluto Press, 1997).

Allen, K., 'Immigration and the Celtic Tiger: A Land of a Thousand Welcomes' in M. Cole and G. Dale (eds) *The European Union and Migrant Labour* (London, Berg, 1999) pp. 91–111.

Alzheimer Society of Ireland, *Caring Without Limits?* (Dublin, Alzheimer Society of Ireland Policy Research Centre, no date).

Amalgamated Transport and General Workers Union, *A New Agenda for Economic Power Sharing* (Dublin, ATGWU, 1999).

Aronowitz, S., *False Promises: The Shaping of American Working Class* (New York, McGraw Hill, 1973).

Bacon, P., *An Economic Assessment of Recent House Price Developments* (Dublin, Stationery Office, 1998).

Bailey, I., and U. Coleman, *Access and Participation in Adult Literacy Schemes* (Dublin, National Adult Literacy Agency, 1999).

Baldwin, R., R. Forslid and J. Haaland, 'Investment Creation and Investment Diversion: Simulation Analysis of the Single Market Programme', CEPR Discussion Paper, no. 1308 (1995).

Baker, C., and K. Weber, *Solidarnosc: From Gdansk to Military Repression* (London, International Socialism, 1982).

Barrell, R., and N. Pain, 'The Growth of Foreign Direct Investment in Europe' *National Institute Economic Review*, no. 160 (1997) pp. 63–76.

Barrett, A., T. Callan and B. Nolan, 'The Earnings Distribution and the Return to Education in Ireland', ESRI Working Paper, no. 85 (June 1997).

Barry, F., J. Bradly and E. O'Malley, 'Indigenous and Foreign Industry: Characteristics and Performance' in F. Barry (eds) *Understanding Ireland's Economic Growth* (Basingstoke, Macmillan, 1999) pp. 45–75.

Bartley, B., 'Spatial Planning and Poverty in North Clondalkin', in D. Pringle, J. Walsh and M. Hennessy (eds) *Poor People, Poor Places: A Geography of Poverty and Deprivation in Ireland* (Dublin, Oak Tree Press, 1999) pp. 225–63.

Bell, D., *The Coming of the Post-Industrial Society* (Harmondsworth, Penguin, 1976).

Bell, G., *The Protestants of Ulster* (London, Pluto, 1976).

Berghman, J., 'The Resurgence of Poverty and the Struggle Against Exclusion: A New Challenge for Social Security in Europe', *International Social Security Review*, 50:1 (1997) pp. 3–21.

Bew, P., E. Hazelkorn and H. Patterson, *The Dynamics of Irish Politics* (London, Lawrence and Wishart, 1989).

Bourdieu, P., *Acts of Resistance: Against the New Myths of Our Time* (Cambridge, Polity, 1998).

Boyd, A., *Have the Trade Unions Failed the North* (Cork, Mercier, 1984).

Breen, R., D. Hannan, D. Rottman and C. Whelan, *Understanding Contemporary Ireland: State, Class and Development in the Republic of Ireland* (London, Macmillan, 1990).

Breen, R., and C. Whelan, *Social Mobility and Social Class in Ireland* (Dublin, Gill and Macmillan, 1996).

Brenner, R., *The Economics of Global Turbulence* (London, New Left Review 229 Special Issue, 1998).

Butler, E., *Milton Friedman: A Guide to His Economic Thought* (Aldershot, Gower, 1985).

Byrne, S., *Wealth and the Wealthy in Ireland: A Review of the Available Evidence* (Dublin, Combat Poverty Agency, 1989).

Callinicos, A., and C. Harman, *The Changing Working Class: Essays on Class Structure Today* (London, Bookmarks, 1987).

Callinicos, A., *Against Post-Modernism: A Marxist Critique* (Cambridge, Polity, 1989).

Cameron, D., *Verbal Hygiene* (London, Routledge, 1995).

Canadian Auto Workers, *Work Re-Organisation: Responding to Lean Production* (Toronto, CAW, 1993).

Carduso, F. H., 'Dependent Capitalist Development in Latin America', *New Left Review*, no. 74 (1972) pp. 83-95.

Cassis, Y., *Big Business: The European Experience in the Twentieth Century* (Oxford, Oxford University Press, 1997).

Chomsky, N., *Rethinking Camelot: JFK, the Vietnam War, and US Political Culture* (London, Verso, 1993).

Clancy, P., 'Education in the Republic of Ireland: The Project of Modernity', in P. Clancy, S. Drudy, K. Lynch and L. O'Dowd (eds) *Irish Society: Sociological Perspectives* (Dublin, Institute of Public Administration, 1995) pp. 467–95.

Clark, D., *Post Industrial America: A Geographical Perspective* (London, Methuen, 1984.

Cliff, T., and D. Gluckstein, *Marxism and Trade Union Struggle: The General Strike of 1926* (London, Bookmarks, 1986).

Cody, S., *Parliament of Labour* (Dublin, Council of Trades Unions, 1986).

Collins, S., *The Haughey File* (Dublin, O'Brien Press, 1992).

Conference of Heads of Irish Universities, *Guaranteeing Future Growth* (Dublin, CHIU, 1999).

Conference of Major Religious Superiors, *Profile of Religious in Ireland* (Dublin, Conference of Major Religious Superiors, 1990).

Conference of Religious in Ireland, *Growing Exclusion* (Dublin, CORI, 1993).

Connolly, J., *Labour, Nationality and Religion* (Dublin, New Books, 1972).

Connolly, J., *The New Evangel* (Dublin, New Books, 1972).

Coogan, T. P., *Disillusioned Decades* (Dublin, Gill and Macmillan, 1987).

Cooney, T., J. McLaughlin and J. Martyn, *Taxation Summary Republic of Ireland 1998/1999* (Dublin, Institute of Taxation in Ireland, 1998).

Corey, L., *The Decline of American Capitalism* (New York, Covici-Friede, 1934).

Coulter, C., 'Hello Divorce, Goodbye Daddy: Women, Gender and the Divorce Debate', in A. Bradley and M. G. Valiulis (eds) *Gender and Sexuality in Modern Ireland* (Amherst, University of Massachusetts Press, 1997) pp. 275–99.

Cousins, C., 'Social Exclusion in Europe', *Policy and Politics*, 26:2 (1997) pp. 127 -45.

Crotty, R., *Ireland in Crisis: A Study in Capitalist Colonial Underdevelopment* (Dingle, Brandon, 1986).

Curry, J., *Irish Social Services* (Dublin, Institute of Public Administration, 1998).

Dalton, M., *Men Who Manage* (New York, John Wiley, 1959).

Danagher, K., *Corporations are Going to Get Your Mama* (Monroe, Maine, 1996).

Davies, J., 'Towards a Theory of Revolution', *American Sociological Review* 27:1 (1962) pp. 5–19.

Department of Education, *Education 2000 International Adult Literacy Survey: Results for Ireland* (Dublin, Stationery Office, 1997).

Department of Industrial Relations, UCD (eds) *Industrial Relations in Ireland* (Dublin, UCD, 1987).

Derrida, J., *Spectres of Marx* (London, Routledge, 1994).

Devlin, P., *Straight Left: An Autobiography* (Belfast, Blackstaff, 1993).

Dicken, P., *Global Shift: The Internationalization of Economic Activity* (London, Paul Chapman, 1992).

Dillon, M., *Debating Divorce: Moral Conflict in Ireland* (Lexington, University Press of Kentucky, 1993).

Drudy, S., and K. Lynch, *Schools and Society in Ireland* (Dublin, Gill and Macmillan, 1993).

Drudy Commission, *Housing a New Approach: Report of the Housing Commission* (Dublin, Labour Party, 1999).

Dublin Transport Office, *Transportation Review and Short Term Action Plan* (Dublin, DTO, 1998).

Durkheim, E., *Suicide: A Study in Sociology* (New York, Free Press, 1966).

Eagleton, T., *Ideology: An Introduction* (London, Verso, 1991).

Eagleton, T., *Marx* (London, Phoenix, 1997).

Edwards, O. D., and B. Ranson (eds) *James Connolly: Selected Writings* (London, Jonathan Cape, 1973).

Elliot, L., and D. Atkinson, *The Age of Insecurity* (London, Verso, 1998).

Ernst, D., and D. O'Connor, *Competing in Electronics: The Experience of Newly Industrialising Countries* (London, Pinther, 1992).

Esping-Andersen, G., *The Three Worlds of Welfare Capitalism* (Cambridge, Polity Press, 1990).

ESRI, *Medium Term Review 1997–2003* (Dublin, ESRI, 1997).

ESRI, *National Investment Priorities for the Period 2000–2006* (Dublin, ESRI, 1999).

Etzioni, A., *Capital Corruption: The New Attack on American Democracy* (New Brunswick, Transaction Books, 1988).

European Commission, *The Economic and Financial Situation in Ireland* (Brussels, European Commission Reports, 1996).

European Commission, *Key Data on Education in the European Union* (Luxembourg, EU Commission, 1997).

Fahey, T., *Social Housing in Ireland* (Dublin, Oak Tree, 1999).

Farrell, M., *Arming the Protestants* (London, Pluto, 1983).

Fogarty, M., D. Egan and W. Ryan, *Pay Policy for the 1980s* (Dublin, Federated Union of Employers, 1981).

Fitzgerald, J., 'Through Irish Eyes: The Economic Experience of Independence in Europe', ESRI Working Paper, no. 89 (October 1997).

Frank, A. G., *Capitalism and Underdevelopment in Latin America* (New York, Monthly Review Press, 1969).

Friedman, M., *Capitalism and Freedom* (London, University of Chicago Press, 1962).

Friedman, M., *There's No Such Thing as a Free Lunch* (La Salle, Open Court, 1975).

Galbraith, J. K., *The Culture of Contentment* (London, Sinclair-Stevenson, 1992).

Gallagher, M., *The Irish Labour Party in Transition 1957–82* (Manchester, Manchester University Press, 1982).

Gallie, D., 'Employment, Unemployment, and Social Stratification', in D. Gallie (ed.) *Employment in Britain* (Oxford, Blackwell, 1990) pp. 465–93.

Geier, J., and A. Shawki, 'Contradictions of the "Miracle" Economy', *International Socialism Review* 2, Fall (1997) pp. 1–15.

Nic Ghiolla Phadraig, M., 'The Power of the Catholic Church in the Republic of Ireland', in P. Clancy, S. Drudy, K. Lynch and L. O'Dowd (eds) *Irish Society: Sociological Perspectives* (Dublin, Institute of Public Administration, 1995) pp. 593–4.

Gilbert, M., *The Italian Revolution: The End of Politics, Italian Style* (Boulder, Westview Press, 1995).

Gilmour, I., *Dancing With Dogma: Britain Under Thatcherism* (London, Simon and Schuster, 1992).

Glacken, J. A., *Chestvale Properties Ltd, Hoddle Investments Ltd, Final Report of John A Glacken, Inspector appointed by the Minister of Industry and Commerce* (Dublin, Stationery Office, 1992).

Gluckstein, D., *The Nazis, Capitalism and the Working Class* (London, Bookmarks, 1999).

Goldring, M., *Belfast: From Loyalty to Rebellion* (London, Lawrence and Wishart, 1991).

Goldthorpe, J., *Social Mobility and Class Structure in Britain* (Oxford, Clarendon Press, 1987).

Goldthorpe J., and C. Whelan, *The Development of Industrial Society in Ireland* (Oxford, Oxford University Press, 1992).

Greaves, C. D., *The Irish Transport and General Workers Union: The Formative Years: 1909–1919* (Dublin, Gill and Macmillan, 1982).

Guiomard, C., *The Irish Disease: And How to Cure It* (Dublin, Oak Tree Press, 1995).

Gyoung-Lee, S., 'The Crisis and the Workers Movement in South Korea', *International Socialism Journal*, no. 78, Spring (1998) pp. 39–54.

Harberger, A., *Economic Policy and Economic Growth* (San Francisco, International Centre for Economic Growth, 1984).

Harman, C., 'State and Capitalism Today', *International Socialism Journal*, no. 51 (1991) pp. 3–54.

Harman, C., *Economics of the Madhouse* (London, Bookmarks, 1995).

Harman, C., 'The Crisis of Economics', *International Socialism Journal*, no. 71, Summer (1996) pp. 3–57.

Harman, C., 'Globalisation: A Critique of the New Orthodoxy', *International Socialism Journal*, no. 73, (1996) pp. 3–35.

Harris, N., *Of Bread and Guns: The World Economy in Crisis* (Harmondsworth, Penguin, 1983).

Haughey, C., *Spirit of the Nation* (Cork, Mercier, 1986).

Haynes, M., and P. Glatter, 'The Russian Catastrophe', *International Socialism Journal*, no. 81 (1998) pp. 45–91.

Healy, S., and B. Reynolds, 'The Future of Work: A Challenge to Society', in B. Reynolds and S. Healy (eds) *Work, Unemployment and Job Creation* (Dublin, Justice Commission, Conference of Major Religious Superiors, 1990) pp. 56–90.

Henwood, D., *Wall St* (London, Verso, 1998).

Herrenstein, R., and C. Murray, *The Bell Curve: Intelligence and Class Structure in American Life* (New York, Free Press, 1996).

Hesketh, T., *The Second Partitioning of Ireland: The Abortion Referendum of 1983* (Dublin, Brandsma, 1990).

Hill, C., *The World Turned Upside Down* (Harmondsworth, Penguin, 1991).

Hill, S., 'The Social Organisation of Boards of Directors', *British Journal of Sociology*, 46:2, June (1995) pp. 245–78.

Hirst, P., and G. Thompson, *Globalization in Question* (Cambridge, Polity, 1996).

Hobsbawm, E., *The Age of Extremes: The Short History of the Twentieth Century* (London, Michael Joseph, 1994).

Holborow, M., *The Politics of English* (London, Sage, 1999).

Holden, W., *Unlawful Carnal Knowledge: The True Story of the Irish 'X', Case* (London, Harper Collins, 1994) pp. 29–30.

Honohan, P., and P. O'Connell, 'The National Development Plan in the Context of Irish Economic Problems', in ESRI, *Economic Perspectives for the Medium Term* (Dublin, ESRI, 1994) pp. 63–77.

Hughes, G., and B. Whelan, *Occupational and Personal Pension Coverage 1995* (Dublin, ESRI, 1996).

Hutton, W., *The State We're In* (London, Cape 1995).

Hyman, R., *Marxism and the Sociology of Trade Unionism* (London, Pluto Press, 1971).

IMF, *International Capital Markets: Developments, Prospects and Policies*, September 1998 (Washington, IMF, 1998).

IMF, *World Economic Outlook*, May 1999 (Washington, IMF, 1999).

Inglis, T., *Moral Monopoly: The Rise and Fall of the Catholic Church in Modern Ireland* (Dublin, UCD Press, 1998).

Inglis, T., *Lessons in Irish Sexual Morality* (Dublin, UCD Press, 1998).

Irish Congress of Trade Unions, *Managing Change: Report of Review Group on Union Involvement in Company Re-structuring* (Dublin, ICTU, 1995).

Irish Congress of Trade Unions, *What People Think of Unions* (Dublin, ICTU, 1998).

Irish Congress of Trade Unions, *Challenges Facing Unions: Irish Society in the Millennium* (Dublin, ICTU, 1999).

Irish National Teachers Organisation, *The Place of Religious Education in the National Schools System* (Dublin, INTO, 1992).

Johnson, H., 'The Market Mechanism as an Instrument of Development', in G. Meir (ed.) *Leading Issues in Economic Development* (Oxford, Oxford University Press, 1989) pp. 516–21.

Kaysen, C., (ed.), *The American Corporation Today* (New York, Oxford University Press, 1996).

Keogh, D., *Ireland and the Vatican: The Politics and Diplomacy of Church-State Relations* (Cork, Cork University Press, 1995).

Kerr, A., 'Collective Labour Law', in T. Murphy and W. Roche (eds) *Irish Industrial Relations in Practice* (Dublin, Oak Tree Press, 1994) pp. 363–77.

Kerrigan, G., *Another Country: Growing Up in 50s Ireland* (Dublin, Gill and Macmillan, 1998).

Kostick, C., *Revolution in Ireland: Popular Militancy 1917–1923* (London, Pluto, 1996).

KPMG, *Study on Urban Renewal Schemes* (Dublin, Stationery Office, 1996).

Krugman, P., *The Return of Depression Economics* (London, Allen Lane, 1999).

Lal, D., *The Poverty of Development Economics* (London, Institute of Economic Affairs, Hobart Paperback, 1983).

Lappe, F. M., J. Collins and P. Rosset, *World Hunger: 12 Myths* (London, Earthscan, 1998).

Lee, J., 'Capital in the Irish Economy', in L. M. Cullen (ed.) *The Formation of the Irish Economy* (Cork, Mercier, 1969) pp. 53–75.

Lee, J., 'Motivation: An Historian's Point of View', in Foras Forbartha (ed.) *Ireland in Year 2000 Towards a National Strategy* (Dublin, Foras Forbartha, 1983) pp. 37–47.

Lee, J., *Ireland 1912–1985: Politics and Society* (Cambridge, Cambridge University Press, 1989).

Lester, R., *As the Union Matures* (Princeton, Princeton University Press, 1958).

Lockwood, D., *The Blackcoated Worker* (London, Allen and Unwin, 1989).

Luibhead, E., 'Irish Immigrants in the United States Racial System', in J. MacLaughlin (ed.) *Location and Dislocation in Contemporary Irish Society* (Cork, Cork University Press, 1997) pp. 253–74.

Lynch, F., 'Health Funding and Expenditure in Ireland', in E. McAuliffe and L. Joyce *A Healthier Future: Managing Health Care in Ireland* (Dublin, IPA, 1998) pp. 92–108.

McCarthy, C., *Decade of Upheaval* (Dublin, IPA, 1973).

McCartney, J., and P. Teague, 'Workplace Innovations in the Republic of Ireland', *Economic and Social Review*, 28:4 (1997) pp. 381–99.

McCraw, T., *America Versus Japan* (Boston, Harvard Business School Press, 1986).

McCutcheon, M., 'The Tax Incentives Applying to US Corporate Investment in Ireland', *Economic and Social Review*, 26:2 (1995) pp. 149–71.

Mahon, E., C. Conlon and L. Dillon, *Women and Crisis Pregnancy* (Dublin, Stationery Office, 1998).

Mair, P., *The Changing Party System: Organisation, Ideology and Electoral Competition* (London, Pinther, 1987).

Mair, P., 'Explaining the Absence of Class Politics in Ireland', in J. Goldthorpe and C. Whelan *The Development of Industrial Society in Ireland* (Oxford, Oxford University Press, 1992) pp. 383–411.

Mantinussen, J., *Society, State and Market: A Guide to Competing Theories of Development* (London, Zed Books, 1991).

Marx, K., *Capital Volume 3* (London, Lawrence and Wishart, 1959).

Marx, K., and F. Engels, *Manifesto of the Communist Party in Selected Works*, vol. 1 (Moscow, Progress, 1977).

Mataloni, R., 'US Multinational Operations in 1996', *Survey of Current Business*, September (1998). (Internet Edition)

Michels, R., *Political Parties* (Glencoe, The Free Press, 1958).

Miliband, R., *The State in Capitalist Society* (London, Weidenfeld and Nicholson, 1969).

Mitchell, A., 'William O'Brien, 1881–1968 and the Irish Labour Movement', *Studies*, Autumn-Winter (1971) pp. 311–31.

Mockler, F., 'Organisation Changes in Fianna Fail and Fine Gael', *Irish Political Studies*, vol. 9 (1994) pp. 165–71.

Moody, K., *Workers in a Lean World: Unions in the International Economy* (London, Verso, 1997).

Mulreany, M., 'Taxation: Ireland and the New Europe', in K. Murphy and M. Mulreany (eds) *Taxation: Ireland and the New Europe* (Dublin, IPA, 1993) pp. 5–30.

Murray, C., *The Emerging British Underclass* (London, IEA, Health Welfare Unit, 1990).

National Economic and Social Council, *Private Sector Investment in Ireland* (Dublin, NESC, 1998).

Nolan, B., and T. Callan (eds), *Poverty and Policy in Ireland* (Dublin, Gill and Macmillan, 1994).

Nolan, B., and G., Hughes, *Low Pay, the Earnings Distribution and Poverty in Ireland, 1987–1994* (Dublin, ESRI, 1997).

O'Carroll, J. P., 'Eamon de Valera, Charisma and Political Development', in J. P. O'Carroll and J. A. Murphy (eds) *de Valera and His Times* (Cork, Cork University Press, 1983) pp. 17–35.

O'Connor, E., *Syndicalism in Ireland 1917–1923* (Cork, Cork University Press, 1988).

O'Connor, J., 'US Social Welfare Policy: The Reagan Record and Legacy', *Journal of Social Policy*, 27:1 (1998) pp. 37–63.

O'Donnell, P., *There Will Be Another Day* (Dublin, Dolmen Press, 1963).

OECD, *Economic Survey: Ireland* (Paris, OECD, 1997).

OECD, *Education at a Glance* (Paris, OECD, 1997).

OECD, *Economic Surveys Ireland 1998–1999* (Paris, OECD, 1999).

O'Grada, C., *A Rocky Road: The Irish Economy Since the 1920s* (Manchester, Manchester University Press, 1997).

O'Hearn, D., 'The Irish Case of Dependency: An Exception to the Exception', *American Sociological Review*, 54:4 (1989) pp. 578–96.

O'Hearn, D., 'Global Re-structuring and the Irish Political Economy', in P. Clancy, S. Drudy, K. Lynch and L. O'Dowd (eds) *Irish Society: Sociological Perspectives* (Dublin, Institute of Public Administration, 1995) pp. 90–132.

O'Hearn, D., *Inside the Celtic Tiger: The Irish Economy and the Asian Model* (London, Pluto Press, 1998).

O'Mahoney, P., 'Punishing Poverty and Personal Adversity', in I. Bacik and M. O'Connell (eds) *Crime and Poverty in Ireland* (Dublin, Round Hall, 1998) pp. 49–68.

O'Malley, E., *Industry and Economic Development: The Challenge of the Latecomer* (Dublin, Gill and Macmillan, 1989).

O'Reilly, E., *Masterminds of the Right* (Dublin, Attic Press, 1988).

O'Toole, F., *Black Hole, Green Card* (Dublin, New Island Books, 1994).

O'Toole, F., *Meanwhile Back at the Ranch* (London, Vintage, 1995).

Partnership 2000 Expert Working Group on Childcare, *National Childcare Strategy* (Dublin, Stationery Office, 1999).

Petersen, W., *Silent Depression: The Fate of the American Dream* (New York, WW Norton, 1994).

Petrella, R., 'Globalization and Internationalization', in R. Boyer and D. Drache *States Against Markets* (London, Routledge, 1996) pp. 62–84.

Praeger, J., *Building Democracy in Ireland: Political Order and Cultural Integration in a Newly Independent Nation* (Cambridge, Cambridge University Press, 1983).

Punch, M., *Dirty Business: Exploring Corporate Misconduct* (London, Sage, 1996).

Reisman, M., *Folded Lies* (New York, Free Press, 1979).

Report of the Tribunal of Inquiry (Dunnes Payments) McCracken Tribunal (Dublin, Stationery Office, 1997).

Report of Inquiry into Industrial Dispute at Dublin Airport (Flynn/McAuley Report) (Dublin, Stationery Office, 1998).

Report of the National Minimum Wage Commission (Dublin, Stationery Office, 1998).

Report on Special Report of the Comptroller and Auditor General on Sale of State Lands at Glen Ding, County Wicklow (Dublin, Stationery Office, 1999).

Report of Investigation into the Administration of Deposit Interest Retention Tax and Related Matters During the Period 1st January 1986 to 1st December 1998 (Comptroller General's Report) (Dublin, Stationery Office, 1999).

Riordan, M., *The Voice of a Thinking Intelligent Movement: James Larkin Junior and the Ideological Modernisation of Irish Trade Unionism* (Dublin, Irish Labour History Society, 1995).

Rose, K., *Diverse Communities: The Evolution of Lesbian and Gay Politics in Ireland* (Cork, Cork University Press, 1994).

Rostow, W., *The Stages of Economic Growth: A Non-communist Manifesto* (London, Cambridge University Press, 1971).

Ruane, F., and H. Goreg, 'The Impact of Foreign Direct Investment on Sectoral Adjustment in the Irish Economy', *National Institute Economic Review*, no. 160 (1997) pp. 76–87.

Ryan, L., 'Irish Emigration to Britain Since World War II' in R. Kearney (ed.) *Migrations: The Irish at Home and Abroad* (Dublin, Wolfhound, 1990), pp. 45–69.

Ryle Dwyer, T., *de Valera: The Man and the Myth* (Dublin, Poolbeg, 1991).

Schor, J., *The Overworked American: The Unexpected Decline of Leisure* (New York, Basic Books, 1992).

Sewn, A., *Irrational Exuberance: The Myth of the Celtic Tiger* (Dublin, Blackhall, 1999).

Shaw, M., and I. Miles, 'The Social Roots of Statistical Knowledge', in J. Irvine, I. Miles and J. Evans *De-Mystifying Social Statistics* (London, Pluto Press, 1979) pp. 27–39.

Smyth, A., (ed.), *The Abortion Papers* (Dublin, Attic Press, 1992).

Smyth, E., 'Labour Market Structures and Women's Employment in the Republic of Ireland' in A. Byrne and M. Leonard (eds) *Women and Irish Society: A Sociological Reader* (Belfast, Beyond the Pale Publications, 1997), pp. 63–81.

Smyth, S., *Thanks a Million Big Fella* (Dublin, Blackwater, 1997).

de Ste Croix, G. E. M., *The Class Struggle in Ancient Greek World* (London, Duckworth, 1981).

Stockman, N., N. Bonney and S. Xuewen, *Women's Work in East and West: The Dual Burden of Employment and Family Life* (London, UCL Press, 1995).

Strauss, E., *Irish Nationalism and British Democracy* (London, Methuen, 1951).

Sweeney, P., *The Celtic Tiger: Ireland's Economic Miracle Explained* (Dublin, Oak Tree, 1998).

Thompson, K., *Emile Durkheim* (Milton Keynes, Open University, 1982).

Trotsky, L., 'The Interaction Between Booms and Slumps', *International Socialism Journal*, no. 20 (1983) pp. 132–44.

UNTCAD, *World Investment Report 1998: Trends and Determinants* (New York, UNCTAD, 1998).

Walsh, D., *The Party: Inside Fianna Fail* (Dublin, Gill and Macmillan, 1986).

Waters, J., *An Intelligent Person's Guide to Modern Ireland* (Dublin, Duckworth, 1998).

Webb, S., and B. Webb, *A History of Trade Unionism* (London, Longmans, 1907).

Weber, S., 'The End of the Business Cycle', *Foreign Affairs*, 76:4, July/August (1997) pp. 65–83.

Wheen, F., *Karl Marx* (London, Fourth Estate, 1999).

Whyte, J. H., *Church and State in Modern Ireland 1923–1979* (Dublin, Gill and Macmillan, 1980).

Wiley, M., *Women and Health Care in Ireland: Knowledge, Attitudes and Behaviour* (Dublin, Oak Tree/ESRI, 1996).

Workers Party, *The Irish Industrial Revolution* (Dublin, Repsol, 1978).

Zuckerman, M. B., 'A Second American Century', *Foreign Affairs*, 77:3, May/June (1998) pp. 18–32.

Index